PLANTS of the BIBLE

A complete handbook

PLANTS of the BIBLE

A complete handbook to all the plants
with 200 full-color plates
taken in the natural habitat

Michael Zohary

Professor of Botany, Hebrew University, Jerusalem

CAMBRIDGE UNIVERSITY PRESS
Cambridge
London New York New Rochelle
Melbourne Sydney

For Magda in gratitude

Michael Zohary
PLANTS OF THE BIBLE

Published by the Press Syndicate of the University of Cambridge
The Pitt Building, Trumpington Street, Cambridge CB2 1RP
32 East 57th Street, New York, NY 10022, USA
296 Beaconsfield Parade, Middle Park, Melbourne 3206, Australia

First published 1982

Library of Congress Catalogue Card Number 82-4535

British Library Cataloguing in Publication Data

Zohary, Michael
Plants of the Bible
1. Plants of the Bible
I. Title
581 QK45.2

ISBN 0 521 24926 0

Photography Michael Zohary
David Darom

Design David Afek
Editor Phyllis Hackett
Editorial Assistant Ronny Stein
Cartography Shaul Shapiro

Typesetting: Ben Zvi Printing Enterprises Ltd., Jerusalem
Color separation: Reshet Kav and Scanli, Tel Aviv
Printed in Belgium by Van Den Bossche, Mechelen

A Note on Transliteration

Certain letters in biblical Hebrew are transliterated as follows:

ḥ denotes ח ; as in Bethlehem (בֵּית־לֶחֶם)
th denotes ת ; as in Bethlehem (בֵּית־לֶחֶם)
ah denotes terminal ה ; as in bathah (בַּתָּה)
tz denotes צ ; as in tzitz (צִיץ)
e in the first syllable denotes the vowel ֵ ; as in Elath (אֵילַת)

All terms taken from languages other than English, such as Accadian, Egyptian, Hebrew, Latin, Greek and Arabic, are printed in italics.

CONTENTS

Preface

I HAVE been privileged to spend a lifetime as a botanist amidst the flora of the Holy Land, exploring the Bible in the light of current botanical research. In writing this book I was motivated by the need for a new scrutiny of the relations between biblical man and his natural environment and for a revision of many accepted 'truths' in the naming and identification of the plants of the Bible.

The translation of many Hebrew plant names into foreign languages is in fact far from satisfactory. Still less so are the numerous books on biblical flora, even when written by qualified botanists or linguists who have gone to great pains to identify all the named plants; since in trying to render every plant mentioned into their own language they may actually 'implant' many alien plants into the Land of the Bible.

Yet this is by no means a research study. It has no claim to exhaust the subject, nor to answer all queries. Quite a number of problems, especially those of nomenclature, remain unsolved. But while the book offers fewer innovations than corrections, it does endeavor to 'weed out' erroneous views and identifications that have become widely ingrained in the study of biblical flora.

The book is divided into two parts. Part one – Biblical Man and His Environment – comprises a comprehensive description of the Holy Land, its landforms, soil, climate and vegetal landscapes, providing an ecologically inclusive view of the interdependency of man and nature, as reflected in the Bible. Particularly stressed is the role of plants in religion and worship, folklore, poetry and art, agriculture and trade. Part two – All the Plants in the Bible – groups them into natural, agricultural, and morphological units. Relevant citations from the Bible accompany the discussion of each plant, and its life history is described in terms of botany, geography, and use.

The idea of writing this book was born in the very surroundings where the plant life of the ancient past still flourishes, where the flowery landscapes of the Bible are still gleaming with that glory which prophets and kings have celebrated in poems and parables and the common people in their songs:

"O Lord, how manifold are thy works! In wisdom hast thou made them all; the earth is full of thy creatures" (Psalms 104:24).

Jerusalem, June 1982

Michael Zohary

Part One
BIBLICAL MAN & HIS ENVIRONMENT

1

Identification of Biblical Plants

THE BOOKS OF THE BIBLE, LANGUAGES & DATES

MORE than one thousand years of oral transmission preceded the setting down of the text of the Hebrew Bible, also known as the Old Testament. Written in the Hebrew language, with the exception of a few parts in Aramaic, it was composed and compiled over a period of several hundred years. The various dates of composition can be distinguished by the various linguistic layers. The Old Testament is traditionally divided into three parts: the Law, also called the Pentateuch; the Prophets; and the Hagiographa, which means 'the Writings.' The canonization of the Law seems to have occurred during the fifth century BC. Parts of the Prophets were compiled as early as the fourth century BC, while the others were apparently canonized in the second century BC, and the Hagiographa between the first and second centuries AD. By this point, all the books of the Bible already constituted a closed collection of sacred literature, so venerated that it was strictly forbidden to change even a single word.

It should be noted that in the middle of the second century AD many other books were in existence, but they were excluded from the canon on the grounds of their secular quality. Most of them are known collectively as the Apocrypha and the Pseudepigrapha. They are somewhat historical in nature, and as such they are invaluable as a source of reference for the names and descriptions so vital for the identification and study of plants. Moreover, the large number of parables, allegories, and idiomatic expressions and phrases in the Old Testament suggests a huge body of extra-biblical folkloristic literature and mythical and legendary works, all of them now lost.

Some of these lost books, however, are mentioned in the Old Testament: "The Wars of the Lord" (Numbers 21:14), "The Book of Jashar" (Joshua 10:13), "The Book of the Acts of Solomon" (I Kings 11:41), and a number of others. The existence of poems or songs is attested by single examples like "The Blessing of Jacob" (Genesis 49), "The Song of Moses" (Exodus 15), and "The Song of Deborah" (Judges 5).

The New Testament was composed by various authors at different times from 66 to 125 AD and canonized at the end of the second century. Although it was set down in Greek, the oral sources of some of the Gospels were in Aramaic and Hebrew, and their influence is still discernible in the Greek text, especially in Mark and Matthew and several of the Epistles.

The names and order of the books of both the Old and New Testaments, still widely disputed, are here, for the sake of simplicity, given in conformity with the Revised Standard Version.

BIBLE TRANSLATIONS AND PLANT NAMING

THE early translations of the Bible into Aramaic, Greek, and Latin, and the comparative study of Semitic languages, are of great importance in identifying biblical plant names. Among the early Semitic languages, the most helpful in deciphering doubtful words in the Hebrew Scripture, whose meaning has been obscured or forgotten during the long period of disuse, are Aramaic – because it was as popular as Hebrew in later biblical times – and Arabic. There are many Hebrew plant names which are identical or cognate with Aramaic and Arabic ones. This, however, cannot be said of Accadian, mother of both, which might have been expected to take the lead in Hebrew linguistics; and Hebrew has been more helpful for deciphering Accadian plant names than vice versa.

The Arabic language, however, serves as a kind of nature reserve for moribund names, assisting at times in the tracing of questionable identifications. This function should be seen in its proper perspective within the context of the events that took place in the Land of the Bible over many generations.

After the fall of the Jewish kingdom and despite the Roman and Byzantine occupations, which lasted for seven centuries (70 BC to 640 AD), many of the Jewish peasants still kept to their land and through all the tumultuous upheavals persevered in tilling their soil. Thus was kept alive a rich vernacular tradition of terms pertaining to plants and agriculture – uninterrupted until the Moslem conquest in 640 AD. Moreover, Jews from Kurdistan still retain in their language names, that were in use at the time of the Babylonian exile.

Adopting the long-established agricultural tradition of the local inhabitants, the Arabs absorbed the various plant names prevailing. These terms gradually infiltrated into their spoken language, thus temporarily storing the original meanings of some words and later serving as a most useful source for tracing uncertain identifications of the biblical plant world. In this manner were preserved in Arabic the names for such species as apple, fig, grape, pistachio, almond, pomegranate, carob, retam, acacia, and others. It should be noted that with the spreading of Arabic, a number of Hebrew-Arabic plant names infiltrated into Ethiopian and the North African languages.

This method of using Arabic as a comparative language, spoken continuously, is advocated by the present writer as a means for shedding more light on some of the most uncertain botanical names.

Of the non-Semitic languages, Greek and Latin have made it possible to translate some obscure expressions and verses in the Bible, because the translation of the Old Testament into Greek was accomplished when Hebrew was still extensively spoken. Although Latin was used only much later for biblical translation, it has assisted in clarifying obscure glosses, thanks to the scrupulous work of the authoritative translator. The fact that most translations of the Bible were made from earlier texts at different dates accounts for their many discrepancies.

The Septuagint – the Greek version of the entire Old Testament – produced in the third century BC, was the first attempt to translate the Bible, including the Deuterocanonical books and several Apocryphal ones, into another tongue. This translation suggests some interpretations that clarify many passages throughout the text.

The Latin translation of the Bible was carried out by St. Jerome in the fourth century AD in Bethlehem. By virtue of his knowledge of the Hebrew language he was able to note the innumerable places where the Greek translation had strayed away from the Hebrew. This mastery of languages promoted his greatest achievement – fidelity to the original. His version is the standard Latin translation, traditionally known as the *Vulgate*, from which were made the first translations of the Bible into most of the West European languages.

The Aramaic text known as the Onkelos translation deals only with the Pentateuch and was recognized as the authoritative Aramaic version. Produced in the second century AD, this work was the result of a long oral tradition. *Targum Yonathan* (Jonathan's Translation), of the first century BC, was considered as the authorized Aramaic version of the Prophets. Both are usually quite reliable, although some plant terms seem to be Aramaization of the Hebrew, probably where the plants in question do not occur in Aramaic-speaking countries outside of Israel.

The Syriac (Eastern Aramaic) **translation** of the Old Testament is the so-called *Pshittah* ('simple'). It appeared in the first century AD and displays a strict adherence to the Hebrew text. A *pshittah* translation of the New Testament also exists. From the end of the third century AD, the Syriac translation became the accepted version of the Bible for the Syrian Church. The Ethiopian, Egyptian (Coptic) and Armenian translations of the Bible all conformed to the Greek and/or the *Pshittah*. The first Arabic translation was made by Saadia Gaon in the tenth century AD.

Owing to inadequate knowledge of the native plants and the tendency, in dubious cases, to assign to the plants of the Bible names familiar to the translators, discrepancies, inaccuracies, and confusion abound in the translations. Even the Septuagint names many plants which are not found in the Land of the Bible but may grow in Greece. The same is true of the Vulgate.

English and other European translations are the worst culprits in this respect, because they give European names to many biblical plants. Chestnut, hazel, boxtree and heather appear in certain English versions, as well as in other earlier translations. Some English versions, furthermore, are inconsistent, calling the same plant by several names (e.g. brier, bramble, thorn and thistle).

Early and later scholars and translators alike were unfortunately not versed in the floral terms of the original Hebrew Scripture. Hence their translations have scarcely any scientific value, but are historically fairly important.

A NOTE ON RESEARCH INTO BIBLICAL FLORA

LONG before the eighteenth century, pilgrim-scholars visited the Land of the Bible in order to study its flora and fauna. Among them were Leonhardt Rauwolf from Holland, who traveled through Arabia, Syria, and other countries (1583-1586). His plant collections were published by J. V. Grenovius in 1775. Most fruitful were the travels of de Tournefort, whose *Relation d'un voyage du Levant* was published in 1717-1718, and of Pier Fôrsskål of Denmark (1761-1762) and F. Haselquist (1777-1778), both students of the famous Swedish botanist Carolus Linnaeus.

Chief among the explorers was the Swiss Edmond Boissier, who collected plants in many countries of the Middle East in 1846, and published in 1867-1888 his monumental *Flora Orientalis* in five volumes with a supplement, still the most reliable source on the flora of the Land of the Bible. Boissier also produced a small but extremely valuable booklet, *Botanique Biblique* (1861), published anonymously in Geneva. Since that time a century has elapsed, during which research into Middle Eastern flora has progressed rapidly. The books and articles of other esteemed botanists and scholars of natural history such as Post, Tristram, Hart, Dalman and Balfour, among others, should also be mentioned here, but they too remained excessively faithful to conventionally accepted interpretations of some plant names.

As to research works on biblical botany, their number is too large to be listed here. They have been written in various languages and published in periodicals, encyclopedias, and dictionaries, and also in some quite voluminous books. The bulk of them are the work of theologians and Bible scholars who were concerned with the proper identification of biblical names for the purpose of translation and study. Publications of this kind first appeared soon after the classical translations of the Bible. Most of them are listed in the fourth volume of E. Loew's *Die Flora der Juden* (1938) and also in H. N. and A. L. Moldenke's *Plants of the Bible* (1952), whose opinion of them is expressed in the following words, published in 1952 and still appropriate today: "Anyone delving even superficially into the literature of Bible plants, will be impressed at once by the striking discrepancies, contradictions, palpable misidentifications, erroneous statements and general confusion which exist there."

Die Flora der Juden is outstanding in its comprehensiveness and philological treatment of the plant names occurring in the Scriptures, and in Talmudic and other Jewish literature. It was published in four volumes between 1924 and 1938. It is strongly analytical and abounds with lists of Hebrew names and their translation, taken from all known sources. Yet, despite its bibliographical breadth and its inexhaustible information about biblical botany, it is inappropriate for general readers and students. Many names are left unidentified and some of the identifications are contextually unacceptable. In the main, however, it will remain forever a masterpiece on biblical botany.

Moldenke was a botanist who never came in touch with biblical flora in their authentic surroundings. Although he was inadequately skilled in the Hebrew language, he contributed largely to the subject by collating all kinds of opinions, versions, translations and interpretations widely dispersed in the literature on biblical botany. Conscientiousness forbade him to reach conclusions in most cases. Accordingly, the one hundred and ten plant names occurring in the Bible are scattered throughout 230 entries in his book.

In Israel, E. and H. Hareuveni have published a number of important papers dealing with biblical plant names and plantlore. Most of these are written in Hebrew and are listed in this book's bibliography.

Recently, J. Felix has published in Hebrew a fairly comprehensive summary of the biblical flora under the title *Olam Ha-tzomeaḥ Ha-mikrai* (The World of Biblical Vegetation). It contains Talmudic and post-Talmudic glosses on the biblical flora, but brings scarcely any new additions or reliable identifications to the many obscure names.

IDENTIFICATION OF BIBLICAL PLANTS

OF the hundred and ten plants named in the Bible, many belong to pre-biblical folklore and phraseology. Some are referred to a hundred times over, others less often, and a few only once, although frequency of reference does not always accord with importance and usefulness. In the total are included unspecified and obscure designations handed down orally through the generations.

This book discusses 128 distinctive plants as belonging to the biblical plant world, a discrepancy of 18 which is accounted for by the fact that the biblical narrators were less interested in individual species than in their significance. Thus, whole groups of plants growing in habitats like swamps, meadows, deserts and salines were lumped together in general categories bearing collective names. Modern botanical knowledge enables us to be more specific in this regard.

Since the general climatic conditions of the country have scarcely changed during the last millenia, its flora and vegetation have not substantially altered either, so that research on the biblical plants can be carried out on a basis of the present-day flora. This, of course, is true only of the native flora. Especially during the last few centuries, the cultivated flora have changed enormously. While there are fewer difficulties in the identification both of the biblical native flora and agriculture, there is a third group of bible plants the identification of which is problematic – that which appears in the Bible as drugs, aromatic oils, incenses and costly timber imported from far away.

The difficulties in the identification of the local flora stem from various sources. To begin with, the designation of a number of biblical plants was not always unequivocal or based on precise knowledge, but rather on symbolic and idiomatic usage. Moreover, biblical names do not all denote specific plants, as is indicated by the twenty names for thorns in the Bible. Although over sixty species occur among the native flora, each of these twenty names could hardly refer to a particular species. Some plant names are undoubtedly homonyms – that is, are given to more than one species. This is best exemplified by the use of *erez* (cedar) for the true cedar, the pine, the tamarisk, and probably the juniper. Other names are presumably polynomials – several names given to one plant species – as in the case of *kotz ve-dardar* and *shamir va-shayith*, both standing for 'thorns'. This is also probably true of *shoshan* and *ḥavatzeleth*, both standing for 'flowers'. (Compare Hosea 14:5 and Isaiah 35:1 with the Song of Solomon 2:1.) Such coupling (hendiadys) is frequent in the Bible and does not apply only to plants. Further difficulties arise from the collective names designating certain plant types rather than a particular species: *kaneh va-suf*, for instance, seems to be a general term for 'reed' and 'rush'. Finally, some plant names are apparently *nomina nuda*, empty names, attached to nothing specific, left over from old lore or obsolete and forgotten phrases, like *rosh ve-laanah* (poisonous plants).

Such relics certainly slipped unawares into the speech of the prophets, especially Isaiah, who has the richest vocabulary of plant names, some of which may never be identified. The prophet himself seems to have been doubtful as to certain common names he mentions. For example, in 41:19 he associates the *shittah* (acacia) with the cedar, to suggest the bringing of joy to the desert – a juxtaposition contextually implausible, since the desert abounds with acacias.

Despite the numerous efforts made by many scholars, among them experts in Semitic languages, and the already great achievements in botanical research, a fair number of biblical plant names have not so far been identified, and some have perhaps no prospect of ever being fully cleared up.

2
The Topography of the Land

THE biblical Land of Israel comprised the areas on both sides of the Jordan, and was adjacent to Assyria in the north and to Egypt in the south – the great powers of the East. Then, as today, the land was a corridor connecting north and south and a crossroads between Asia and Africa.

The environmental factors of the country are extremely diverse in terms of topography and climate, owing primarily to the contrasting altitudes, ranging from 2,800 m. in the north (Mt. Hermon) to 396 m. below sea-level in the south (Dead Sea area). These variegated landforms have decisively influenced the conditions and way of life of the people and molded much of the country's history.

The salient topographical feature is the elevated ridge system stretching like a backbone all along Cisjordan, sloping steeply down eastwards and gently towards the sea in the west – forming the four longitudinal topographic belts: the Coastal Plain, the Hill Country, the Rift Valley and the Transjordan Plateau. These belts are fairly well marked by differences in their geomorphological features, their climatic conditions and their plant-life. This overall configuration has scarcely changed during the last million years, and looked in biblical times as it does today. All these longitudinal belts are split into latitudinal units. Two of the larger valleys across the hill belt are the Esdraelon Valley in the north and the Beer Sheba Valley in the south.

THE COASTAL PLAIN

THE Coastal Plain is a rather wide undulating strip, divisible from west to east into a sandy zone covered by sand plains and shifting dunes. Eastwards, a zone of sandy-calcareous hills runs intermittently along a belt of red loam, and farther east is an almost continuous belt of dark soil, varying in width, which has always been the most fertile part of the country and its main granary. This plain – in its greater part subject to a true Mediterranean climate and harboring its characteristic flora and vegetation – is twice interrupted by mountains that converge upon the sea, once at the Ladder of Tyre in the north and once at Mt. Carmel farther south. It abounds with lateral brooks and rivulets, permanent in the north and seasonal in the south. Ever since biblical times this plain has been transversely subdivided into four districts: the Negev and the Philistia Plains in the south, the Sharon and the Zebulun Plains in the north.

The shifting dunes seriously obstructed the agricultural use of sizable sections of the Coastal Plain, impeding the flow of water to the sea and turning great stretches of land into marshes. Much of it has therefore remained unsettled; at least a part of it – the Sharon, between Jaffa and Haifa – was, until the last century, rich in natural oak forests.

THE HILL COUNTRY

THE Hill Country, whose tallest peaks are Mt. Meron in Upper Galilee (1,208 m.) and Mt. Ramon in the Negev (1,010 m.), is also divided from north to south into latitudinal districts known since days of old as the Galilee – enjoying the highest amount of rainfall and therefore the most fertile; Samaria – including Mt. Gilboa and Mt. Carmel; and Judea, farther south. From Beer Sheba, the vast deserts of the Negev extend southwards. During the biblical era, the slopes of the mountain ridges were the main areas of typical terraced Mediterranean dry-farming agriculture, yielding summer and winter crops and fruit orchards.

Fertility decreases as the annual rainfall diminishes from north to south. In Judea the

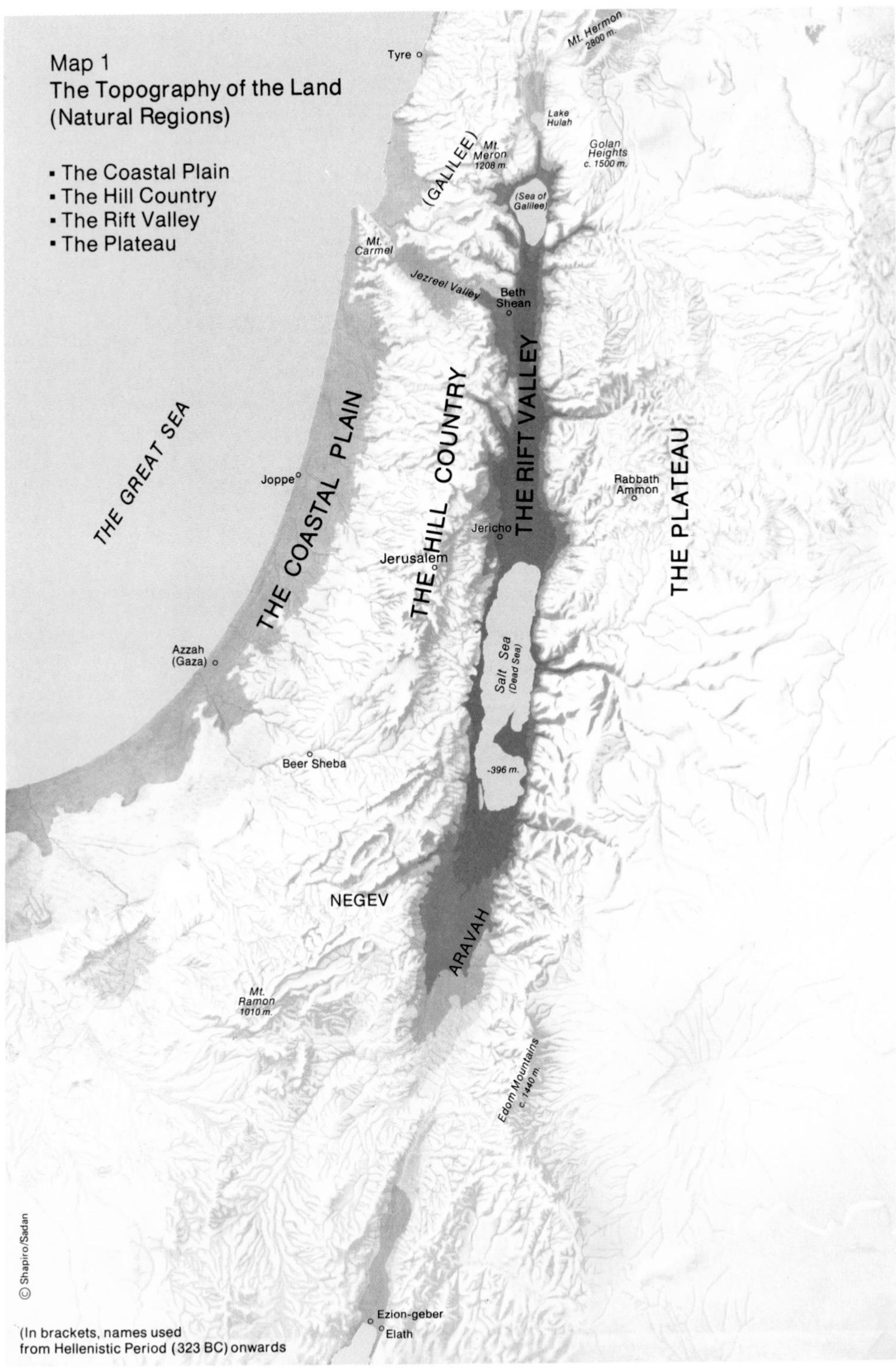
Map 1
The Topography of the Land
(Natural Regions)
▪ The Coastal Plain
▪ The Hill Country
▪ The Rift Valley
▪ The Plateau
Tyre
Mt. Hermon 2800 m.
Lake Hulah
Golan Heights c. 1500 m.
(GALILEE)
Mt. Meron 1208 m.
(Sea of Galilee)
Mt. Carmel
Jezreel Valley
Beth Shean
THE RIFT VALLEY
THE HILL COUNTRY
THE COASTAL PLAIN
THE GREAT SEA
THE PLATEAU
Joppe
Rabbath Ammon
Jericho
Jerusalem
Azzah (Gaza)
Salt Sea (Dead Sea)
-396 m.
Beer Sheba
NEGEV
ARAVAH
Mt. Ramon 1010 m.
Edom Mountains c. 1440 m.
Ezion-geber
Elath
© Shapiro/Sadan
(In brackets, names used
from Hellenistic Period (323 BC) onwards

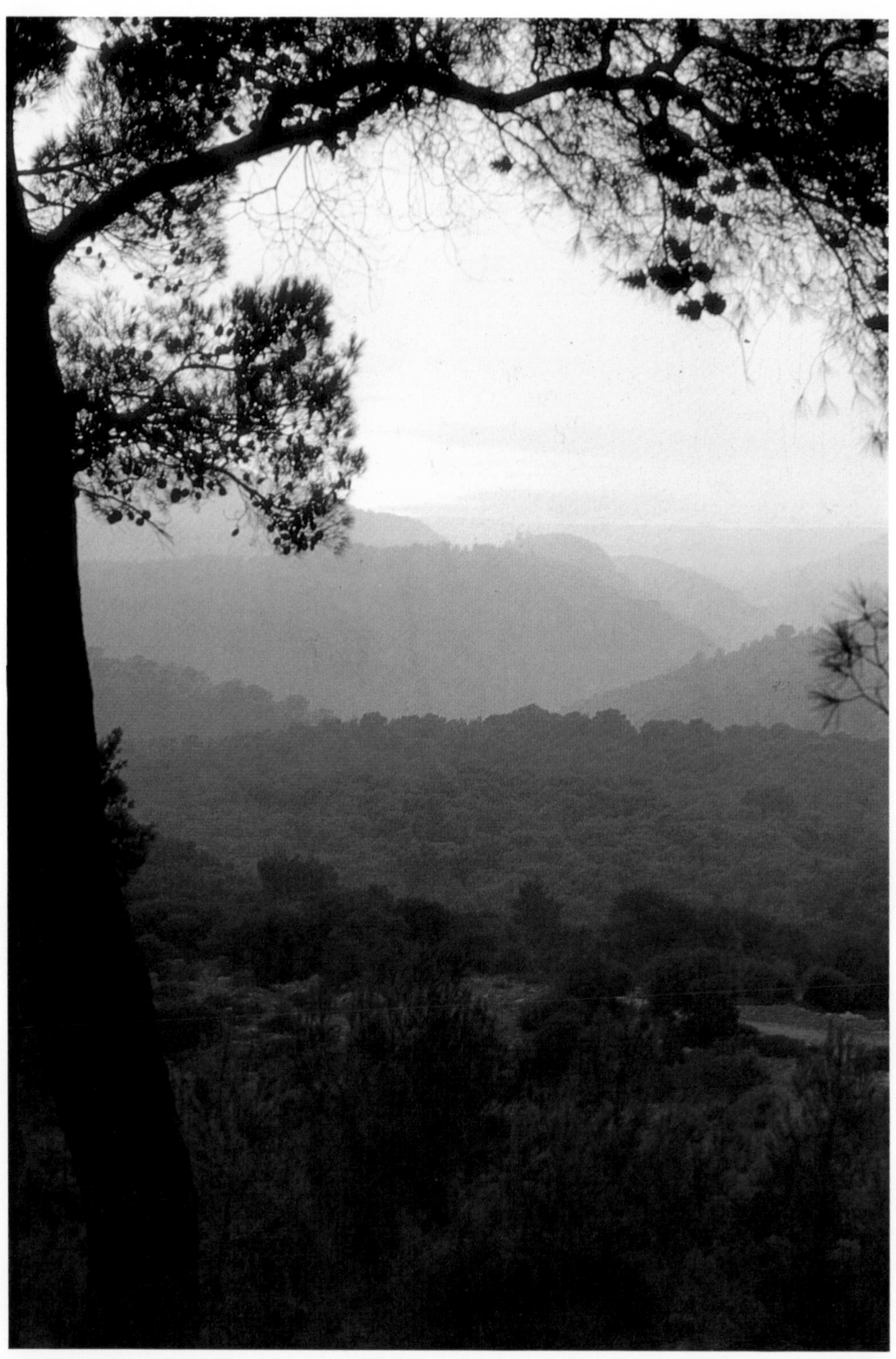

Mt. Carmel in the Hill Country; its rich and variegated forests and maquis – notably of oak and Aleppo pine – have scarcely changed since biblical times (left).

The environmental factors of the country are extremely diverse in terms of topography and climate, owing primarily to the contrasting altitudes, ranging from 2800 m. at snow-clad Mt. Hermon in the north (above) to 396 m. below sea-level at the Dead Sea in the south (below).

The acacia tree dominates the landscape in the Aravah Valley, which runs from south of the Dead Sea for 180 km., between the Negev mountains in the west and those of Moab and Edom in the east.

The biblical 'jungle of the Jordan' – the riverine Jordan forest – is dominated mainly by the Euphrates poplar and the tamarisk, both of which tolerate a high degree of salinity.

high mountain ridge intercepting the rains from the west cuts off the eastern slopes and turns them into the Judean shadow-desert. Up to the latitude of Daharie (about 20 km. south of Hebron), the whole mountain-ridge sustains rain-fed agriculture and displays a natural though heavily devastated arboreal vegetation, but farther south the rainfall is too sparse and irregular to support permanent farming.

The Negev is, generally speaking, a desert, parts of which are well suited to pasture and to sporadic agriculture. The severe floods occurring almost every year and running down the mountain slopes have facilitated the development of a special kind of terrace agriculture fed by run-off water, even in the dreary desert. The idea of farming parts of the Negev through utilization of these water resources was of deep concern to the Israel monarchy. One of the outstanding masters in this regard was King Uzziah (eighth century BC). This type of run-off water agriculture was later highly developed by the Nabateans in the first centuries AD, gradually declining with the conquest of the Negev by the Arabs in the seventh century AD. It then lay desolate until the middle of this century, when efforts to revive this vast wasteland were put into effect.

THE RIFT VALLEY

THE Rift Valley has its own characteristics. Starting in northern Syria and terminating at the source of the Zambesi in Africa, it runs the length of Israel and can be divided into five different parts. The northernmost section, usually called the Dan Valley, is an exceedingly fertile plain rich in springs and traversed by three brooks which merge to form the Jordan River. Southwards lies the Ḥulah Plain, a flooded depression which until recently included the largest papyrus swamp in the Middle East. Except for a small nature reserve, the swamps have now been drained. Both plains are all but entirely within the area of the Tabor oak forests. South of the Ḥulah, the Jordan makes its way along a deep bed cut through a plateau to empty into the Sea of Galilee, which is bordered by most fertile plains.

The Lower Jordan Valley from Beth Shean to the Dead Sea owes its poverty of vegetation to the low rainfall. The salt content of the Jordan increases southwards and the one significant vegetal feature here is the riverine Jordan forest, dominated mainly by the Euphrates poplar and the tamarisk, both of which tolerate a high degree of salinity. This forest, the biblical "jungle of the Jordan (Jeremiah 49:19), reaches the northern foreshore of the Dead Sea, where the land is vegetated by saline plants, extending to the steep slopes of the mountains on either side. From north of Jericho southward, a string of fresh-water springs and brooks empties into the Jordan and the Dead Sea, accounting for the great oases of Naaran, Faria, Jericho, Nimrim, En Gedi and Zoar. South of the Dead Sea, the broad, 180 km. long Aravah Valley runs between the mountains of the Negev in the west, and those of Moab and Edom in the east.

Its extremely variegated soil and microtopography are built up of desert pavement, sand fields and dunes, salines, and gravelly, fan-shaped wadi outlets. During the biblical era, sparsely settled by desert nomads, it was the valley along which the trade routes passed from the Red Sea harbors (Ezion Geber) to the country's inland centers.

THE PLATEAU

THE Transjordan Plateau is naturally divided into three significant latitudinal blocs: the Bashan, north of the Yarmukh River; Gilead and Moab, between the Yarmukh and the Zered Brook; and Edom, between Mt. Seir and the Gulf of Elath. The rivers traversing the blocs are the Yarmukh, the Yabok, the Arnon and the Zered, which flow into the Jordan, the Dead Sea and the Aravah Valley.

Transjordan's two highest peaks are remote from each other: the northernmost reaches a height of about 1,500 m. in the Golan and the southernmost 1,734 m. in Edom; the plateau in general exceeds in altitude that of the Cisjordanian ranges. A dominant characteristic of Edom is the overlay on the igneous massif of Nubian sandstone, which has created huge sandy deserts and the mighty layers of rocks from which Petra, the picturesque Nabatean capital, was carved.

3
The Sown Land and the Desert

THE occurrence of so great a number of plant communities in Israel, even within climatically uniform zones, is due to the great diversity of soil types and their properties.

The word *adamah*, occurring in the Bible over two hundred times, refers both to land and to soil. *Karka* indicates in the Bible only the ground floor of a building, although in post-biblical Hebrew it refers to soil as well.

While climatic diversity and concomitant seasonal and annual changes are conspicuous in many chapters and verses of the Bible, little mention is made of soil varieties, which are second in importance only to climate. Indeed, the country's soil is extremely variegated, ranging from deep, fine-grained, and very fertile, to dry stony desert. The dominant soil types of Israel are:

Terra Rossa, the commonest and most characteristic soil type in the Mediterranean part of the country. Derived from the hard limestones and dolomites of the Upper Cretaceous and the Eocene, and red to brown in color, it occurs in a number of varieties and is, on the whole, one of the most fertile soils, especially in the lowlands. Although shallow in the mountains, it supports most of the natural forests and woods.

Rendzina, a gray to grayish-white soil derived from soft chalky rocks or marls; it occurs with *terra rossa* and under the same climatic conditions. It has a high moisture capacity and is fairly fertile in a Mediterranean climate. It varies greatly in color and is agriculturally more workable than *terra rossa.*

Sandy Soils, limited to the Coastal Plain and consisting mainly of silica grains carried by onshore winds. They occur in a variety of forms, from calcareous sandstone and sandy clay, to sandfields and dunes. These are light soils, easily workable agriculturally.

Alluvial Soils, usually transported from the uplands by erosion or found in areas inundated by rivers. They are deep, heavy, and fine-grained, with a high moisture capacity, and are limited to plains and inter-mountain valleys. They are the most fertile soils in the country and have been intensively cultivated since ancient times.

Gray Steppe Soil, a semi-desert type, derived mainly from soft chalk where there is little rain, and especially characteristic of the eastern and southern margin of the regularly sown Mediterranean area. It also occurs in the western Judean Desert and the northern Negev, never supports arboreal vegetation and is uncultivable.

Loess Soil, confined chiefly to the northern Negev and southern Transjordan. Transported by dust storms from plantless regions and deposited in plains and inter-mountain valleys, it is the most valuable soil of the desert and in certain regions has been cultivated for millennia.

Hammada, a desert soil whose cover of coarse stones conceals a gray or brownish, stone-mixed earth, sometimes salty, sometimes altogether saltless. On the whole barren, it can, under special conditions, support a sparse growth of low shrubs.

Reg, a desert soil limited to the desert plains and valleys. Regs are vast, extreme desert flats, densely covered with angular rubble and pebbles. The soil beneath this stony cover is fine-grained, often rich in salt and gypsum. Its extreme dryness makes it absolutely sterile.

Swamps and Salines, both more or less richly vegetated by particular kinds of plants.

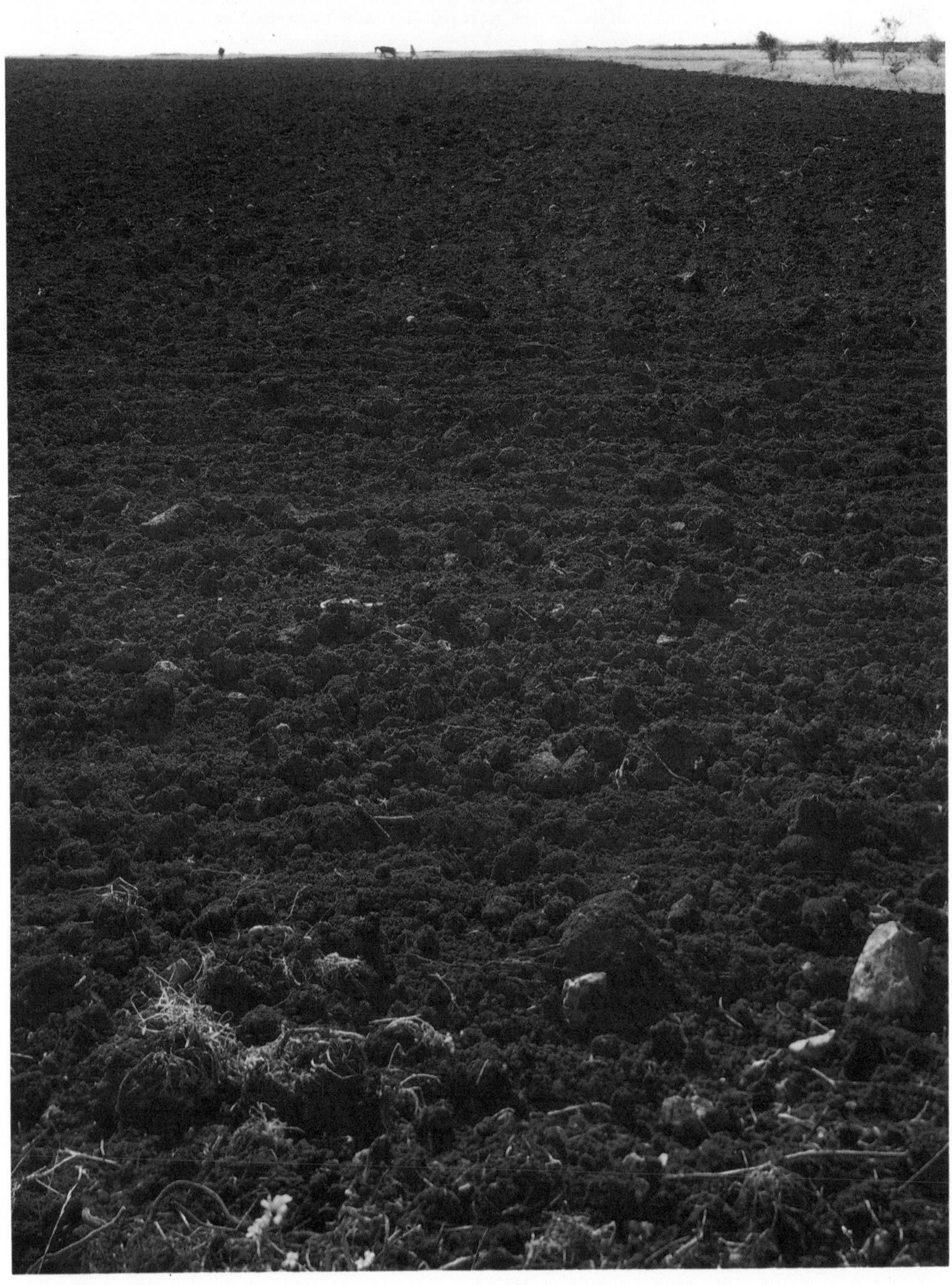

The highly fertile Terra Rossa soil in the northern lowlands of the country; red to brown in color, it is the commonest and most characteristic soil in the Mediterranean part of the Land.

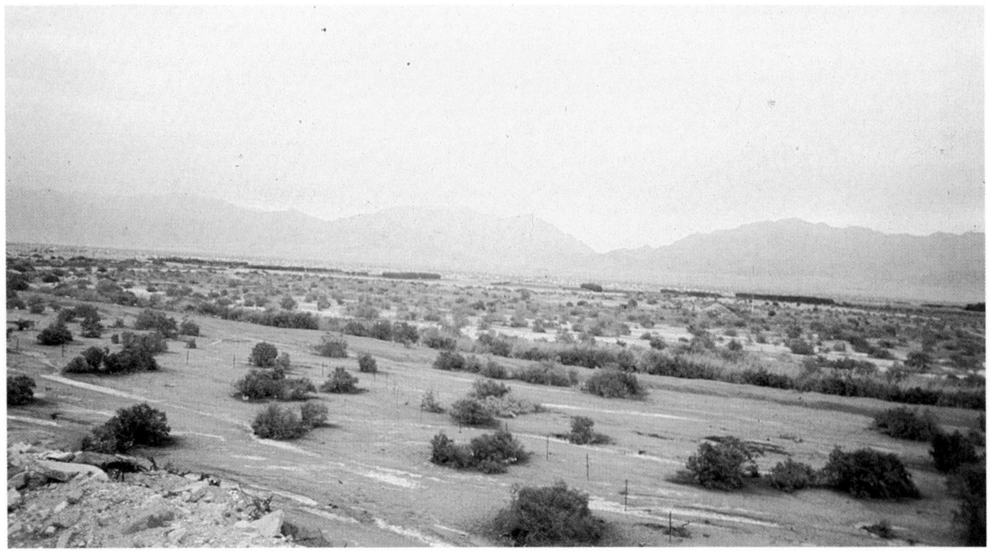

The 'salt land of the Bible' – part of the Aravah Valley south of the Dead Sea – displays a large, fairly dense tamarisk forest mingled with arthrocnemum, both typical of saline vegetation.

The mountains that separate the sown land and the desert; here, uncultivable gray steppe soil on the eastern slopes of the Judean mountains, descending from Jerusalem into the desert towards Jericho and the Dead Sea. On the hillock lies Jerusalem with Mt. Scopus on the right and the Mount of Olives in the center.

Shifting dunes in the Negev, caused by dust storms from plantless regions; these picturesque hills form one variety of the many sand soils, some of them light and easily workable agriculturally.

Deeply furrowed soil in the Esdraelon Valley in the north; heavy and fine-grained with a high moisture capacity, this alluvial soil - limited to plains and inter-mountain valleys - is the most fertile in the country and has been intensively cultivated since ancient times.

4
Seasons and Climate

THE topographical diversity of the Land is reflected in the extreme climatic differences, ranging from temperate sub-humid in the north to sub-tropical hyper-arid in the south. This and the drastic fluctuations of the climate have had such an impact on the individual and communal life of its people that rain and drought, heat and cold, figure in the Bible as central themes in poetry, proverbs, sermons, curses and blessings. Hunger and famine appear over a hundred times in the Bible and were clearly the most feared disaster. Indeed, the foremost factor in the climatic conditions in Israel is the precipitation of rain, so much so that in biblical times, when man's very existence hung upon the agricultural yields, precipitation could mediate between life and death.

Seasons. The country's climatic pattern is characteristically Mediterranean in the sense that the year is divided into two seasons: a mild and rainy winter, beginning with the first rain in October, and a hot and dry summer, beginning in May: "Cold and heat, summer and winter" (Genesis 8:22); Spring and autumn, being too brief, are seldom mentioned in the Bible as proper seasons.

The duration of the seasons and the quantity of rain change strikingly with latitude and altitude and from one year to another. In a country situated at the very rim of the Afro-Asian desert belt, precipitation is uncertain not only in amount but also in distribution. The 'sown' land and the 'desert' are separated by a belt changing in width from year to year; the Negev, generally considered a very dry desert, sometimes blooms – "like the crocus it shall blossom abundantly" (Isaiah 35:1–2) – whereas great portions of the sown land are sometimes rainless. While the mean annual rainfall in some places in Upper Galilee amounts to 1000 mm., it drops to 600 mm. and 700 mm. in Samaria and Judea; to 400 mm. in southern Judea and in the northern Negev to 200 mm.; while the southernmost Negev has an average of 25 mm. and may be rainless for several consecutive years. The amount of rainfall is not proportional to latitude. In the southern latitudes the curve of decrease is much steeper than in the northern part of Israel. Its instability in time, quantity and heaviness make rain the supreme local climatic element, as aptly expressed by the Bible: "but the land which you are going over to possess is a land of hills and valleys, which drinks water by the rain from heaven" (Deuteronomy 11:11).

Rain. The amount of annual rainfall has divided the country into wheat land and barley land. Barley cultivation can be maintained with a minimal rainfall of 200 mm., depending on stability. As a matter of fact, in areas where 200 mm. is the annual mean, only 50 mm. of rain may fall in one year and 400 mm. in another. Such irregularity is responsible for the frequency of drought and famine, and is the reason why wheat crops, which require at least 400 mm., ripen a month or more later than the barley. Accordingly, the sheaf of the first harvest – brought to the Temple at Passover – consisted of barley, while the wheat harvest was celebrated at Pentecost, seven weeks later.

Dew, another kind of precipitation, is deemed a heavenly blessing too, and is indeed vital for the maintenance of summer crops, especially in the Negev, the Coastal Plain and elsewhere, where about 250 annual dew-nights have been counted. The snow that falls almost every year on the Judean and Upper Galilean mountains, however scarce, also provides effective precipitation.

Temperature, although generally considered second only to rainfall in importance, has less influence on the climatic pattern and is therefore less frequently mentioned in the Bible as a vital factor. Nevertheless it is of major concern for seasonal harvests of field crops. The mean annual temperature varies widely from north to south. Its monthly mean drops in January, the coldest month, to 7°C in Galilee, 8°C in Jerusalem, 11°C in Beer Sheba and about 16°C in the Dead Sea area. Even more dramatic are the mean maxima in July, the hottest month, when temperatures range from 20°C to 38°C.

The very existence of tropical plants in our native flora and vegetation depends upon the high winter temperatures found here. The warm temperatures in the lower Jordan Valley, the Aravah Valley, and the Coastal Plain have fostered the growth of sub-tropical crops there since ancient times.

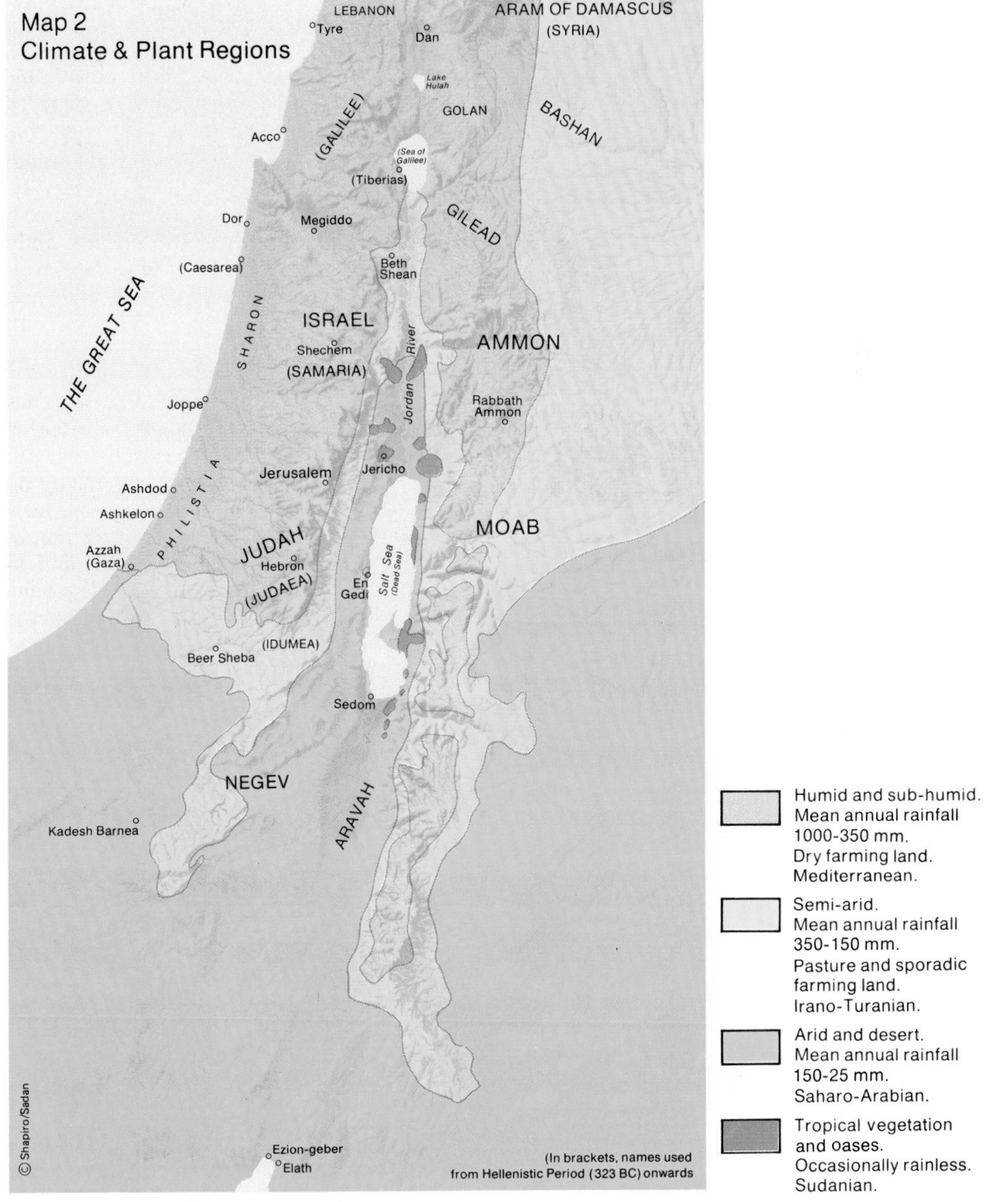

5

Vegetal Landscapes of Biblical Times

THE land of Israel harbors about 2,600 plant species, an extraordinary number considering the size of the area and the fact that roughly half of it is desert. It has therefore long attracted the attention of scholars in natural history, particularly during the last two centuries. There are four geographical elements in the flora: Mediterranean, Irano-Turanian (Oriental steppe), Saharan – all temperate – and Sudanian (tropical Sudanian-Zambesian). Each prevails in different areas, which are characterized by appropriate climatic conditions.

In view of the richness of local plant species in this country it is surprising to find no more than 110 plant names in the Bible, which might suggest that the biblical writers and the people they describe had little interest in their natural surroundings. This, however, is untrue. The Bible is perhaps the most pervaded with nature of all scriptures or ritual-historical works. We shall return later to the theme of response to and love of nature, and simply point out here that though the Bible is primarily concerned with plants associated with agriculture, religion and ritual, plants appear in the poetic and proverbial literature as well, and the biblical flora also includes a dozen or more plants used for healing, incense, and cosmetics. It should be stressed that even in ordinary non-professional secular literature, one does not find so high a proportion of reference to plants related to various aspects of life as that which appears in the Bible.

The main vegetal landscapes of the country, largely unchanged since biblical times, include forest, maquis, shrubbery, swamp, desert and saline. The Bible gives collective names to the various physiognomic plant formations: *yaar* and sometimes *ḥoresh* denote 'forest' and 'woodland', while *bathah* denotes 'shrubbery'. The number of tree species does not exceed three percent of the total flora; about half are deciduous, the remainder evergreen.

FOREST & WOODS

EVIDENCE that forests and woodland trees were much more abundant in the past than they are today is provided by some localities which bear the names of trees and forests but are now entirely devoid of arboreal vegetation, because forests were usually destroyed to extend agricultural areas.

Israel and the adjacent Lebanon were once the main source of wood for some of their timberless neighbors, as ancient documents dealing with the export of timber from Canaan amply demonstrate. Since then, however, the forests have largely been destroyed, but the vestiges that remain still preserve the principal characteristics of their remote past, and some forests known from biblical times still flourish today.

The Common Oak Forest is the most familiar and important type of local arboreal vegetation. Apart from the common oak itself (*Quercus calliprinos*), the dominant constituent of this type, there are the Palestine terebinth (*Pistacia palaestina*), the laurel (*Laurus nobilis*), the strawberry tree (*Arbutus andrachne*), the common hawthorn (*Crataegus aronia*), and the carob tree (*Ceratonia siliqua*).

Displaying a tremendous resistance to axe, fire, and animal browsing, this type of forest has managed to survive in part, despite the incessant destructive action of man and his flocks.

The common oak – of shrubby stature in the maquis – can under certain conditions grow to an impressive height and reach a remarkable

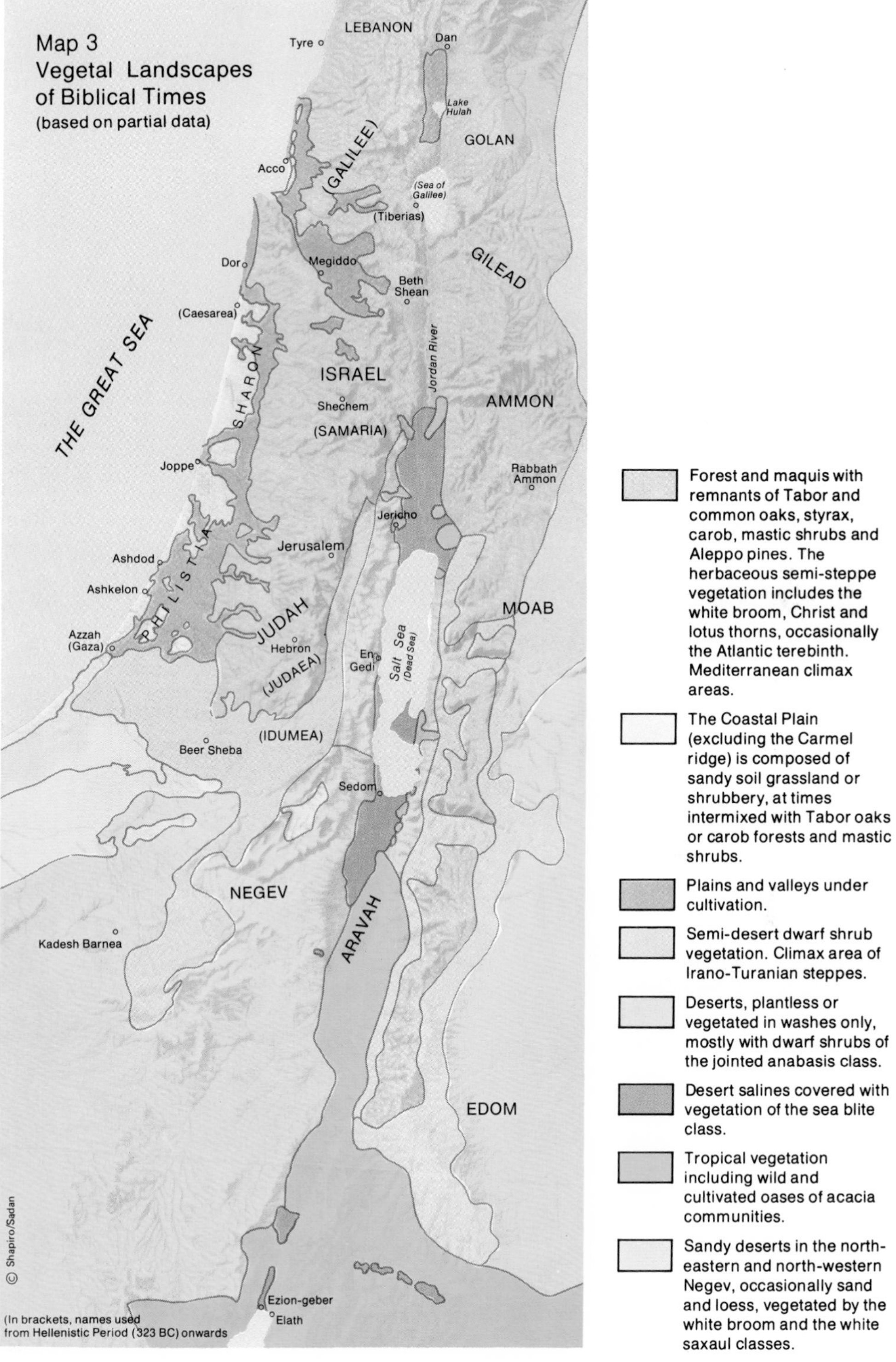
Map 3
Vegetal Landscapes of Biblical Times
(based on partial data)
LEBANON
Tyre
Dan
Lake Hulah
GOLAN
Acco
(GALILEE)
(Sea of Galilee)
(Tiberias)
Dor
Megiddo
Beth Shean
GILEAD
(Caesarea)
THE GREAT SEA
SHARON
Jordan River
ISRAEL
Shechem
(SAMARIA)
AMMON
Joppe
Rabbath Ammon
Jericho
Jerusalem
PHILISTIA
Ashdod
Ashkelon
MOAB
Azzah (Gaza)
JUDAH
Hebron
(JUDAEA)
En Gedi
Salt Sea (Dead Sea)
Beer Sheba
(IDUMEA)
Sedom
NEGEV
ARAVAH
Kadesh Barnea
EDOM
© Shapiro/Sadan
Ezion-geber
Elath
(In brackets, names used from Hellenistic Period (323 BC) onwards
Forest and maquis with remnants of Tabor and common oaks, styrax, carob, mastic shrubs and Aleppo pines. The herbaceous semi-steppe vegetation includes the white broom, Christ and lotus thorns, occasionally the Atlantic terebinth. Mediterranean climax areas.
The Coastal Plain (excluding the Carmel ridge) is composed of sandy soil grassland or shrubbery, at times intermixed with Tabor oaks or carob forests and mastic shrubs.
Plains and valleys under cultivation.
Semi-desert dwarf shrub vegetation. Climax area of Irano-Turanian steppes.
Deserts, plantless or vegetated in washes only, mostly with dwarf shrubs of the jointed anabasis class.
Desert salines covered with vegetation of the sea blite class.
Tropical vegetation including wild and cultivated oases of acacia communities.
Sandy deserts in the north-eastern and north-western Negev, occasionally sand and loess, vegetated by the white broom and the white saxaul classes.

Most of the Coastal Plain looks like these sand plains; at Caesarea they display a kind of savannah forest dominated by the conspicuous carob tree and the mastic pistacia (above).

The dense oak forest in the northern part of the Hill Country - here, the western Galilee - enjoys the highest amount of rainfall and is therefore the most fertile (left).

Under the extremely arid climate and the poor soil in this desert land - Mt. Ramon in the central Negev - only widely scattered dwarf shrubs and herbs of desolate monotony can grow, such as these low bushes of white wormwood providing the background for the more conspicuous Atlantic terebinth (below).

Rich riverine vegetation along the banks of a Jordan rivulet, just before it empties into the northeastern waters of the Sea of Galilee. Dominant among these water plants is the oleander (pink flowers in the background). In front of the oleander are the ever-present reeds, and in the foreground the dark green bushes of the scentic mint.

On the edge of the desert, a typical dwarf-shrubbery, the most striking feature in the Mediterranean part of the Land. Here, on the eastern slopes of the Judean mountains on the way to Jericho, the thorny burnet is the dominant plant.

age. It was therefore widely revered or even deified. In its shade, the Hebrews of the past, and later the Arabs, buried their esteemed and beloved dead.

The Tabor Oak Forest is deciduous, limited to the Sharon, Lower Galilee, and the Ḥulah and Dan Valleys. It is dominated by a broad-leaved oak known as the Tabor oak. From its remnants, three varieties can be distinguished: the forest-park of the Sharon Plain, where the dispersed oaks were accompanied by a cover of grass reminiscent of a savannah; the oak in the Lower Galilee, accompanied by several arboreal components of the maquis, very often the styrax tree (*Styrax officinalis*); and in the Ḥulah-Dan Valley and on the adjacent mountain-slopes, the Atlantic terebinth (P. *atlantica*), the principal cohabitant of the Tabor oak. Both trees can attain great stature and relatively old age. They are the trees (*allon* = oak; *elah* = terebinth) which so often in the Bible symbolize strength and splendor.

The Aleppo Pine Forest. Here the Aleppo pine (*Pinus halepensis*) predominates, mingling with a few species of the common oak maquis. This type of forest needs a soft, grayish-white chalky soil and was once much more common. Remnants can be found in Galilee, Samaria, and Judea, as well as in Gilead, and there are still fairly large stands on Mt. Carmel.

Carob and Mastic Pistacia Scrub Forests. A type of evergreen scrub forest, dominated by the carob tree (*Ceratonia siliqua*) and the mastic pistacia bush (*Pistacia lentiscus*), grows in the foothills west of the mountain range, from Judea to the border of Lebanon, on the clay hills of calcareous sandstone (*kurkar*) and consolidated sand dunes of the northern Sharon, as well as on some of the eastern slopes of the mountains of Galilee and Samaria. This scrub forest, which usually climbs the mountains no higher than 300 m., has in some places been totally destroyed; in others the carob tree alone has been spared for its fruit, edible by man and cattle.

These forests and scrub forests are the characteristic feature of Mediterranean vegetation, and formed originally a more or less continuous arboreal mantle. But since the soil and climate of the area have always been suitable for permanent agriculture, man has persistently interfered with the natural vegetation, mainly in order to expand his farming and pasture area, but also to obtain building materials and fuel for his fire. Some woods have nevertheless survived by virtue of natural conditions and the sturdiness of the trees, which regenerate after cutting and burning. Where man refrains from damaging them, natural rehabilitation takes place in successive stages, each stage producing vegetation of higher stature and different composition until a true forest or shrub forest emerges.

Hydrophytic Vegetation. Swamps and river-banks are centered mainly on the Coastal Plain and in the Jordan Valley, and abound in water plants. Some dominant ones among them are the reed (*Phragmites australis*), papyrus (*Cyperus papyrus*), clammy inula (*Inula viscosa*), prickly sea rush (*Juncus acutus*), bramble bush (*Rubus sanguineus*), oleander (*Nerium oleander*), etc. On the banks of permanent rivers, riverine forest vegetation comprises species of willow (*Salix*) and oriental plane tree (*Platanus orientalis*). Particularly notable are the banks of the Jordan with remnants of thick forests of Euphrates poplar (*Populus euphraticus*) and tamarisk (*Tamarix spp.*).

SHRUBBERIES

Dwarf Shrubbery *(bathah).* The most important phase in the process of re-establishing primary vegetation after its devastation by man is the appearance of a dwarf-shrub formation. This biblical *bathah* soon covers deforested or abandoned areas; it may exist for a longer or shorter period without the concomitant return of arboreal vegetation, which must await soil improvement; finally it is replaced by maquis or forests. Since forest destruction continues unabated, the dwarf-shrub takes up more and more space and eventually becomes the most striking vegetal feature in the Mediterranean part of Israel. Leading the several plant communities of the *bathah* is the thorny burnet (*Sarcopoterium spinosum*). Another group of dwarf-shrubs not associated with the above burnett leads communities of its own. Legions of annual plants with colorful flowers and many grasses of the dwarf-shrubbery bloom in the rainy season.

Besides typical Mediterranean dwarf-shrubberies, the eastern and southern limits of the Mediterranean area produce a kind of herbaceous *bathah* which is fairly rich in species but is scantier, has fewer shrubs, and can never develop into arboreal vegetation. It is a semi-steppe formation, also harboring species which have penetrated from the adjacent steppe.

Sand Vegetation. A belt of light soil, mainly composed of sand, spreads all along the Coastal Plain. Its special vegetation is dominated by shrubs – perennial herbs and grass – able to inhibit the movement of the sand, like marram grass (*Ammophila arenaria*), white broom (*Retama raetam*), Palestine knotweed (*Polygonum palaestinum*) and wormwood (*Artemisia*). These plants live with many other annuals and perennials adapted to the extreme conditions of on-shore winds and soil movement. When the sand is stabilized and the soil consolidated, the carob and mastic pistachia scrub forest finally take possession in the middle and northern parts of the coastal belt.

Behind the sand dunes are broad stretches of sandy clay and hills of calcareous sandstone, where special plant communities of shrubs, dwarf-shrubs and many sand-favoring herbs grow. The sandy clay ground is characterized by a community of the bipinnate spring grass (*Desmostachya bipinnata*), which comprises dozens of annual species, and often includes scattered trees of the Tabor oak.

DESERT VEGETATION

Steppe and Desert Vegetation. About half of the Land is steppe and desert, which never, except under special conditions, maintain wood vegetation. Both the Irano-Turanian and the Saharo-Arabian territories are essentially pastureland and support no agriculture except in valleys and depressions, near river estuaries or on flooded beds of ephemeral wadis. Under the extreme climate and poor soil only widely scattered low bushes, dwarf-shrubs and herbs of desolate monotony can grow. A striking feature is the many tiny annuals which complete their life-cycle within the few weeks of the rainy season. Perennial plants are fewer in number and are mostly equipped with physiological and anatomical means for withstanding the drought of the long summer.

The steppes and deserts of the country can be classified according to the type of soil on which their vegetation depends.

Gray-Soil Steppes. Close to the southern and eastern borders of the Mediterranean territory are areas of gray calcareous soil containing no injurious salts. The chief feature of the vegetation is the white wormwood (*Artemisia herba-alba*), accompanied by other low and mostly gray dwarf-shrubs and, in the spring, by numerous annuals. This type characterizes the western part of the Judean Desert and the northern and central Negev.

Loess Steppes. Stretches of loess soil, especially in the plains and valleys of the northern Negev, encourage a particular segetal vegetation – weeds together with field crops – dominated by santolina milfoil (*Achillea santolina*). Within it are numerous other weeds found nowhere else in the country. Where the loess is not cultivated, a blackish-green dwarf-shrub, the black hammada (*Hammada scoparia*), dominates much of the steppe.

Gravel Deserts. These comprise wide areas of the central and southern Negev, where vegetation is extremely poor and largely confined to runnels and wadi beds that cross the plains. In these areas the gravelly hills and their slopes display scattered bean caper bushes (*Zygophyllum dumosum*), associated with a few other dwarf-shrubs and herbs, or are altogether plantless. The banks of the dry riverbeds and depressions are dominated by the community of jointed anabasis (*Anabasis articulata*), shaggy sparrow-wort (*Passerina hirsuta*), white broom (*Retama raetam*), tamarisk (*Tamarix*), and other plants. The dry soil of the slopes in some parts of the Judean Desert and elsewhere is high in gypsum and other salts and is poorly and sparsely vegetated, mainly by succulent dwarf-shrubs like the Dead Sea blite (*Suaeda asphaltica*), chenolea (*Chenolea*), reaumuria (*Reaumuria*), and the bluish-green orache (*Atriplex glauca*).

Sand Deserts. The sand-dune belt of the western Negev joins that of the Mediterranean territory, but because of low precipitation, the plant cover is poorer. Apart from sand wormwood (*Artemisia monosperma*) and white broom bushes, such perennial grasses as the triple-awned grass (*Stipagrostis scoparia*),

One of the string of oases punctuating the desert region of the Jordan and Aravah Valleys; this wild oasis of date palms and tamarisks, in the Aravah, adheres to the mouth of a brackish river.

Pennisetum divisum and the turgid panic grass (*Panicum turgidum*) grow in thick clumps. In the western Negev, the loess is covered by a layer of sand which not only improves soil quality but retains more moisture, so that vegetation density increases accordingly and differs considerably in composition from that of the dunes. In the Aravah Valley, the vegetation of the dunes (which are derived mainly from the weathered Nubian sandstone) consists of bushes and small trees, like white saxaul (*Haloxylon persicum*), white hammada (*Hammada salicornica*), caligonum (*Caligonum comosum*), and white broom.

The Salines. Although saline soils also occur in the coastal territory, they are characteristic of the deserts. Found mainly in the Aravah Valley and the lower Jordan Valley, their presence is caused by drainless basins, high ground-water levels, and saline springs. The most important plants of the Aravah salines include many species of tamarisk, shrubby blite (*Suaeda fruticosa*), arthrocnemum (*Arthrocnemum*) and saltwort (*Salsola*). In the flood regions north and south of the Dead Sea there is a large, fairly dense tamarisk forest characteristic of salines. Considerable areas exist, however, in which the salt concentration (mainly sodium chloride) is so great that no plant can grow. This is the 'Salt-land' (*Eretz mleḥah*) of the Bible.

The Tropical Vegetation of the Aravah and Jordan Valleys. The string of oases punctuating the desert region of the Jordan and Aravah Valleys contains about a dozen tropical tree species, which because they need a high temperature and humidity adhere to the mouths of tributaries of these valleys. Among them are acacia (*Acacia*), ban tree (*Moringa*), toothbrush tree (*Salvadora persica*), and the Jericho balsam (*Balanites aegyptiaca*). Besides these, many tropical annuals and perennials grow in wadi beds, rock crevices, and other sites. Species of lavender (*Lavendula*), cassia (*Cassia*), rattlebox (*Crotolaria*), hoary pea (*Tephrosia*), cenchrus (*Cenchrus*), ginger grass (*Cymbopogon*), rose mallow (*Hibiscus*), Indian mallow (*Abutilon*), caperbush (*Capparis*), cleome (*Cleome*), morettia (*Morettia*), etc., can all be found there.

6
Agriculture in the Bible

CULTIVATED LANDSCAPES

MAN'S interference with nature is as old as man himself. For more than half a million years he has roamed the Near East, and within this enormous span, he must, however few his numbers, have markedly altered the composition and dominance of some parts of the local vegetation, by the daily use of plants for his livelihood.

The 8,000 to 10,000 years that have elapsed since the invention of agriculture have sufficed to destroy or devastate much of the original vegetation from many areas which lent themselves to agriculture. The great fertile plains, and even smaller areas in the inter-mountain valleys, were the first to be materially affected. The non-arable land was also seriously damaged both by man and by his domesticated animals in their continuous cuttings, grazings, and burnings. Nor is the present desert vegetation in its primary composition, for it too has been grievously used. The heedless removal of shrubs and trees from the mountain slopes and the torrential rains have in many places eroded the soil to the point of leaving the rocks bare.

But all this has not totally affected the basic pattern of the primary vegetation. Vestiges of forest and other plant formations have remained here and there as indications of the past plant cover, or have been preserved by the local population, which since ancient times has admired and deified trees and buried their honored dead in the woods or under a single majestic tree. These scattered trees or stands, sometimes conspicuous for the pieces of cloth hung on their branches by visiting Arabs, reveal to botanists the type of past vegetation in areas which are now completely timberless.

Hundreds of wild plants provided the elements of man's diet many millennia before the invention of agriculture. This land was surely among the countries which participated in the domestication of cultivated plants and animals. Remnants of cultivation dating back to the seventh millennium BC have been found in Jericho, Mt. Carmel and elsewhere. Thus, by the time of the Bible, a long series of agricultural plants was already flourishing throughout the Middle East. Moreover, Israel and the neighboring countries are the home of a score or so of ancestors of cultivated plants – among them bread plants, pulses and fruit trees – which have largely influenced the history of man and his culture. The date palm and the olive tree have been known here from the fourth millennium BC. At the period of the Exodus, the Land of Canaan was a thriving agricultural country blessed not only with the biblical 'seven species' but with many others, mentioned or not mentioned in the Bible.

AGRICULTURE IN THE BIBLE

SCARCELY does any other ancient book offer so rich and vivid a picture of agricultural life as the Bible. Besides numerous rituals and social and agrarian laws, in themselves testimony to high cultural standards, a number of popular customs were linked with agriculture as man's central and daily occupation. The social structure, livelihood, and domestic life of the ancient Israelite family revolved almost exclusively around agriculture, whose various activities are frequently mentioned in biblical parables. Words connected with 'root', 'fruit', 'seed', 'harvest', 'blossom' and so on provide endless metaphors, as in, for example, Psalms 92:7; Proverbs 22:8, 31:16; Jeremiah 31:29; Ezekiel 34:31; Hosea 8:7, 10:1; and Amos 6:12.

The cultivated landscape of the first centuries of the post-biblical era remained much the same as in the biblical period. Some tracts of the

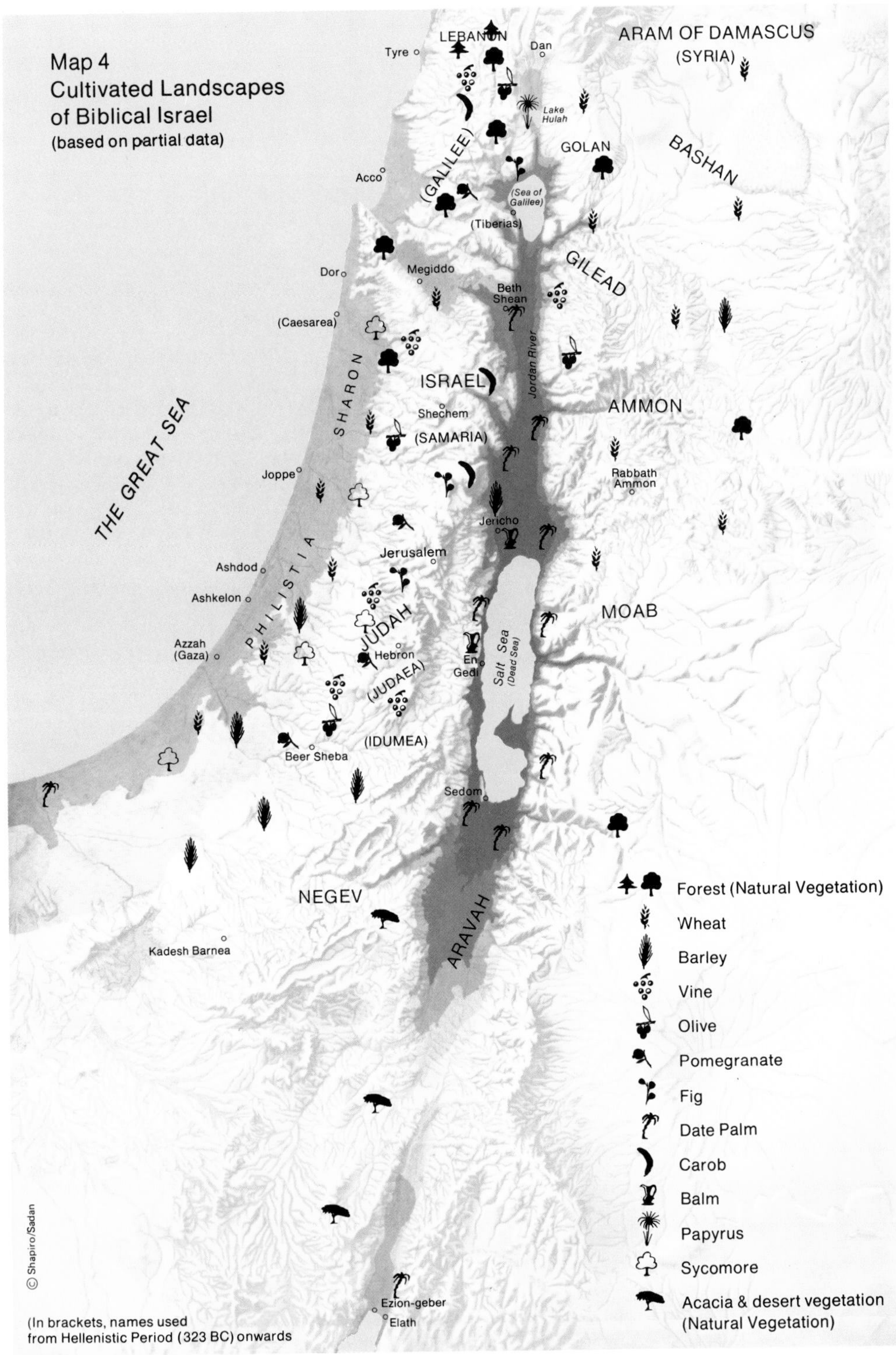

Map 4
Cultivated Landscapes
of Biblical Israel
(based on partial data)
LEBANON
Tyre
Dan
ARAM OF DAMASCUS
(SYRIA)
Lake
Hulah
GOLAN
BASHAN
Acco
(GALILEE)
(Sea of
Galilee)
(Tiberias)
GILEAD
Dor
Megiddo
Beth
Shean
(Caesarea)
Jordan River
SHARON
ISRAEL
Shechem
(SAMARIA)
AMMON
THE GREAT SEA
Joppe
Rabbath
Ammon
Jericho
Jerusalem
Ashdod
Ashkelon
PHILISTIA
JUDAH
MOAB
Azzah
(Gaza)
Hebron
En
Gedi
Salt Sea
(Dead Sea)
(JUDAEA)
(IDUMEA)
Beer Sheba
Sedom
NEGEV
ARAVAH
Kadesh Barnea
Ezion-geber
Elath
Forest (Natural Vegetation)
Wheat
Barley
Vine
Olive
Pomegranate
Fig
Date Palm
Carob
Balm
Papyrus
Sycomore
Acacia & desert vegetation
(Natural Vegetation)
(In brackets, names used
from Hellenistic Period (323 BC) onwards
© Shapiro/Sadan

"You shall not plow with an ox and an ass together" (Deuteronomy 22:10).

Traditional agriculture in Judea and Samaria still makes use of the same age-old methods as in the early days of the Land of Israel; a pair of oxen draws a wooden plow with a metal blade, the seeds are sown by hand and reaped with a sickle, the crops are threshed with a threshing sledge and winnowed with a hayfork.

A watchman's stone lodge in the orchards of the Judean mountains. Fruit tree orchards and vegetable gardens were cultivated on the terraced hill slopes. The ancient Hebrews achieved a high standard of terrace cultivation by improving the techniques for utilizing mountainous terrain (above, right).

"And they came to Bethlehem at the beginning of barley harvest" (Ruth 1:22).

"He is winnowing barley tonight at the threshing floor" (Ruth 3:2).

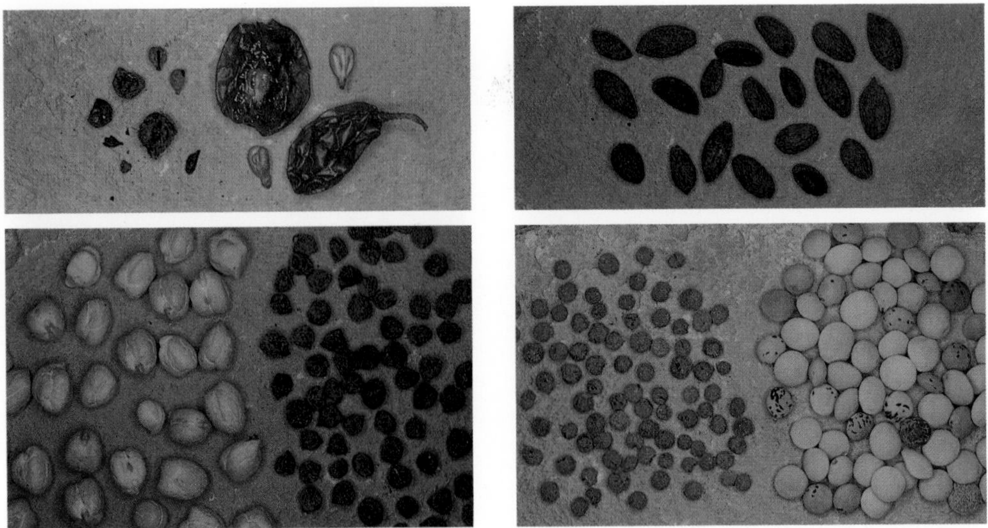

Carbonized remnants unearthed in archaeological excavations: raisins - Arad, Bronze Age (upper left); olives - Golan Heights, Chalcolithic Period (upper right); chick-peas - Arad, Bronze Age (lower left); lens - Arad, Bronze Age (lower right).

Grains of primitive cereals, very similar to those of biblical times, which can still be found in some fields in the Holy Land. Unlike the modern cereals, these grains still bear their shaft after threshing. From left to right, the ripe grains of barley, emmer wheat and einkorn wheat.

Talmud constitute a major source of information here, especially *Zeraim*, whose discussion of agricultural law and rituals discloses the strongly differentiated methods of cultivation and crop treatment then current.

The standard of biblical agriculture seems to have been relatively high, as indicated by the rich vocabulary of terms designating crop habitats: *kerem* (vineyard, olive grove), *gan* (garden), *ginah* (vegetable garden), *pardes* and *mata* (orchard), *mikshah* (gourd-field), *sadeh, shdemah* (field), *nir* (arable land), and others. Even more striking is the abundance of botanical terms concerning the various parts of the plant and the clear distinctions between different kinds of stems, branches, flowers, and fruits – *anaf, bad, zmorah, sarafah, ḥoter, netzer, shluḥah*, and *zalzal*, for example, are all terms for different kinds of branches.

Agriculture was based on dry-farming and fed by the winter rains which sustained not only the winter crops but also some summer crops. There must also have been some irrigation in the non-rainy areas: "And Lot lifted up his eyes, and saw that the Jordan valley was well watered everywhere, like the garden of the Lord, like the Land of Egypt" (Genesis 13:10). The agricultural inventory was not rich but was adequate to sustain life's needs, especially since the non-arable mountains provided abundant pasture for stock. Such bi-seasonal dry-farming was for millennia the main form of agriculture in most Mediterranean countries and still predominates in the Arab villages in Israel. After the exile and return (c. 597–515 BC), agriculture flourished again in Judea and in Galilee; orchards, vineyards and grainfields were spread in new areas. The precious balm tree growing in En Gedi and Jericho was in great demand and exported to many countries.

The cultivated flora consisted of plants domesticated *in loco* or in nearby countries, like wheat, barley, lentil, pea, fig, olive, carob, date palm, sycamore, and plants introduced from fairly remote countries, like the pomegranate, walnut, vine, apple, mulberry, and pistachio. Quite a number of plants have never grown in the Land, but were imported as drugs or spices – like nard, myrrh, galbanum, cinnamon, saunders, and others.

Field crops consisted of winter cereals, mainly wheat (emmer and durum wheat) in the rainier areas, and barley in semi-arid parts and run-in valleys of the desert. Of the summer cereals, a single crop is mentioned in the Bible, presumably a kind of sorghum (*doḥan*), which thrives well even in the mountains, without irrigation. While the area was the home of wheat and barley, sorghum was introduced from Egypt along with melons. The rendition of *doḥan* as 'millet' is less plausible.

Cereal fields, on terraces of the mountain slopes and in inter-mountain valleys, were then as today the most salient features of the cultivated land. Some terraces were later ruined by desert herdsmen, and the natural vegetation, except for some trees and shrubs left to secure the stony terrace walls, was totally eradicated.

Gardens and Orchards. Next in importance to cereals were the pulses, often sown as field crops but also appearing in gardens near the houses. The Bible mentions lentils, broad beans, and chick-peas, but bitter vetch and garden peas as well as fenugreek were probably grown too; all of them most likely domesticated from native species in neighboring countries.

Vegetables were grown in small gardens near the houses with or without irrigation. They included a few species of the onion family (onion, leek, garlic) as well as coriander, cummin, and fitches, and condiments such as dill and a kind of mint (Matthew 23:23).

Although there were no root vegetables like turnips, beets or cabbages, the gardens may have had carrots, since *jizer* (a word retained in Arabic for 'carrot') is the name of a famous site in biblical Israel. Root salads and pot-herbs were and still are gathered by peasant women for home use and marketing. Scores of edible wild herbs still grow as in prehistoric times, despite continuous plucking.

The cultivated landscape was especially notable for its fruit-tree gardens. Each kind of fruit tree – date palm, olive, fig, walnut, almond, pomegranate, and sycamore – lends its unique shape and color to the landscape.

7

Trade: The Ancient Ways

ANCIENT Israel – with its harbors on two seas, the Mediterranean and the Red Sea, and the two great highways traversing its length – was a crossroads of international commerce connecting north, south and east and leading to the great kingdoms of the Orient. Known as the 'Via Maris', 'the Way of the Sea', passing Israel along the coast, and the 'King's Highway' crossing Transjordan, these transport routes through Israel extended to Assyria in the north, to Mesopotamia in the east, to Sheba, south of Arabia, in the south, and as far as Ophir in East Africa.

Long-distance trade in biblical times was a monopoly of kings and the trade routes were protected by royal strongholds. King David established the first bonds of commerce with Tyre, then a great maritime power. During the reign of King Solomon, Israel's wealth was primarily due to its control over the main transport routes between Egypt, Mesopotamia, and Assyria – the caravan routes from the oasis of Tadmor to the south of Arabia and the inland link between the Mediterranean and the Red Sea.

Through the flourishing commercial ties between King Solomon and King Hiram of Tyre Israel provided Tyre with wheat and oil in exchange for cedar and cypress wood, gold, brass and iron, and also skilled seamen to sail the fleet. The commercial relations of King Solomon with King Hiram, the Queen of Sheba, the King of the Hittites, and the kings of Egypt and other neighboring countries are extensively described in I Kings 9. After Solomon, other kings of Judah and Israel strove to maintain these commercial ties.

The Holy Land's main exports of cereals, olive oil, wine, honey, condiments, and wooden ware, some destined for Egypt, were shipped through the bustling international trade routes. Luxury commodities were imported: precious stones, drugs, copper, iron, lead and gold, ivory, frankincense, and other incenses.

Sea trade was carried through North African and East Mediterranean coastal countries. This busy sea-route was plied first by the Canaanites and later by the conquering Phoenicians, with whom Israel's trade was well developed. Also important were the trade ways passing through the Red Sea and further east to southern India, then a large center of commerce connecting the western and Far Eastern trade routes.

Of the trade routes which led from southern Arabia, biblical Ophir and Sheba, one has been extensively described by such scholars of the ancient Orient as Thomas (1932), Bowen-Albright (1958), and Van Beek (1960). This is the so-called 'Incense-Route'; along its busy ways precious drugs and every variety of frankincense, balm, myrrh, and other incenses were carried to the Land of Israel by camel caravans and further to the commercial centers in Egypt and the Fertile Crescent.

Another route, inland from Elam (Babylon) via Tadmor to Damascus and Gilead, seems to have been used to transport other kinds of merchandise, including nuts and tragacanth: "Then they sat down to eat; and looking up they saw a caravan of Ishmaelites coming from Gilead, with their camels bearing gum, balm, and myrrh, on their way to carry it down to Egypt" (Genesis 37:25).

Local trade was limited to agricultural products and locally manufactured domestic utensils. Inland routes were traversed by camels and donkeys. Markets for retail trade were often located at the town and city gates and wares were probably displayed on stalls, as they still are in oriental markets.

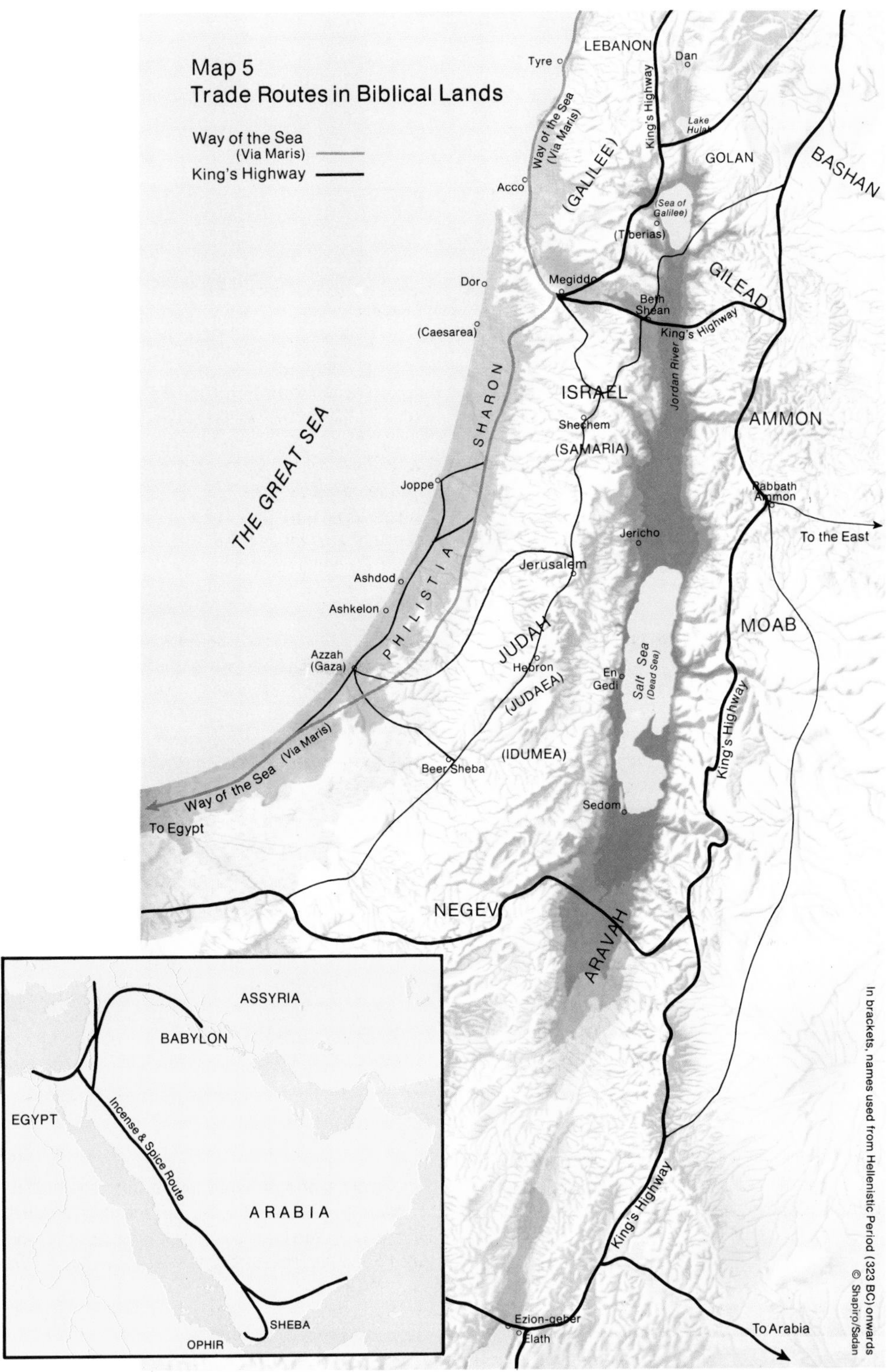
Map 5
Trade Routes in Biblical Lands
Way of the Sea
(Via Maris)
King's Highway
LEBANON
Tyre
Dan
Way of the Sea (Via Maris)
King's Highway
Lake Hula
(GALILEE)
GOLAN
BASHAN
Acco
(Sea of Galilee)
(Tiberias)
GILEAD
Megiddo
Dor
Beth Shean
King's Highway
(Caesarea)
Jordan River
SHARON
ISRAEL
AMMON
Shechem
THE GREAT SEA
(SAMARIA)
Joppe
Rabbath Ammon
Jericho
To the East
Jerusalem
Ashdod
PHILISTIA
Ashkelon
MOAB
JUDAH
Azzah
(Gaza)
Hebron
En Gedi
Salt Sea
(Dead Sea)
(JUDAEA)
King's Highway
(IDUMEA)
Beer Sheba
Way of the Sea (Via Maris)
Sedom
To Egypt
NEGEV
ARAVAH
ASSYRIA
BABYLON
EGYPT
Incense & Spice Route
ARABIA
SHEBA
OPHIR
King's Highway
Ezion-geber
Elath
To Arabia
In brackets, names used from Hellenistic Period (323 BC) onwards
© Shapiro/Sadan

Some ancient coins bear motifs from the plant world. Left: three ears of barley, representing the bounty of the land, are depicted on a bronze coin minted in Jerusalem during the reign of Agrippa I (42 AD). Right: the date palm was so strongly established as a symbol for the people of Israel that after conquering the Land, the Romans minted several bronze coins depicting a mourning woman seated under a palm, symbolizing the fallen Jewish state and bearing the inscription *IVDAEA CAPTA* (Judea in Captivity). This coin was minted by Vespasian (71 AD) after the destruction of the Second Temple.

The domestication of the camel (c. 13th century BC) made available a most useful means of travel and transport over long distances inland. A steady, slow-moving animal especially suited to level ground and sands, the camel easily adapts itself to severe desert conditions and has therefore been acclaimed as 'the ship of the desert'. Camel caravans played an important role in the import of perfumes, balms and spices from southern Arabia, and promoted commercial ties among the ancient kingdoms of the Fertile Crescent, contributing particularly to the legendary riches of biblical Ophir and Sheba.

8
Plants in Religion and Worship

RARELY has an ancient nation attributed holiness to so many plants as did the Hebrews during the biblical period. Scripture abounds with rites, feasts, and commands associated with plants and their cultivation. Numerous passages indicate that trees and woods were used as places of worship (Deuteronomy 12:2, 16:21; II Kings 16:4, 17:10. to name a few).

The first reference to plants as God's creatures is in the first chapter of the first book of the Bible: "And God said, 'Let the earth put forth vegetation, plants yielding seed, and fruit trees bearing fruit in which is their seed, each according to its kind'" (Genesis 1:11).

Mighty and aged trees were adored and deified, serving as symbols of godliness and divine power. The Hebrew *allon* (oak) and *elah* (terebinth) are identical or cognate with the words for 'god' and 'goddess' and are probably the source of the post-biblical collective designation *ilan* for 'tree'. Perhaps the crowning example of the association of plants with holiness is embodied in the story of the 'burning bush' (Exodus 3:2-6), where God made his revelation to Moses (see 'Senna Bush').

The tasks of the sages of the cities were performed in the trees' shade, judgement was passed there (Judges 6:11; I Kings 13:14), and kings were enthroned. Later trees (or in desert places, shrubs) also served for the burial-sites of great figures (I Chronicles 10:12). Some communities still gather by holy trees to conduct memorial services and to pray.

The ties with the plant world found their strongest expression in the timing of the three great festivals in accordance with the agricultural calendar. Passover (*Pesaḥ*) occurs in spring, when the barley begins to ripen and its first sheaves (*omer*) should be offered as a sacrifice (Leviticus 23:10).

Pentecost (*Shavuoth*), the 'harvest festival', occurs at the onset of summer, at the time of wheat harvest; and this was associated with the law of offering the first fruits (*bikurim*) to the Lord (Deuteronomy 26:2).

The third festival, called Tabernacles (*Sukkoth*), is the feast of 'ingathering of the fruit', occurring in the fall, when the fruit is picked and the agricultural cycle draws to its end (Exodus 34:22). It is at this feast that the Hebrews were commanded to take 'four species', as a symbol of thanksgiving to God for the fertility of the Land: "And you shall take on the first day the fruit of goodly trees, branches of palm trees, and boughs of leafy trees, and willows of the brook; and you shall rejoice before the Lord your God seven days" (Leviticus 23:40).

Many religious laws centered mainly around agriculture and its products. During the harvest season, fallen sheaves had to be left for the poor to collect and the corners of fields left unreaped for the same purpose. All crops, fruits, and land's yield were tithed for the priests, for maintaining the Temple. From a service to the priests and their households, this later became a compulsory gift to the poor. Other laws of a more ecological nature were those which forbade the collection of fruit during the first three years after planting and the crossbreeding of different species, and established every seven years the *Shmittah*, a Sabbatical year in which cultivation was prohibited so that the natural yield of the land should be free to every one and the land itself might rest.

An important religious role was also attached to incenses, prepared from costly resins, balms and other drugs produced from trees and shrubs mostly imported from far-away countries.

A Palm Sunday procession in Jerusalem, rooted in an ancient tradition arising from the welcome the people of Jerusalem gave Jesus on his entry to the city: "So they took branches of palm trees and went out to meet him, crying, "Hosanna! Blessed is he who comes in the name of the Lord, even the King of Israel!" (John 12:13).

The Feast of Tabernacles offers thanksgiving to God for the bounteous yield of the earth. The Israelites were commanded to take 'four species': "And you shall take on the first day the fruit of goodly trees, branches of palm trees, and boughs of leafy trees, and willows of the brook; and you shall rejoice before the Lord your God seven days" (Leviticus 23:40). Here, a celebrating crowd at the Western Wall in Jerusalem; branches of the 'four species' are held together in dry palm brackets and lifted in prayer (right).

Mighty and aged trees were adored and deified as symbols of divine power, and also served as the burial-sites of great figures. Some communities still gather at holy trees to conduct memorial services and to pray. The cloths hanging on this tree are a tribute to a venerated Bedouin (below, right).

9
Plantlore and the Arts

INNUMERABLE biblical allusions, parables, and metaphors proclaim the vital significance of plants in the daily existence of the ancient Israelites and indicate how intimate was nature's proximity to man.

One of the profoundest expressions of this awareness is the sophisticated and poetic parable of Jotham: "Then all the trees said to the bramble, 'Come you, and reign over us.' And the bramble said to the trees, 'If in good faith you are anointing me king over you, then come and take refuge in my shade; but if not, let fire come out of the bramble and devour the cedars of Lebanon!'" (Judges 9:14–15).

Similarly impressive is the song of the vineyard in Isaiah 5:1–2: "My beloved had a vineyard on a very fertile hill. He digged it and cleared it of stones, and planted it with choice vines; he built a watchtower in the midst of it, and hewed out a wine vat in it; and he looked for it to yield grapes, but it yielded wild grapes"; while the Song of Solomon, included in the canon only after a long dispute, provides clear evidence of the existence of a body of folk songs, pastoral love-tales and plantlore outside of Scripture but sung and recounted in secular life. This book, comprising a string of dialogue fragments between a loving couple, a shepherd and a shepherdess, or a prince and a princess, is charged with emotion, fragrance and beauty, arising in part from the charm lilies, roses, balms and costly perfumes held for the ancients.

Numerous Hebrew proper names are taken from the plant world, including *Elah* (terebinth), *Allon* (oak), *Assa* and *Hadassah* (myrtle), *Oren* (laurel), *Bosmath* (balm), *Dilan* (gourd), *Diklah* (palm), *Tamar* (date palm), *Zait* (olive), *Livneh* (a derivation of styrax), and *Kotz* (thorn). Towns, villages and districts were also named for trees, shrubs, herbs, and parts of plants.

Trees and fruits lent themselves as symbols of beauty and bounty: "The righteous flourish like the palm tree, and grow like a cedar in Lebanon" (Psalms 92:12). Peace and prosperity were expressed by tranquil picturesque scenes: "But they shall sit every man under his vine and under his fig tree" (Micah 4:4).

The candelabrum of the Tabernacle, in the earliest days of the Israelites, had six branches carved as flowers; the priestly garments had a pomegranate pattern running along the hem. At the Temple itself, visited at each festival, the candelabrum (as in the Tabernacle) was modeled on the shape of a tree with a trunk and lateral branches bearing buds and flowers and ornamented with almonds. Trees were planted in the Temple court (Psalms 92:13) and all the furniture, ornaments, and decorations in King Solomon's temple were made of costly wood. At the portico of the Second Temple, renovated and elaborated by King Herod, was a golden vine whose clusters reached the height of a man. Synagogues dating from the first centuries AD have been found decorated with motifs of plants, leaves, flowers and fruit on their friezes, lintels, pillars, and mosaic floors. One such synagogue shows a zodiac with the four seasons, a basket of fruits, *ethrog* (citron), *lulav* (palm branch), vine leaves and tendrils, and olive leaves, side by side with traditional ritual implements such as the candelabrum and the *shofar* (ram's horn). Floral designs, olive twigs, clusters of grapes, figs, pomegranates, and palms occur on ossuaries and sarcophagi from the last centuries BC and the first centuries AD.

Nor were plant motifs reserved only for solemn or religious occasions. They have been discovered on the decorated floors and tiles of royal palaces and wealthy homes. Plants even entered into the world of commerce, for first-century coins bear the images of barley, pomegranates, palms and grapes.

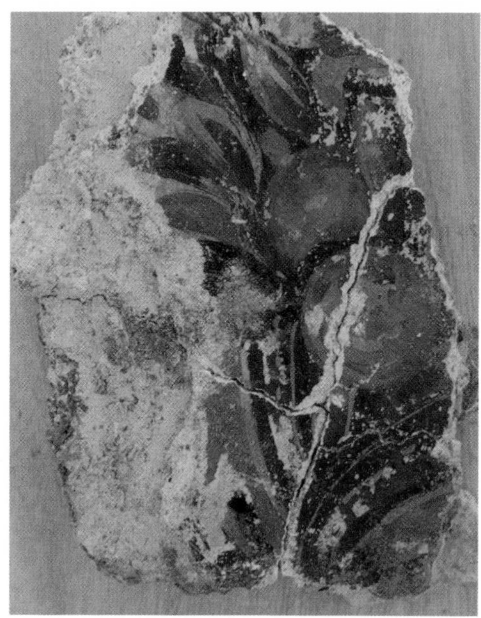

Motifs drawn from the plant world were often used for ornamenting everyday utensils. This pottery oil lamp, found in a burial cave south of Jerusalem (c. 70–135 AD), displays symmetrical grape clusters and vine leaves. The two branches near the handle are probably those of a palm tree (above, left).

A rare and well-preserved fragment of a thin plaster fresco, showing pomegranates and leaves. This slab, together with others, was unearthed in a house excavated in the Upper City of Jerusalem (Herodian Period, 1st century BC). The novelty of these fragments lies in the choice of motifs from the plant world, depicted in particularly lively colors (above, right).

The remnants of stone reliefs found in the synagogue of Capernaum – one of the most splendidly designed synagogues of the Galilee – depict, apart from the traditional Jewish ritual vessels, many motifs drawn from the plant world. Among these are clusters of grapes, figs, pomegranates, palm branches and dates, flowers, tendrils, garlands and branches. One of these richly decorated friezes is ornamented with acanthus leaves and various floral shapes, notably the recurring six-petaled rosette. All the leaves are spread flatly over the surface, giving a lace-like effect (c. 2nd century AD).

Part Two
ALL THE PLANTS IN THE BIBLE

1
Fruit Trees

FRUIT trees and cereals were the chief agricultural crops in the time of the Bible. The two together often represented the blessing of God: "Then I will give you your rains in their season, and the land shall yield its increase, and the trees of the field shall yield their fruit" (Leviticus 26:4). Fruit was of special importance because it could be stored in times of plenty to assuage hunger in times of want; figs, dates and grapes could be dried and olives processed. Widely consumed were the various by-products of fruit, such as wine - made from grapes and pomegranates - and honey, made from dates, figs, and grapes. Dried fig cake was very popular. Also common in the market were pistachios and almonds.

Poetry and song celebrate trees and their fruit, which symbolize prosperity and peace. The date palm was so strongly established as a symbol for the people of Israel that after conquering the land, the Romans issued coins showing a mourning woman underneath a palm - *Judea Capta* (Judea in Captivity). Small wonder, then, that it was forbidden to cut down fruit trees: "When you besiege a city for a long time, making war against it in order to take it, you shall not destroy its trees by wielding an axe against them; for you may eat of them, but you shall not cut them down" (Deuteronomy 20:19).

Vine

Vitis vinifera L.

For the Lord your God is bringing you into a good land, a land of brooks of water, of fountains and springs, flowing forth in valleys and hills, a land of wheat and barley, of *vines* and fig trees and pomegranates, a land of olive trees and honey.

Deuteronomy 8:7–8

Behold, the days are coming, says the Lord, when the plowman shall overtake the reaper and the treader of *grapes* him who sows the seed; the mountains shall drip sweet wine, and all the hills shall flow with it.

Amos 9:13

I am the true *vine*, and my Father is the vinedresser. Every branch of mine that bears no fruit, he takes away, and every branch that does bear fruit he prunes, that it may bear more fruit.

John 15:1–2

FROM the dawn of man's history the vine and its fruit were widely cultivated in the Old Testament world: "Noaḥ was the first tiller of the soil. He planted a vineyard" (Genesis 8:20). The high standard of viticulture in Canaan prior to the Israelite conquest is evident from the story of the spies sent by Moses to explore the land, returning with "a cluster of grapes and they carried it on a pole between the two of them" (Numbers 13:23). In those early days wine, the choicest of drinks, was offered to honored guests: "Melchizedek King of Salem [Jerusalem] brought out bread and wine to Abram" (Genesis 14:18).

The importance of viticulture in the Land of Israel during biblical times was manifested in the vintage season, a yearly feast of joy and gladness. The youth would then spread out in the vineyard, where, according to tradition, the girls selected their husbands, all celebrating in song and dance. Moreover, the prosperity of the Land is symbolized in the blessing of Judah: "Binding his foal to the vine and his ass's colt to the choice vine, he washes his garments in wine and his vesture in the blood of grapes" (Genesis 49:11–12).

So the vine became an image of bounty and the blessing of God in the future (Amos 9:13). On the other hand, the blessing of abundance could be reversed into a curse of desolation and national punishment, as indeed Isaiah prophesied: "And joy and gladness are taken away from the fruitful field; and in the vineyards no songs are sung, no shouts are raised; no treader treads out wine in the presses; the vintage shout is hushed" (Isaiah 16:10). Thus, the vine, one of the 'seven species' with which the Land was blessed, was regarded as a national emblem. It appeared on mosaic floors, murals, and portals of synagogues, on pottery, furniture, tombs and coins; even in exile, the Israelites still cherished the grapes of Judah, chiseling their shape on tombstones in foreign lands.

The identification of the Hebrew *gefen* with 'vine' is as unquestionable as *kerem* with 'vineyard' and *anavim* with 'grapes'. Innumerable words in the Bible are associated with planting, pruning, vintage and wine production, and various terms designate the parts of the plant and its fruit varieties.

In the New Testament, spiritual meanings are attributed to the vine, and the most significant of them is recorded in John when Jesus identifies himself with this plant.

The vine is a climbing shrub from whose base numerous slender branches sprout, straggling along the ground or climbing by means of long entwined tendrils. The plant simultaneously produces sterile and fertile branches, the latter growing so fast that they sometimes attain a length of two or four metres during a single season. Since they are too weak to support themselves and their heavy load of grapes, they are usually held up on sticks. The leaves, which are divided into five-toothed lobes, unfold in early spring and drop off late in summer. The minute, greenish flowers, in thickly branched clusters, shed their hood-like cover when they open. Pollination is induced by bees, which gather both pollen and nectar from the flowers. The fruit, whose color comes from the membranous skin but whose flesh itself is colorless, is a berry containing two seeds in each of its two cells. In the wild species, the berries are dispersed by birds.

The vine is one of the 50 species of the common *Vitis*, all of them indigenous to temperate regions. The species discussed here is native to southern Europe and was introduced into cultivation very early. Whereas viticulture was established in Israel, Syria and Egypt in the Early Bronze Age, pips of grapes have been discovered in northern Greece from as early as 4500 BC, possibly offshoots of the wild vine species *Vitis sylvestris* native to the southern European countries, altogether unknown in ancient Israel.

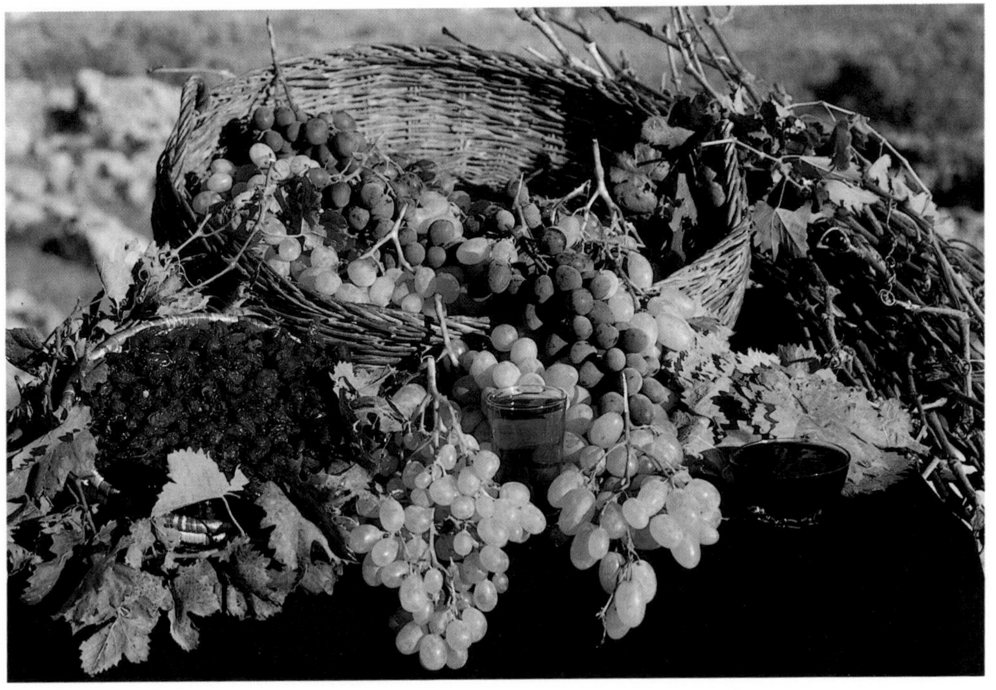

Olive

Olea europaea L.

The trees once went forth to anoint a king over them; and they said to the *olive tree*, **'Reign over us.' But the olive tree said to them, 'Shall I leave my fatness, by which gods and men are honoured, and go to sway over the trees?'**

Judges 9:8–9

But if some of the branches were broken off, and you, a wild olive shoot, were grafted in their place to share the richness of the *olive tree*, **do not boast over the branches.**

Romans 11:17–18

FLOURISHING among the rocks and on poor soil, rich groves of olive trees are scattered on the mountain slopes of Galilee, Samaria and Judea, crowned by the Mount of Olives in Jerusalem. The olive, also numbered among the 'seven species' of the Land, abounded in biblical days both in the mountains and in the Coastal Plain.

The olive leaf has symbolized peace and heralded new life and hope ever since the early history of mankind, as so aptly expressed in the biblical story of the flood: "And the dove came back to him in the evening and lo, in her mouth a freshly plucked olive leaf; so Noaḥ knew that the waters had subsided from the earth" (Genesis 8:11). It was to this gnarled age-old tree that the other trees first appealed for reigning over them in the parable of the trees (Judges 9:8–9). The righteous as an individual and the integrity of the People of Israel were metaphorically likened, in the Bible, to this evergreen tree.

So popular were the tree and its fruit that, apart from the daily diet, the oil was used in holy ointments of kings and priests, and for anointing the sick, for lighting at home and in the Temple, and as a solvent of various spices, incenses and aromatics used as perfumes and in cosmetics. The tree's richly grained wood had its uses for devising various products like wooden ornaments and household utensils, although it was unsuited for the manufacture of furniture, owing to the trunk's hollowness.

The fruit itself was ingathered when fully ripe in the autumn. Then, as today, the branches were beaten with a long stick and the falling olives collected in baskets. The oil was processed from the olives by crushing them with a revolving stone. A stream of oil spouted from underneath the stone into a cistern dug in the ground. At the foot of the Mount of Olives were such oil presses in old days. So exuberantly did the oil flow there, and so picturesque were the surrounding olive groves, that this site derived its name therefrom: Gethsemane (Hebrew: *Gat-Shmanim* = oil-press).

The olive tree is precisely identifiable with the Hebrew *zayit* or *etz-zayit*, and its agricultural significance during biblical times is evident from the many Scriptural references to olive groves, olive trees and olive oil.

The tree, a very slow grower, achieves great age and bears fruit even after the trunk is hollow. In fact, some olive groves in Israel are believed to be more than a thousand years old. The olive seems to have been cultivated more

widely in the past than it is today, as oil presses discovered in densely bushed areas testify.

In Israel and other Mediterranean countries the tree often grows wild and is considered a variety of the cultivated species known as *O. Europaea* L. var *oleaster*, which is not uncommon in the local evergreen bush, and thought to be the wild progenitor of the cultivated olive. Although there is uncertainty as to where it was first cultivated, the fact that it has been unearthed in Israel at what is so far the earliest prehistoric evidence of the Chalcolithic (3700 BC) layers - north of the Dead Sea - allows us to assume that this country cradled the cultivated olive tree. Olive pits, furthermore, have been found in variously dated excavations and sites.

The tree belongs to the Olive family, of which there are 400 species thriving in temperate and tropical climates. Because the genus *Olea* comprises 35 species mainly African, Indian and Australian, *O. europaea,* the only Mediterranean species, is in a sense an outsider. A stately tree with a gnarled gray trunk, growing 5-8 m. tall and up to 1 m. wide, it is richly branched and abundantly covered with oblong-lanceolate evergreen leaves, gray below and blue-green above. Its clusters of small, white flowers appear in spring and are shed soon after pollination. The fruit is a one-seeded drupe which ripens fully in the autumn and is black or bluish in maturity and green earlier in the season.

Fig

Ficus carica L.

So when the woman saw that the tree was good for food, and that it was a delight to the eyes, and that the tree was to be desired to make one wise, she took of its fruit and ate; and she also gave some to her husband, and he ate. Then the eyes of both were opened, and they knew that they were naked; and they sewed *fig* leaves together and made themselves aprons. Genesis 3:6–7

For lo, the winter is past, the rain is over and gone. The flowers appear on the earth, the time of singing has come, and the voice of the turtledove is heard in our land. The *fig tree* puts forth its figs.

Song of Solomon 2:11–13

From the *fig tree* learn its lesson: as soon as its branch becomes tender and puts forth its leaves, you know that summer is near.

Matthew 24:32

THE fig is the first fruit to be mentioned by name in the Bible, in the story of Adam and Eve. Dried figs dating from the Neolithic Age (5000 BC) were uncovered at the excavation of Gezer, a major city of ancient days, located on the western slopes of the Judean mountains; and the fig was also grown in ancient Egypt. The Hebrew for 'fig tree' in the Bible is *teenah*; for the fruit, *teenim*; *develah*, often in the plural, is 'a cake of dried figs'; and derivatives are also proper names for people and places.

The fig played an important part in daily nutrition in biblical and post-biblical times. Owing to its high sugar content it could be dried, made into pressed cakes, and stored for the fruitless season, like the raisins and other delicacies that were offered as gifts. It is often linked in the Bible with the vine, both being numbered among the 'seven species' and symbolizing prosperity and peace (Micah 4:4).

In the Mediterranean countries, the fig is characteristic of dry-farming agriculture. It is about 3–5 m. tall and has palmate leaves, large, rough to the touch and prominently nerved, which fall at the beginning of winter and unfold in early spring. The latex in all parts of the tree is a skin irritant and may cause a kind of dermatosis. The numerous minute flowers of the fig are enclosed in an apple- or pear-shaped fleshy container called 'syconium.'

The fig occurs in two sexual forms, the 'wild' or male, called *caprificus*, and the 'cultivated' or female. Wild figs have many female flowers and fewer male ones, while the 'female' fig tree has female flowers only. The pollination of the female figs by the pollen of the male is a complicated process. A minute wasp, *Blastophaga psenes*, deposits its eggs in the ovaries of the caprifig's flowers and turns them into galls. The female wasps which develop from the galls are fertilized by the males and leave through a small opening at the top of the fig. On the way out they must pass the male flowers and thus be

dusted with pollen. They then make their way to the female figs, again by means of a minute opening, and, heavy with pollen, fertilize the stigmas of the female flowers and bring about fertilization and seed-setting. Because their ovipositors are too short, they cannot oviposit in the ovaries; while in the caprifig the ovaries are within the reach of the ovipositors and are therefore turned into galls yielding inedible figs. The fig, thus, is a dioecious tree, which means that only females set seeds and produce edible fruit. Its fruit production is totally dependent upon the wasp as a vector of the pollen from the male figs.

There are, however, varieties of fig trees of the same species which produce delicious fruit independent of pollination. This is a common natural phenomenon in horticulture called parthenocarpy (production of seedless fruits).

Not unlike the date palm, the fig tree digresses heavily in distribution from the area of the 1,000 mostly tropical species included in the genus. Although its origin is disputed, it is now reliably believed that the fig growing in the jungles of the Caspian foreshore, northwest Turkey, and probably elsewhere in these surroundings, is the ancestor of the one domesticated by man.

Date Palm

Phoenix dactylifera L.

The righteous flourish like the *palm tree*, and grow like a cedar in Lebanon. They are planted in the house of the Lord, they flourish in the courts of our God. They still bring forth fruit in old age, they are ever full of sap and green.

Psalms 92:12–14

The next day a great crowd who had come to the feast heard that Jesus was coming to Jerusalem. So they took branches of *palm trees* and went out to meet him, crying, "Hosanna! Blessed is he who comes in the name of the Lord, even the King of Israel!"

John 12:12–13

THE date palm is one of the Holy Land's most ancient fruit trees. Its significance in the cultural and agricultural life of the Bible can be measured by the numerous times its fruit is mentioned, and the people and places that bear its Hebrew name *tamar* - unquestionably identified with date palm. In Judges (4:5) Deborah sat under the palm tree, which served in poetry as a symbol of upright stature, justice and righteousness. Its leaves are among the 'four species' for the Feast of Tabernacles (Nehemiah 8:15), and it continues to symbolize holiness and resurrection in Christian worship. Although not explicitly named among the 'seven species' with which the Land has been blessed, it is believed that *dvash* (honey) in Deuteronomy 8:8 refers to it. Jericho, thought to be the oldest city in the world, is called in the Bible "the city of palm trees" (Deuteronomy 34:3). Ancient Palmyra (Tadmor) bespeaks palms, and the Arab town in Sinai, El Arish, stands for 'huts' - huts made entirely of palm leaves.

Palm trees and leaves were used as motifs by King Solomon in Temple engravings and sculptures. In the Capernaum synagogue have been found some friezes on which are carved palm branches (third century AD). The Maccabees (second century BC) used the palm as the emblem of victory on their coins, while Roman coins of the first century AD depicted a woman seated under a palm as an image for the captured Judea.

Apart from the palm's role in the service of spiritual imagery throughout the Bible, it had manifold practical uses: the fruit is sustaining, its honey refreshing; from the tree's trunk a tasty juice could be made. The leaflets were woven into mats, baskets, and other household utensils, while its wood served for fences, roofs, and rafts.

The date palm is primarily a tree of the desert oases. The earliest remains of cultivated dates have been found in the Ubaidian (about 4000 BC) and Chalcolithic (3700 BC) strata at several sites in the Near East, mainly in tropical areas. Much has been written about the wild progenitors of the date palm, but it is now fairly well established that wild date palms are widely dispersed near brackish rivers and springs all along the Sahara from the Atlantic Ocean to the Persian Gulf, forming wild oases inhabited by saline or semi-saline plant communities. It was from these incipient oases - with which the Aravah Valley abounds - that the palm tree was taken into cultivation.

As a tree of plains and valleys, the date palm is intensively cultivated nowadays in the Jordan and Aravah Valleys, the Dead Sea area and the Coastal Plain, mainly in the El Arish and Gaza districts. It is an important part of the agriculture in the hot and warmer parts of Israel, and different varieties have adapted themselves to the particular climatic conditions of each region.

The genus *Phoenix*, whose name probably derives from the date palm cultures of the coastal region of Phoenicia, comprises about 30 species, only a few of which yield edible fruit. It is a remarkable fact that, like the cultivated olive tree, the date palm is a geographic digression of an almost exclusively tropical palm family – the *Arecaceae* – comprising about 4,000 species growing in both the Old and the New Worlds.

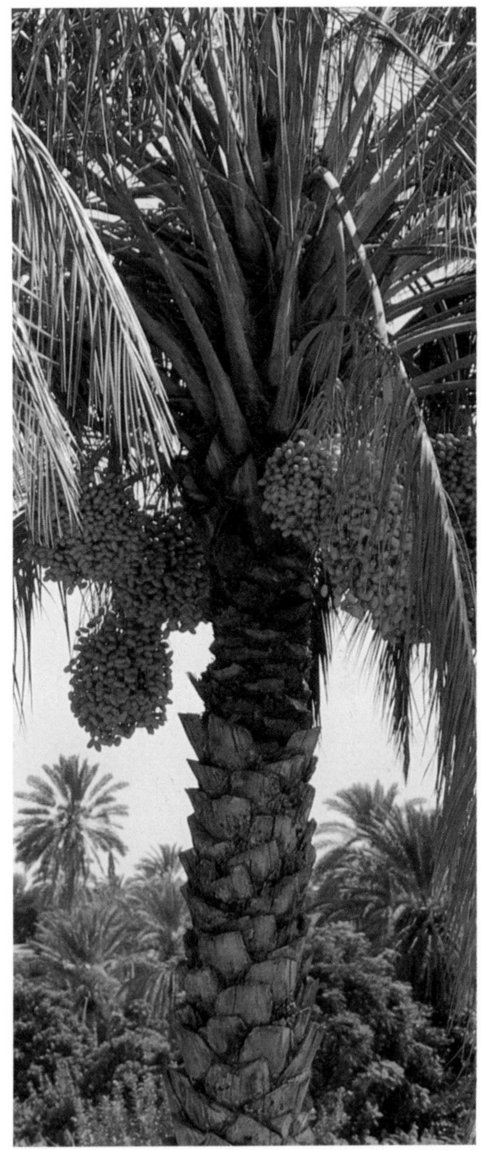

The date palm is a dioecious species attaining a height of 10–20 m. At the top of its straight, unbranched stem it produces a cluster of pinnate leaves 2–3 m. long, which are shed annually after they have been replaced by another cluster. The younger leaves are folded and resemble a stick (the *lulav* of the 'four species' of Leviticus 23:40), and the flowers of both male and female trees grow in dense numerous clusters covered by a woody spathe which splits into boat-shaped valves at blossom time. Although the flowers are usually pollinated by the wind, man, even in ancient times, and ignorant though he was of pollination processes, took the male flower cluster and deposited its pollen on the female.

Beginning to bear fruit at the age of five years, the tree flowers in the spring and its fruit ripens at the end of the summer. The fruit is a berry 2–4 cm. long, with a sweet, fleshy pulp and a large seed. Since the palm-grower is interested only in fruit-bearing trees, he propagates the trees by suckers, which sprout at the base of the stem after fruit-setting, rather than by seeds, which would produce groves about half of whose trees would be male. Since a single male tree can supply enough pollen to fertilize 25–50 females, not very many are needed. Propagation of this kind, furthermore, is vital for keeping the crop genetically pure.

Pomegranate

Punica granatum L.

And they came to the Valley of Eshcol, and cut down from there a branch with a single cluster of grapes, and they carried it on a pole between two of them; they brought also some *pomegranates* **and figs.**

Numbers 13:23

Your lips are like a scarlet thread, and your mouth is lovely. Your cheeks are like halves of a *pomegranate* **behind your veil.**

Song of Solomon 4:3

MANY praises are bestowed indirectly upon the pomegranate in the imagery of the Song of Solomon, for the woman's beauty is likened to its beautiful shape, its many seeds symbolize fertility, its delicious red juice figures as the lovers' nectar, and so lovely and odorous are its blooming flowers that they stand for the awakening of spring and its loveliness. The pomegranate gave its perfect shape to the golden bells that ornamented the Temple, to its furniture, embroidery, and carved column-capitals, and to the priestly garments (Exodus 28:33–34).

Together with grapes, it was chosen to represent the bounty of the Land by the spies sent by Moses to explore Canaan. However, although the fruit is numbered among the 'seven species' with which the land has been blessed, it was not, like the date or the fig, a staple article of diet.

The Hebrew *rimmon* is an authentically identified plant frequently mentioned in the Bible as a tree and also as a proper name for people and places.

Parts of the pomegranate were once used medicinally, and its bark and rind, once ingredients of ink, are still used for tanning. Pomegranate rinds were found in the excavation of Neolithic Gezer. The seeds are eaten fresh or as a confection and can be made into a spiced wine. It is because of these seeds, delectable and refreshing in summer, that the tree has been cultivated for thousands of years. Although nowadays it is giving way to more profitable fruit trees, it was once abundant in the local orchards.

The pomegranate is the only genus of the *Punicaceae* family and consists of two species: the common pomegranate, a widely cultivated fruit tree or shrub, and *P. protopunica* a dwarf-shrub with small flowers and fruits. We are concerned here with the first, which is a small deciduous tree whose stem is richly branched and whose leaves are oblong and entire. Its showy crimson flowers appear late in spring and at the end of summer; the fruit is red and the size of an apple or larger.

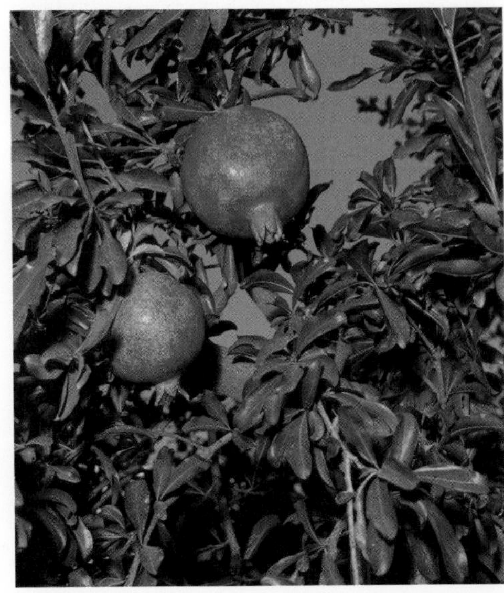

Carob

Ceratonia siliqua L.

Now John wore a garment of camel's hair, and a leather girdle around his waist; and his food was *locusts* and wild honey.
Matthew 3:4

And he would gladly have fed on the *pods* that the swine ate; and no one gave him anything.
Luke 15:16

THE carob tree, annually producing quantities of sweet fruit, is native to Israel and is important in the local vegetation. It is astonishing that although it has undoubtedly been common in the Land since ancient times, it is not mentioned in the Old Testament and is only hinted at in the New Testament, although its Hebrew name *ḥaruv* often appears in the Mishnah and the Talmud and is also preserved by the Arabs of southwestern Asia and North Africa. Nor is there linguistic or contextual evidence for assigning one of the few biblical tree names to the carob. The identity of the carob with the 'locust' in Matthew and the 'pods' in Luke (see above) is still disputed, in spite of contextual plausibility and the similarity of the Hebrew *ḥagavim* (locust) to *ḥaruvim* (carob).

The story of John (which gave rise to the carob's other name – St. John's Bread) recalls the story in the Talmud about the Jewish sage Rabbi Shimeon Bar-Yoḥai, who while hiding in the Galilean caves with his son, for fear of capture by the Romans, was said to have been sustained for twelve years on carobs alone.

Significant in many plant communities, the carob tree is common in the Coastal Plain and the adjacent foothills, and on the eastern slopes of Galilee and Samaria.

The carob tree is a medium-sized evergreen, its trunk often gnarled and densely branched on top to form a globular to somewhat oval crown. The leaves are divided into two to four pairs of ovate, entire leaflets. The flowers are unisexual, males and females growing on different trees and crowded in short spikes on old thick branches. They are small and greenish and appear in autumn, but the fruit does not mature until late in the following summer. It is a dry, fleshy, indehiscent, many-seeded brown pod, shed when ripe. The sweet pulp, from which a kind of syrup is prepared by the Arabs, may contain as much as fifty percent sugar and is edible by man and livestock.

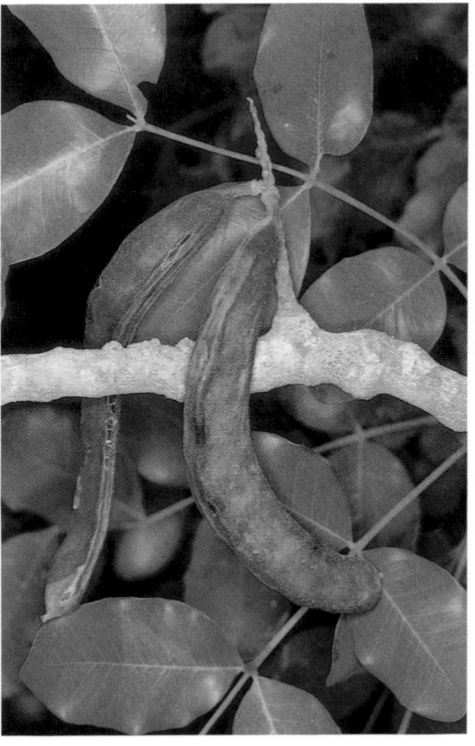

Walnut

Juglans regia L.

I went down to the *nut* orchard, to look at the blossoms of the valley, to see whether the vines had budded, whether the pomegranates were in bloom.

Song of Solomon 6:11

IT was once thought that the walnut tree might have grown only in the imaginary garden of the Spouse in the Song of Solomon – like the "nard and saffron, calamus and cinnamon, with all trees of frankincense, myrrh and aloes, with all chief spices" (4:13), since the verse in the heading is the sole biblical mention of *egoz* – 'walnut'. But this is untrue, as Josephus Flavius praised the fruitful valley of Genesareth for its abundance of walnut trees, among other plants, and post-biblical literature often adverts to the walnut as a tree important in legend and ritual. A wealth of sayings and proverbs attests to its use not only for nuts but for oil, tannin and timber, and for wood for the altar fire in the Temple. Single walnut trees are still grown in all parts of Israel and there is even a place called the Valley of Walnuts in eastern Jerusalem.

The name *egoz* is unequivocally identified and is preserved in Arabic as *goz* or *jauz*.

The walnut is native to southeastern Europe, the Caucasus, northern Turkey, Persia, and other West Asian countries, where it often forms steppe forests. It was already cultivated in biblical times and along with other trees, such as the white poplar, the pomegranate, the pistachio and the mulberry, was probably introduced into Canaan from Persia or Turkey.

The generic name *Juglans* is corrupted from *Jovis glans* or 'Jupiter's nut'. The genus includes about 40 species, spread throughout the temperate regions of the Old and New Worlds. In Europe and western Asia, only one species is cultivated, but in America and elsewhere also other species of *Juglans* with similar nuts are grown.

The walnut, or Persian walnut, is a stately tree, often 6–8 m. tall, and 20 m. around the crown. Its leaves are composed of two to five pairs of large, entire and fragrant leaflets which are shed in the winter. The flowers appear before the leaves unfold; the male flowers grow in long catkins and the female in clusters. They are small and green and are pollinated by the wind. The globular fruits ripen at the end of summer. The outer cover or husk is astringent and blackens the hand when peeled. While it is still on the tree it cracks open, letting the nuts fall to the ground. The wooden shell encloses the edible kernel, about sixty percent of which consists of fat.

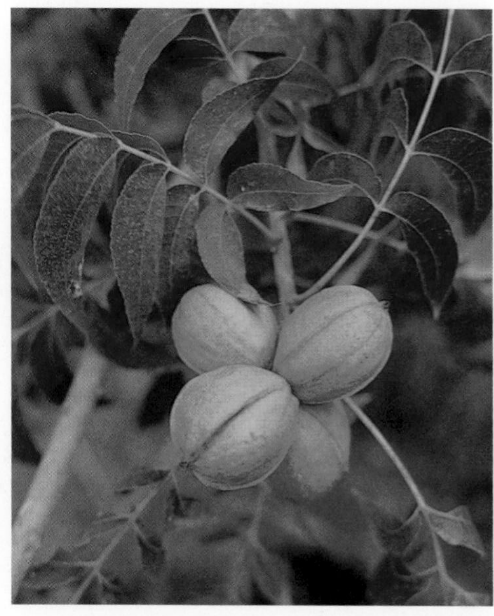

Pistachio

Pistacia vera L.

Then their father Israel said to them, "If it must be so, then do this: take some of the choice fruits of the land in your bags, and carry down to the man a present, a little balm and a little honey, gum, myrrh, *pistachio nuts*, and almonds."

Genesis 43:11

PISTACHIO nuts (*botnim*) are mentioned only once in the Bible, in a list of appropriate gifts for an esteemed man, and so they must have been considered one of the Land's most delicious fruits. The place name Betonim (Joshua 13:26), in the district of the tribe of Gad in southern Transjordan, an area suited to the pistachio, is probably derived from *botnim*. These two passages and a reference in the Talmud make it clear that the tree has long been cultivated in Israel; a pistachio nut has in fact been found in the late Neolithic stratum in Greece.

There is no doubt of the identification of the pistachio with *botnim*. The Arabic *butm*, or its cognate *botnim*, also refers to other species of *Pistacia* such as *P. palaestina* and others, while the modern Hebrew *elah* stands for all of them.

The pistachio is a small deciduous tree whose trunk has a multitude of branches and whose leaves consist of two or three pairs of rather large, ovate leaflets with minute unisexual flowers, male and female on different trees. The fruits are one-seeded nuts with a hard shell which splits along a lateral suture. The tasty, fatty kernel is about 1 cm. long.

The pistachio is a steppe tree, growing wild in semi-arid countries of southwest Asia amid a steppe-like dwarf shrubbery. It was probably introduced into Israel from Syria or directly from Persia, along with other cultivated plants.

Almond

Amygdalus communis L.

And on the morrow Moses went into the tent of the testimony; and behold, the rod of Aaron for the house of Levi had sprouted and put forth buds, and produced blossoms, and it bore ripe *almonds*.

Numbers 17:8

They are afraid also of what is high, and terrors are in the way; the *almond tree* blossoms, the grasshopper drags itself along and desire fails; because man goes to his eternal home, and the mourners go about the streets.

Ecclesiastes 12:5

AS the first tree to flower before the end of winter, the almond tree in ancient days symbolized the hastening of events. It is indeed the herald of spring in Israel.

The Hebrew *shaked* appears in the Bible as an almond tree or branch and as a fruit; the term 'almond-shaped' (*meshukadim*), together with *kaftor* (flower-bud), *gavia* (calyx), and *peraḥ* (probably corolla), is used three times in Exodus in connection with the almond-flower ornamentation of the candelabrum for the Tabernacle in the Sinai Desert. Flowering almonds are not found in the Sinai today, but they may once have been, especially in its mountainous regions, since they do grow in the hills of the Negev. It is possible that other trees with similar flowers (e.g. the Sinai hawthorn, *Crataegus sinaica*) were used as models for the candelabrum and also figured in the story of the almond rod in Numbers 17:8 and in Jeremiah 1:11–12, although these are seemingly legendary and symbolic.

Genesis 30:37 gives the name *luz* for 'almond tree'. *Luz* also appears as a place-name in Samaria (Genesis 28:19; Joshua 16:2), probably indicating a wealth of almond groves. Since *shaked* is rendered *luz* in Aramaic and other Semitic languages, the correspondence between the two is unquestioned. That both of them mean 'almond' is equally sure, especially since *luz* or *lauz* is still used by Arabs and Kurdish Jews as the name for the tree.

The genus *Amygdalus* comprises about 40 species, confined mainly to southwestern and Central Asia. There are at least 15 species in Persia, and two wild bitter-seeded and one cultivated sweet-seeded species in Israel. We are concerned here with the last, a medium-sized tree, whose oblong-lanceolate leaves are shed at the beginning of winter. It starts to flower in the first half of February and continues to do so for about a month, producing a mass of blossoms, mainly before leaf-setting, like a snow-white cloud in the landscape. The flowers each have a bell-shaped calyx and a spreading corolla, 15–20 stamens, and a pistil. Honey-bees collect the pollen and nectar.

About ten weeks after the flowers appear, the fruit starts to ripen. The fleshy pericarp dries up and splits into valves, releasing the seed, which

falls to the ground. Within the shell, the kernels are coated by a delicate brown skin and are eaten raw or roasted, or are ground for food. They contain about 50% fat and have been cultivated here since early prehistory. The local bitter strains have, no doubt, been used as stocks for the grafting of sweet-seeded varieties. The fact that Israel harbors two or three wild species of almonds very close in habit to the cultivated tree suggests that it might have been one of the original countries in which the almond was domesticated.

Sycomore

Ficus sycomorus L.

And the king made silver as common in Jerusalem as stone, and he made cedar as plentiful as the *sycamore* of the Shephelah.
I Kings 10:27

The bricks have fallen, but we will build with dressed stones; the *sycamores* have been cut down, but we will put cedars in their place.
Isaiah 9:10

And he sought to see who Jesus was, but could not, on account of the crowd, because he was small of stature. So he ran on ahead and climbed up into a *sycomore tree* to see him, for he was to pass that way.
Luke 19:3–4

THE sycomore tree of the Scriptures is a species of *Ficus* not unlike the fig tree in its fruit, which it is said to bear several times a year, although its main crop matures in early summer and secondary crops somewhat later. Its figs, although much inferior in taste and sugar content to the true fig, were in ancient times widely consumed by the poor and even marketed. The sycomore very abundant and characteristic of the Coastal Plain, was not as important for its fruit as for its wood, used as building timber. Its light weight and porous structure made it especially suitable for ceilings. Ancient Egyptian coffins attest to the fact that it was proof against damp and rot.

Although other identifications have been made, 'sycomore' is the only correct rendition of *shikmim* or *shikmoth*, a word that appears seven times in the Bible and only in the plural. Some scholars assume that the species was introduced from Africa, perhaps by Natufian Man (about 10 000 BC) bringing seeds or cuttings. This seems improbable because its fruit was not valued and could never have rivaled the fig, which thrives in the same area, the Coastal Plain. Although its timber was valuable, there is no evidence that it was imported into this country.

In my opinion, it was never in fact 'introduced' into Israel, but remained as a tertiary relic of the earlier tropical flora, not unlike other vestiges (*Acacia albida, Ziziphus spina-Christi*), which since the Natufian period have mainly been vegetatively planted and propagated from native stands.

The fig and the sycomore are representatives of the genus *Ficus*, which comprises about 1,000 mainly tropical species. Unlike the fig, the sycomore is a robust tree, attaining a height of 10 –15 m. and a crown circumference of 20–25 m. with a trunk sometimes 1–2 m. in diameter. Its leaves recall those of the mulberry but are shed only in extremely cold winters. Like many other tropical trees, it bears its fruit in grape-like clusters which spring from the main stem or the older branches, a phenomenon known as cauliflory. The syconia of the sycomore consist of a globular receptacle lined on its inner side with succulent hairs, among which the minute male and female flowers are inserted. At the top of the fig is a very narrow opening (*ostium*), encircled with tiny scales, through which certain wasps enter for purposes of oviposition. Of these, the *Sycophaga sycomori* is the main species. In the lower part of the fig are the female flowers, which are far more numerous than the males in the upper part near the *ostium*. The whole rather complicated story of pollination is not unlike that of the true fig tree.

The fertilization of the sycomore by wasps is vital to the ripening of the fruit, but no seeds can be produced thereby, since the ovaries are converted into galls which make the figs inedible for man. To prevent the setting of this type of fruit, the ancient Hebrews incised the fig before maturity with a special knife. Such gashing is called *balos* in Hebrew, an operation to which the prophet Amos was presumably referring when he said: "I am no prophet, nor a prophet's son; but I am a herdsman, and a dresser of sycamore trees" (Amos 7:14). Other countries used the same method, and Egypt and Cyprus, among others, do so still.

For reasons not clearly understood, the variety so dependent upon the wasp was replaced in this country by a parthenocarpic variety, which has no need of the wasp for ripening its seedless figs.

The many solitary examples of the species, which thrive here despite the obstacles of sand dunes and stormy sea winds, support the assumption that the tree is indigenous to the southern part of the Coastal Plain. Since it cannot be reproduced by seeds, its survival is now solely dependent upon man, or, more bluntly, it is man who has saved the sycomore from extinction.

Apple

Malus sylvestris Mill.

Sustain me with raisins, refresh me with *apples*; for I am sick with love.

Song of Solomon 2:5

The vine withers, the fig tree languishes. Pomegranate, palm, and *apple*, all the trees of the field are withered; and gladness fails from the sons of men.

Joel 1:12

DESPITE the widespread tradition that apples were the forbidden fruit of the Garden of Eden, they are not in fact mentioned in the narrative. The Hebrew *tappuaḥ* occurs five times in the Bible as an apple tree or its fruit, six times as a place name (as in Joshua 15:33), and once as a proper name (I Chronicles 2:43). Biblical botanists have strenuously debated the identification of *tappuaḥ*, which, for reasons not sufficiently clear, has sometimes been rendered 'apricot' (*Armeniaca vulgaris*) or 'bitter orange' (*Citrus vulgaris*), although these plants were introduced much later than the apple, which dates in Europe from the Neolithic Age.

Although no trace of the apple has yet been discovered among the prehistoric remains of the Middle East, indirect evidence, especially the fact that the Arabic *tuffaḥ* refers exclusively to the apple tree, justifies its identification with the Hebrew *tappuaḥ*. Ancient Egyptian papyri of the period of Ramses II (1298–1235 BC) disclose that the fields of the Nile delta were full of fine plants – pomegranate, apple (*taph*), olive, and fig trees. Pliny's *Historia Naturae* mentions many apple varieties, including the red and the white from Syria.

A few varieties of *Malus sylvestris* in fact grow wild in Turkey, where the author has found a variety of this species among forest trees. They might once have been native to Lebanon as well, a country famous for its apple groves.

According to Goor (1968), apples might have been introduced into Israel and Egypt from Iran or Armenia (and, in my opinion, from Turkey and Syria) at about 4000 BC. In the early days of agriculture, fruit trees like the walnut and the mulberry, and even such timber trees as the white poplar, were customarily introduced from neighboring countries.

The apple tree is stately, reaching a height of 8–12 m. It has elliptical or roundish leaves and white flowers, 3–4 cm. in diameter, growing in clusters of four to six. The fruit is a small, globular, green-yellow to reddish pome, 3–4 cm. across. Because of its occurrence in the Middle East, this species seems to have been widely bred and domesticated so that hundreds of strains were developed and are now grown throughout the temperate regions of the globe.

Black Mulberry

Morus nigra L.

He who is *impoverished* **chooses for an offering wood that will not rot; he seeks out a skilful craftsman to set up an image that will not move.**

Isaiah 40:20

They showed the elephants the juice of grapes and *mulberries*, **to arouse them for battle.**

I Maccabees 6:34

The apostles said to the Lord, "Increase our faith!" And the Lord said, "If you had faith as a grain of mustard seed, you could say to this *sycamine tree*, **'Be rooted up, and be planted in the sea,' and it would obey you."**

Luke 17:5–6

WHILE the rendition of *tut* in Maccabees as 'mulberry tree' raises no questions, the words *sycamine* in Luke and *mesukan* in Isaiah, though etymologically cognate, can less certainly be identified with the mulberry. Yet *mesukan* is clearly related to the Sumerian *messikanu* or *sukannu*, identified by Thompson (1949) as 'mulberry' and contextually satisfying in the passage from Isaiah; *sycamine* may have the same origin.

The genus *Morus* consists of ten species which range from China to North America. In the Mediterranean countries, the two species which have been cultivated for centuries are the white mulberry (*M. alba*) and the black (*M. nigra*); the white having been introduced from China and grown mainly for its leaves, which nourish the silkworm and assure silk production. Although silk is mentioned several times in the Bible, neither biblical nor post-biblical literature refers to its production, despite the cultivation until recently of the white mulberry in Lebanon, Syria and sporadically also in Israel.

The black mulberry, possibly a derivative of the white, grows wild in northern Persia, on the shores of the Caspian Sea and in ancient Colchis, whence it was introduced long ago into the lands of the Bible. Such early introduction from Persia and its neighbors was true of the apple, the pomegranate, the fig and the pistachio.

The black mulberry is medium-sized, deciduous and dioecious, and flowers in the spring either before or together with the unfolding of the mostly lobed and dentate leaves. The flowers are minute, green, and wind-pollinated, the male growing in pendent catkins and the female in globular or ovate heads. After pollination, the groups of female flowers become black, berry-like fruits made of fleshy drupes. They have a sweet-sour taste, but because of their low nutritional value the tree is not often grown.

2
Field Crops & Garden Plants

THE importance of the field crops in ancient Israel can be measured by the daily consumption of bread, which was the major constituent of the meal of the poor, the rich, and the king alike: "And at mealtime Boaz said to her, 'Come here, and eat some bread, and dip your morsel in the wine'" (Ruth 2:14). Bread also had its place among the offerings to God and was called 'the Showbread': "You shall serve the Lord your God, and I will bless your bread and your water" (Exodus 23:25). The utter dependence of human existence upon bread is also attested to by the place bread occupied in the symbolic realm. Ears of barley, representing bounty, were a motif on Jewish coins (first century AD) and on oil lamps.

The biblical field crops were wheat, emmer, barley and sorghum. Wheat and barley were the most important and accordingly are mentioned first among the 'seven species' with which the Land of Israel was blessed; the others are fruits – grapes, figs, pomegranates, olives and dates (honey).

Most of the field crops were cereals, which except for sorghum, a summer crop, were grown in winter. Since the techniques of growing summer crops were certainly known to the people of the Bible, it is probable that both irrigated and non-irrigated summer crops existed, though on a small scale. Wheat was grown in great abundance in all the rainy districts of the Mediterranean area, mainly in valleys and mountain terraces; the extensive wheat belts of the Coastal Plain were in great part within the boundaries of Philistia.

Then, as today, barley was grown on the margins of the Mediterranean area, near the desert or in favorable desert lowlands where the rainfall is not sufficient to sustain wheat. Barley is much inferior to wheat and, although used for bread, has always been the bread of the poor. Emmer, too, though less productive than wheat, was fairly common.

The multiplicity of terms relating to field cultivation and harvesting tools, parts of plants and bread-making, testifies to the high standard of agriculture in biblical and earlier times. Indeed, agricultural methods and a rich apposite vocabulary antedated by millennia the conquest of the land by the Israelites, as probably do also some ritual and rural habits and laws connected with agriculture.

Garden Plants

THE vegetable garden of biblical times was woefully lacking in variety. Without radishes, turnips, rapes, lettuce, beans, or cucumbers in his garden, man must have depended on the wild vegetation for much of his vegetable diet. The term *esev ha-sadeh* (grass of the field) presumably refers to edible herbs, pot-herbs and other plants, which are still collected and marketed by peasants. Among the local flora are scores of such useful plants, which have in part satisfied man's need for vegetables.

The four groups into which the biblical garden plants can be divided are: vegetables – onions and leeks; pulses – lentils, broad beans and chick-peas; gourds – watermelon, muskmelon and probably bottle gourds; and the condiments – mint, marjoram, coriander, cummin, fitches, and probably dill.

Industrial Plants

NOT all the species included in this chapter are referred to in the Bible as industrial plants. Flax, however, is frequently mentioned. It was probably widely cultivated in biblical times for weaving linen, and used for priestly vestments as well as for ordinary clothing. Despite the skill and effort required to manufacture it, it was the only fiber plant grown.

Cotton was not cultivated in the Holy Land, although it appears as one of the royal textiles listed in the Book of Esther: "There were white cotton curtains and blue hangings caught up with cords of fine linen and purple to silver rings" (1:6).

The castor bean plant was very common in its wild state, but never cultivated except where it was grown for its valuable oil, in countries such as India and Egypt. In the Bible this plant is described only in a legendary context (Jonah 4:6–11).

Linen fibers were actually obtained by cutting the fruiting flax plants and steeping them in water for a few weeks. Thus the fibers were separated from the soft tissues, and were then dried and bleached in the sun.

Wheat

Triticum durum Desf.

A land of *wheat* and barley, of vines and fig trees and pomegranates, a land of olive trees and honey.

Deuteronomy 8:8

So Hiram supplied Solomon with all the timber of cedar and cypress that he desired, while Solomon gave Hiram twenty thousand cors of *wheat* as food for his household, and twenty thousand cors of beaten oil.

I Kings 5:10–11

THE main field crop of biblical times was wheat. The fields were not irrigated and were fully dependent upon the highly unstable annual rainfall, which was sometimes so scanty that the fields did not 'yield their crops'. Disastrous famine years are frequently mentioned in the Bible, which speaks of Egypt as a wheatland with abundant water for irrigation, a granary for its famine-afflicted neighbors.

There were two species abundantly cultivated in Israel and the neighboring countries, both tetraploid, one the so-called durum wheat (*T. durum*), the other emmer (*T. dicoccum*) Schult). The former is still, as it was in the time of the Bible, the dominant field crop grown commonly for bread in the warm-temperate countries. Its grains are free (not hulled), hard, rich in gluten and supply excellent flour. It is sown before or after the early rains and harvested in June or July. Besides bread, it was used in numerous specific recipes and as a cereal offering to God – the 'Showbread'. Wheat, the Hebrew *ḥittah*, is probably included in the generalizing terms *bar* (Genesis 41:49), *dagan* (Numbers 18:27), and *kamah* (Judges 15:5), and *avur, omer, geresh, carmel* and others, all through the Old Testament.

Wheat is a member of the Grass family. Its species are all annual, with erect culms ending in an ear of spikelets along the central axis (rhachis). Each spikelet has three to seven flowers, of which only a few produce grains. These, the fruit of the wheat, contain a single seed with a minute embryo and a large body of endosperm storing about seventy percent of starch and about ten percent of proteins. The coats, or outer layers of the seeds, are bran, which is most nutritive for cattle and poultry.

The other species, emmer, also a tetraploid, was widely grown in Israel and in other Near Eastern countries (including Egypt) from the seventh millennium BC. But it was greatly inferior to the durum wheat, at least with respect to its hulled grains, which could not be freely threshed.

Hard (durum) Wheat *Triticum durum*

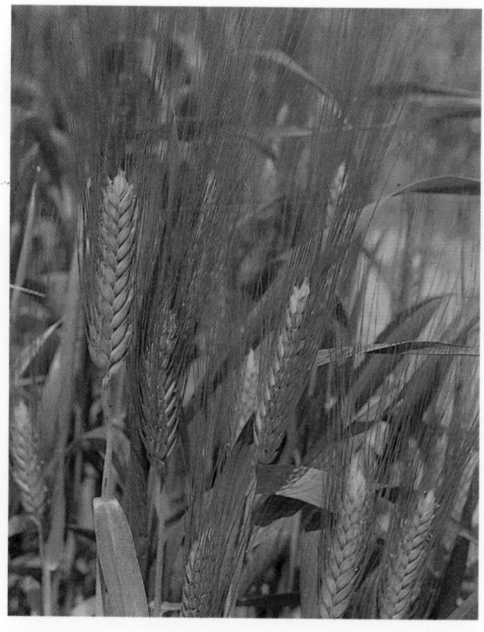

It was emmer that bore a name of its own and was not included in the term *ḥittah*. As *kussemeth* (or *kussemoth* or *kussmim*), it is mentioned three times in the Bible along with *ḥittah*: "But the wheat and the spelt [*kussemeth*] were not ruined, for they are late in coming up" (Exodus 9:32; see also Isaiah 28:25 and Ezekiel 4:9).

The rendition of 'spelt' for *kussemeth* is erroneous, since spelt denotes a hexaploid wheat variety (*T. aestivum* L. var spelta) which does not grow in Israel.

The wild progenitor of emmer wheat and durum wheat is the species known as *Triticum dicoccoides* (Koern.) Aaronsohn, which is native to Israel and the neighboring countries. It resembles the cultivated species, but its mature ears are brittle and disarticulate into single spikelets which fall to the ground, whereas the cultivated ears are tough and remain so until harvested. This characteristic, so important for reaping, was sought for by farmers through millennia until they found a special mutation whose individuals produced tough ears. From then on only these were sown and bred – simple words that indicate the epic story of the domestication of wheat, which took place about 8,000 years ago in one or more of the most primitive agricultural villages of the Assyrian mountains (Jarmo in Iraq), and probably in the Land of Israel as well, where the culture is even older and the wheat ancestor more abundant.

Wild Wheat *Triticum dicoccoides*

Barley

Hordeum vulgare L.

So Naomi returned, and Ruth the Moabitess her daughter-in-law with her, who returned from the country of Moab. And they came to Bethlehem at the beginning of *barley* harvest.
Ruth 1:22

One of his disciples, Andrew, Simon Peter's brother, said to him, "There is a lad here who has five *barley* loaves and two fish; but what are they among so many?"
John 6:8–9

BARLEY can be definitively identified as the Hebrew *seorah* (pl. *seorim*), mentioned more than thirty times in the Bible and no fewer than thirteen times in company with wheat. Although one of the 'seven species' with which the Land was blessed, barley was considered inferior to wheat, as Revelation 6:6 clearly attests. The poor people's bread, barley was limited to areas with sparse rainfall, like semi-arid margins of the mountains and sections of the northern Negev. Since it ripens a month or more before wheat, it was taken for the *omer* offerings at the Passover feast while the first grains of wheat were offered at the Feast of Pentecost.

The cultivation of barley ranges from the polar regions to the tropics. Because its soil and moisture requirements are rather modest, it also occurs in semi-arid countries, and, since the 16th century, has been grown not for bread but essentially for forage. Its ancestral wild form and the region and time of its first domestication are now clear. It has been acceptably argued that the cultivation of barley began at about 8000 BC in southwest Asia, where the wild progenitor of the two-rowed barley – the Tabor barley (*Hordeum spontaneum*) – is widespread.

The genus *Hordeum* consists of 18 species, of which only the two-rowed (*H. distichum*) and the more prevalent six-rowed barley (*H. hexastichum*) are cultivated. According to some botanists the two species are varieties of the common barley (*H. vulgare*), an erect annual grass, very leafy along the main and the secondary culms. Each culm terminates in an ear made up of numerous spikelet groups bearing three flowers each; in the two-rowed barley, only one flower of each spikelet group is fertile, or grain-producing, while in the six-rowed, all three spikelets develop into grains.

Common Millet

Panicum miliaceum L.

Sorghum

Sorghum bicolor (L.) Moench

And you, take wheat and barley, beans and lentils, *millet* and spelt, and put them into a single vessel, and make bread of them. During the number of days that you lie upon your side, three hundred and ninety days, you shall eat it.

Ezekiel 4:9

THE Hebrew *doḥan*, here 'millet', although mentioned only once in Scripture, seems to have been more common post-biblically. In Arabic the two species mentioned above are called, among other names, *duḥn, doḥna* and related names. They may well have been cultivated in biblical times, but there are no historical records.

Millet, believed to derive from a wild Ethiopian species, *Panicum callosum* Hochst, was taken very early into cultivation and relics of it in Mesopotamia date back to about 3000 BC, though no such early traces have so far been found in Israel. It is a summer crop which in Israel requires irrigation.

Sorghum, locally named *durrah*, though so far not documented archeologically, is known to have moved from East Africa via southwest Asia to India, where archeological findings confirm its cultivation at about 2000 BC. It is better suited than millet to the climate and agricultural conditions of Israel, where it thrives both in the lowlands and in the mountains as a most productive non-irrigated summer crop.

An erect and rather tall plant, sorghum has many broad leaves spread along its several culms, which end in a thick, densely-branched panicle of flowers producing globular whitish grains used for stock feed and, in some countries, for a crude kind of bread.

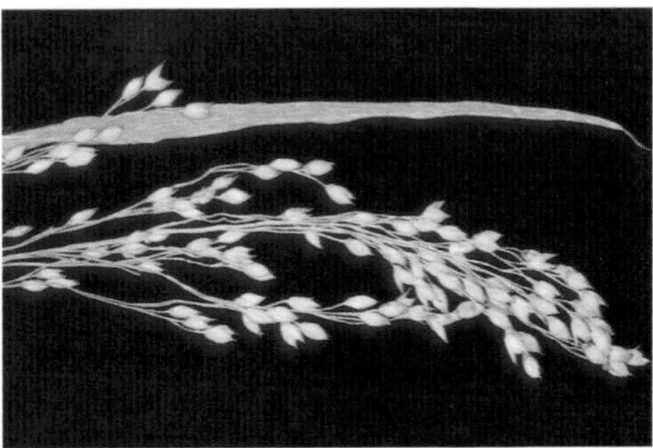

Common Millet *Panicum miliaceum*

Sorghum *Sorghum bicolor*

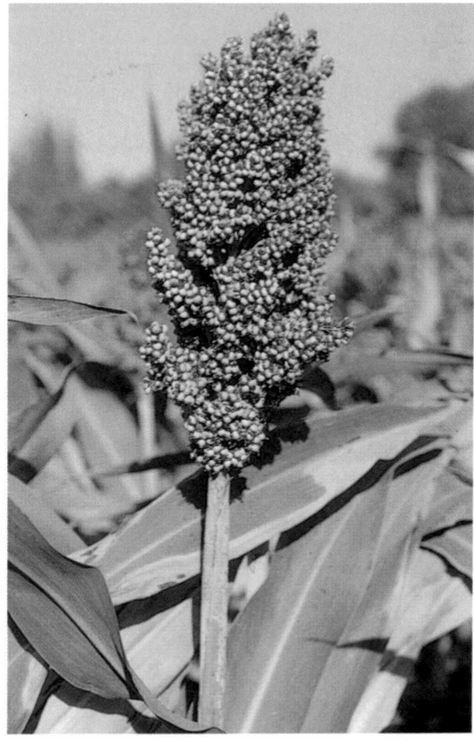

Flax

Linum usitatissimum L.

The *flax* and the barley were ruined, for the barley was in the ear and the flax was in the bud.

Exodus 9:31

They took the body of Jesus, and bound it in *linen* cloths with the spices, as is the burial custom of the Jews.

John 19:40

FLAX fibers for spinning, the linen thus produced, and the flax plant itself are the three meanings of the Hebrew *pishtah.* Since the word is mentioned several times in the Bible, flax must have been intensively cultivated. Although *pesheth* and *pishtah* and other cognates are used for 'flax' in Hebrew and other languages of the ancient Middle East, they have sometimes been replaced by the Accadian *kitu*, Phoenician *kittan* and Arabic *kettan*, used for both 'flax' and 'cotton'. In the Bible the word is inherent in *kutoneth*, 'a linen shirt'.

The Gezer Calendar, which was found at the ancient site of the city of Gezer, dating back to the beginning of the Israelite kingdom (c. 10th century BC), includes references to the cultivation of flax, which, together with wool, was the chief material for weaving cloth for garments and linens.

The flax plant, one of about 200 species of the genus *Linum*, is grown not only for its fibers but also for its seeds, which are rich in oil. At the time of the Bible and earlier, however, it was exclusively a fiber plant. Cultivation dates back to 5000 BC in the countries of the Middle East, including the Land of Israel, where flax probably originated and where its wild progenitor, *Linum bienne*, still occurs in the native flora.

The cultivated flax is an annual herb 50 cm. or more in height; its erect stem branches toward the top. Its branches have long, narrow leaves and showy blue flowers consisting of five sepals, five petals, five stamens and an ovary with a long style. The fruit is a globose capsule containing several oleiferous seeds.

Cotton

Gossypium herbaceum L.

And when these days were completed, the king gave for all the people present in Susa the capital, both great and small, a banquet lasting for seven days, in the court of the garden of the king's palace. There were white *cotton* curtains and blue hangings caught up with cords of fine linen and purple to silver rings and marble pillars, and also couches of gold and silver on a mosaic pavement of porphyry, marble, mother-of-pearl and precious stones.

Esther 1:5–6

COTTON, the Hebrew *karpas*, is mentioned only once in the Bible. It was presumably not grown in the Land of Israel in the early biblical period but was cultivated in the last centuries BC. It was called *tzemer-gefen* (vine wool) because its leaves resemble those of the vine.

Gossypium is a genus of the *Malvaceae* family, whose 30 species or so of annual herbs and tree-like perennials are all tropical or subtropical. Only four species are cultivated, two in the Old World and two in the New, where cultivation goes back to ancient times. Five-thousand-year-old cloth fragments of the Old World species (*G. herbaceum* and *G. arboreum*) have been found in the Indus Valley of Pakistan; cotton was also cultivated in America long before Columbus; remains of it from 4500 BC have been found in central coastal Peru.

The local cotton is an annual herb, up to 1 m. tall, with large 3-5 lobed leaves. In their axils are long stalks bearing large red or cream-colored flowers, accompanied by three large, deeply-cut green leaflets. The fruit is a many-seeded capsule which opens by means of three valves. The seeds are covered with long, dense, white or yellowish hairs, whose length depends on the particular variety. It is these hairs for which cotton is grown and has reached world-wide distribution in the textile industry, pushing flax entirely aside.

Leek

Allium porrum L.

Onion

Allium cepa L.

Garlic

Allium sativum L.

We remember the fish we ate in Egypt for nothing, the cucumbers, the melons, the *leeks*, the *onions*, and the *garlic*; but now our strength is dried up, and there is nothing at all but this manna to look at.

Numbers 11:5–6

IT is amazing that these three vegetables, so frequently mentioned and commented upon in post-biblical literature, appear in the Bible only in the passage quoted, where the longing of the Israelites of the Exodus for remembered foods is articulated.

Onions, leeks and garlic belong to the genus *Allium*, which is a member of the large Lily family and comprises approximately 600 species, about thirty of them native to the land. Most *Allium* species are limited to the temperate zones of the Old and New Worlds. While no wild ancestor has been found for the onion so far, one which has been suggested for leek and garlic (*Allium ampeloprasum*) is native to Israel. Although they were known in ancient Egypt as early as 3200 BC, onions, leeks and garlic were not domesticated there. The two former originated in Central Asia, and only garlic is believed to be of East Mediterranean origin.

Leek

THE leek (rendered as *ḥatzir* in Numbers) differs from garlic and onions in the shape of the leaf. While its open leaves are more akin to those of garlic, they tend not to form a bulb at the base. Like the onion, the leek is widely cultivated, and is indeed the most precious of the few cultivated species of *Allium*.

Onion

THE common garden onion is a bulbiferous herb up to 1 m. tall, whose large bulb consists of tunicate scales which are the fleshy bases of the leaves. The numerous tunics surround each other and serve as storing organs where reserve substances accumulate. The outer membranous coats of the bulb are tunics which have been emptied of their substances. The leaves are hollow and approximately the length of the stalk, which is also hollow, swollen in the middle, and terminating in a head of flowers. These have a perianth of six leaves, six stamens and three styles; the ovary develops a three-chambered seed-bearing capsule. The onion is extensively cultivated throughout the world. The Hebrew *betzalim* (sing. *batzal*) is clearly 'onions'.

Garlic

THE correct translation of *shumim* is 'garlic', and, like the word for 'onion', it appears in the plural. The Talmud refers to the seasoning of a number of foods with garlic, and it is also used in medicine as a digestive, stimulant, diuretic, and anti-spasmodic agent. Its solid stem bears flat leaves, some of which thicken at the base to become fleshy tunics in whose axils large bulbs are developed, forming the cloves by means of which, unlike the leek and the onion, the plant is exclusively propagated. The small flowers are grouped into heads, where small bulbs, instead of flowers, sometimes appear.

Leek *Allium porrum* (above, left).
Onion *Allium cepa* (above, right).
Garlic *Allium sativum* (below).

Lentil

Lens culinaris Medic.

Then Jacob gave Esau bread and pottage of *lentils*, and he ate and drank, and rose and went his way.

Genesis 25:34

And you, take wheat and barley, beans and *lentils*, millet and spelt, and put them into a single vessel, and make bread of them.

Ezekiel 4:9

THE first of the pulses mentioned in the Bible, Israel's ancient agriculture gave an important place to lentils. They were indeed a popular and important food during the biblical and post-biblical periods.

There is no doubt that the four references in the Bible to the Hebrew *adashim*, the several references in post-biblical literature, and the Arabic word *adas* all mean 'lentil'.

The lentil may be as old as cultivation itself. The cultivated lentil seems to have originated and been domesticated in the Near East. Carbonized seeds have been found in the earliest farm villages, dating back six or seven millenia BC, and since the Bronze Age, lentils have been frequent associates of wheat and barley. They occur in Israel also in a wild state, probably as escapees from cultivation.

The lentil is a nutrient pulse, used in soups, pastes and purées. The seed has two lens-like cotyledons which separate in threshing. Combined with other grains, it is ground into flour and used for cakes.

The genus *Lens* comprises a few species with numerous varieties and scores of strains, essentially limited to the Near East. One of them is the widely known *Lens culinaris*, an annual, much-branched plant, with rather low and weak stems. Its leaves end in a tendril. The fruit of the little pink-to-whitish flowers is a small, single-seeded pod. The lentil grows in various soils as a winter crop from sea-level to 1,200 m., but it needs a mild winter and sufficient rain.

Chick-Pea

Cicer arietinum L.

And the oxen and the asses that till the ground will eat salted *provender*, **which has been winnowed with shovel and fork.**

Isaiah 30:24

THE chick-pea is a pulse widely cultivated, especially in eastern Mediterranean countries and India, for its seeds, which are eaten roasted and ground and from which several dishes are prepared. Since its closest relatives grow in Turkey and in some neighboring countries, it was without question originally domesticated there and has indeed been found in the pre-pottery Neolithic levels of some prehistoric sites, in the Early Bronze Age deposits of Jericho, in Iraq and elsewhere. Its earliest records are from a site in Turkey dating from 5000 BC.

In the quoted passage, the biblical *ḥamitz*, cognate with the Arabic *ḥumus* and the Aramaic *ḥimtza*, means 'chick-pea'. *Ḥimtza* is currently used also in modern Hebrew for *Cicer arietinum*. (The RSV translation as 'provender' is mistaken).

The chick-pea is 30–35 cm. tall, an annual with an erect, heavily-branched stem and pinnate leaves with five to eight pairs of ovate to oblong, acutely dentate leaflets. Stem and leaves are densely covered with glandular hairs and are very viscid. The flowers are usually solitary and borne on a long stalk; the white, pink or blue corolla is about 1 cm. long. The pods, which are swollen, oblong and often 1–2.5 cm. long, house one or two angular seeds, 0.5 cm. in diameter. The flowers are usually self-pollinating. Relatively drought-resistant, the chick-pea is the latest of the spring pulses and is not harvested much before mid-summer.

The common garden pea, *Pisum sativum* L., was undoubtedly grown in Israel during and long before biblical times. It has been found in Early Neolithic farming villages in Israel and the neighboring countries, dating back to 7000–6000 BC. Moreover, the wild ancestor of the garden pea, *P. syriacum* (Berg.) Lehm., grows in Israel. It is therefore amazing that this pulse is nowhere mentioned in the Bible.

Broad Bean

Vicia faba L.

When David came to Mahanaim, Shobi the son of Nahash from Rabbah of the Ammonites ... brought beds, basins, and earthen vessels, wheat, barley, meal, parched grain, *beans* and lentils, honey and curds and sheep and cheese from the herd, for David and the people with him to eat.

II Samuel 17:27–29

WIDELY cultivated in biblical times, the broad bean was an important article of diet, as it still is in Egypt today, on account of its manifold uses. The beans are pounded in mortars for meal and sometimes mixed with millet, to make porridge and purées, or a kind of coarse bread. They are frequently cooked and eaten whole. Their cultivation is declining, however, to make way for other more delicate pulses.

The Hebrew *pol* is contextually common in post-biblical literature and is certainly 'beans'. Beans flourished during biblical times and have been found in the Neolithic levels in Jericho, where they are still cultivated. Their general distribution as a garden pulse is world-wide. Although the plant has long been thought to have originated in the Middle East, where some of the species in the local flora closely resemble the broad bean, careful research has recently refuted the assumption of its origin from local relatives. The plant itself has thus far nowhere been found in a wild state, and it is quite possible that the wild ancestor has with time become extinct.

The broad bean belongs to the huge leguminous family and is a somewhat isolated member of the genus *Vicia*, which numbers 200 species. It is an erect annual plant up to 1 m. tall; its stem - sometimes hollow - is angled and branches mainly in its upper part. The leaves are without tendrils and have two large ovate to oblong leaflets. The big white flowers, with brown-spotted wings, bloom in late spring and ripen their large pods, each with three to six ovate seeds, in summer.

Watermelon

Citrullus lanatus (Thunb.) Mansf.

We remember the fish we ate in Egypt for nothing, the cucumbers, the *melons*, the leeks, the onions, and the garlic; but now our strength is dried up, and there is nothing at all but this manna to look at.

Numbers 11:5–6

The watermelon has been known in Egypt since the Bronze Age and probably much earlier. Because three species of the genus *Citrullus* are native to Africa (Kalahari and Namibia), the watermelon can reasonably be said to have been domesticated in Africa in the Neolithic period.

THIS species has a multitude of varieties, differing in color, shape, markings, and consistency of fruit. Its cultivation is widespread throughout the warmer countries of the globe.

The translation of the Hebrew *avatiḥim* should be 'watermelons', not 'melons', since this meaning has been preserved for centuries by Arab villagers.

The watermelon is a slender, hairy annual, with long, weak branches spreading over the ground. Its large, hairy leaves are split into three or four pairs of lobes and the flowers are unisexual, solitary and axillary. The corolla is deeply fivefold, pale yellow, 2–3 cm. in diameter. The fruit is globose or oblong, varying in size from 10 to 60 cm. or more. Its flesh is red, green or yellow, and is sweet when ripe.

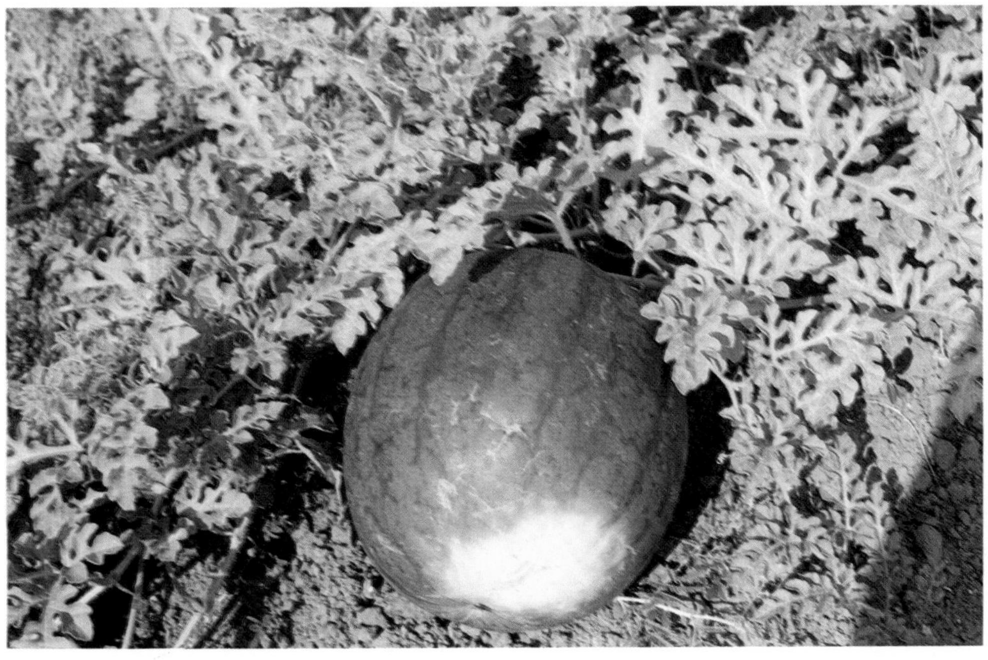

Muskmelon

Cucumis melo L. var. chatae Nand.

We remember the fish we ate in Egypt for nothing, the *cucumbers*, the melons, the leeks, the onions, and the garlic.

Numbers 11:5

And the daughter of Zion is left like a booth in a vineyard, like a lodge in a *cucumber field*, like a besieged city.

Isaiah 1:8

THE correct rendition of the Hebrew *kishuim* and *mikshah* must be 'muskmelons' and not 'cucumbers', since garden cucumbers did not exist in Egypt in biblical times. *Mikshah* is thus 'a melon-field'. The "lodge in the cucumber field" was the booth of twigs or mats still used today in the gourd-field to guard against theft.

The muskmelon and all other species of *Cucumis* – except the garden cucumber (*Cucumis sativus*) and its relatives, which are native to northern India – are tropical plants from East Africa, home of more than a score of wild *Cucumis* species. This suggests that the wild muskmelon was originally cultivated in East Africa. Among the many varieties of *C. melo* are forms with long and narrow fruits, superficially resembling the garden cucumber.

The muskmelon is a trailing, hairy annual, with roundish or ovate to kidney-shaped leaves, angled to shallowly lobed, 8–15 cm. across, borne on long stalks. The tendrils are simple and the flowers unisexual, female and male on the same plant. The corolla is yellow and deeply fivefold, about 2 cm. long. It has three free stamens and an ovary of three to five united carpels. The fruit varies in size (10–40 cm.), and shape, and is usually yellow, or light green.

Many varieties of muskmelon are cultivated in the Near East and throughout the warm countries; in Israel, where a few new strains have been developed, it is grown mainly in the Coastal Plain and other plains as a dry-farmed summer crop.

Bottle Gourd

Lagenaria siceraria (Mol.) Standl.

Zenan, Hadashah, Migdal-gad, *Dilean*, **Mizpeh,Ioktheel, Lachish.**

Joshua 15:37–38

THE town-name of Dilean is undoubtedly derived from *delaath*, a term occurring in post-biblical literature for the bottle gourd, then the principal gourd field-plant (and one which has been long and extensively cultivated) – in addition to cucumbers, which were introduced rather later, muskmelon and watermelon.

The bottle gourd or calabash, a single species of its genus, was cultivated very early in Africa and other regions of the Old World, not as food but as a container for liquids after the bitter flesh and seeds (by which it is propagated) had been scooped out. Specimens have been found in Egyptian tombs dated about 3500–3000 BC. Specimens of this same gourd have also, astonishingly, been found in Peruvian and Mexican caves; the findings date back to about 7000 BC. Scientists now have no doubt, after experimental proof, that, like the coconut, these bottle-shaped gourds floated from Africa to the other side of the Atlantic, their seeds remaining viable after two years on the ocean.

The gourds alluded to in the Bible are exclusively African; other kinds of gourd, like squashes and pumpkins, could be introduced only after the discovery of the New World.

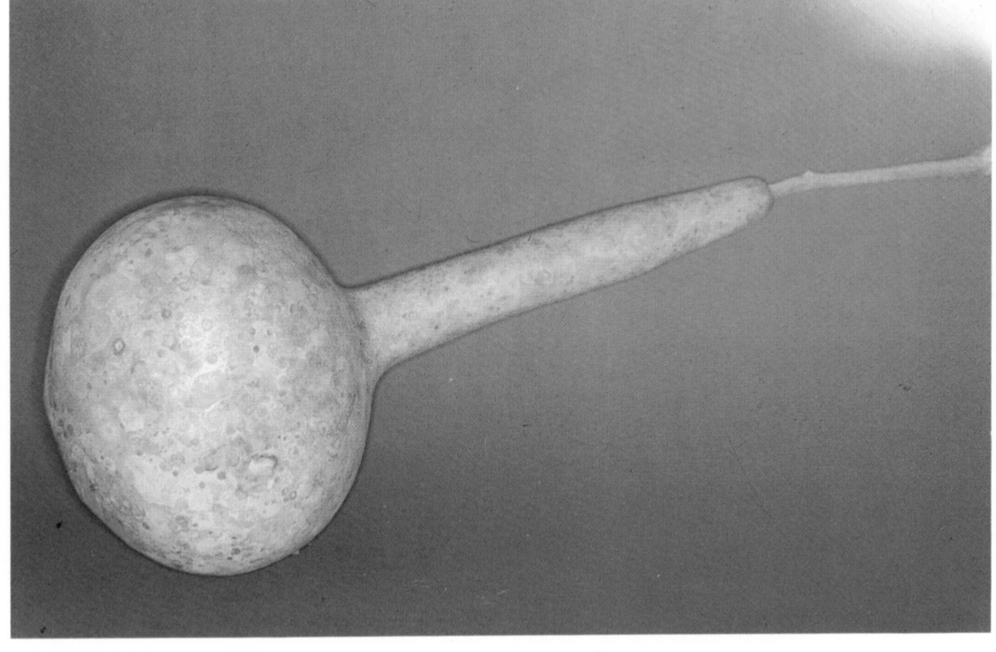

Mint

Mentha longifolia L.

Cummin

Cuminum cyminum L.

Dill

Anethum graveolens L.

Woe to you, scribes and Pharisees, hypocrites! for you tithe *mint* and *dill* and *cummin* and have neglected the weightier matters of the law, justice and mercy and faith; these you ought to have done, without neglecting the others.

Matthew 23:23

MINT grows in the Holy Land along ditches and water courses and in swamps. Commonly used as a condiment because of its aromatic oil and as seasoning for meat, it was probably far more popular in the past when people tried to flavor their tasteless food.

Of the three species of *Mentha* in Israel, *M. longifolia* is the most common, and is used medicinally in infusions considered carminative and stimulating, as well as for headaches and general pain. Since mint is listed along with other garden condiments, it is quite possible that one of the local native plants was grown in the garden.

The mint is a perennial herb, 40–100 cm. tall, covered with tiny hairs. Its main stem branches abundantly in the upper section, each branch terminating in a spike of minute purplish-pink flowers. The leaves are grayish-green, lanceolate, and toothed along the margin. Like other water-plants, it grows most luxuriously in the summer.

Cummin

THERE is no problem in identifying the Hebrew *kamon* as 'cummin', in accordance also with the Arabic *kemun*, the Accadian *kemum*, and the Greek translation. Undoubtedly native to the Middle East, the plant has not yet been found wild, with the exception of a hairy variety from Turkestan.

Cummin is an annual herb with an erect stem branching above; each branch terminates in a composed umbel of minute flowers. The leaves are deeply incised into long capillary lobes. The small, elliptical and hairy fruits consist of two carpels which are the cummin grains, widely used for flavoring bread and dishes. It is also used in folk-medicine as an anti-spasmodic, and its oil is an ingredient of perfume.

Dill

DILL is mentioned only once in the New Testament. Together with mint and cummin, it appears in connection with the accusation that the Pharisees deal diligently with minor points of the law, while neglecting much weightier matters.

In post-biblical literature dill is named *sheveth*, which is identical with its Arabic name *sabth*. Grown in the Bible Lands since ancient times, dill has a number of uses. Its aromatic fruits (seeds) are used for flavoring food and an essential oil is extracted from them. The leaves are widely used for seasoning pickles; the ripe seeds are also used medicinally as a carminative.

Dill is cultivated in gardens and also found as an escapee in the wild or even as a weed among crops. It is a hardy annual of the Carrot family. Its stem is about half a metre tall and branches richly above. It is densely clad with dark green leaves finely dissected into filiform lobes.

In some translations of Matthew, dill is rendered as 'anise'. This is a common name for *Pimpinella anisum* L., an annual with greenish-white flowers cultivated in more temperate countries as a condiment and flavorer. However, it is more than doubtful whether anise has ever been grown in the biblical countries.

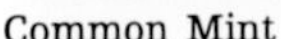

Common Mint *Mentha longifolia*

Cummin *Cuminum cyminum*

Dill *Anethum graveolens*

Common Rue

Ruta chalepensis L.

But woe to you Pharisees! for you tithe mint and *rue* and every herb, and neglect justice and the love of God; these you ought to have done, without neglecting the others.

Luke 11:42

RUE appears only once in the Scriptures (Luke 11:42), under its Greek name *peganon*; in post-biblical literature it is mentioned more than once as *pigam*, closely cognate with the Arabic *fegan*; another Arabic name for it is *saadab*.

Luke mentions rue and mint together as herbs. A similar phrase is found in Matthew 23:23, but rue is not specifically listed there (see 'Dill').

Frequently grown in home gardens, both as an ornamental plant and as a condiment, rue contains an essential oil which is distilled from its leaves and other green parts. Medicinally it is used as an antispasmodic, and also for several home remedies.

A dwarf-shrub native to Israel and other Mediterrranean countries, the common rue grows in the *bathah* (dwarf-shrubbery) formations where its yellow flowers and heavy scent render it very striking. It is a richly-branching plant with abundant dissected leaves covered throughout with oil-bearing glands. Its flowers have a green calyx and 4–5 yellow fringed petals about 1 cm. long. The fruit is a small capsule with dark seeds.

Black Cummin

Nigella sativa L.

***Dill* is not threshed with a threshing sledge, nor is a cart wheel rolled over cummin.**
Isaiah 28:27

THE identity of the Hebrew *ketzaḥ* with 'black cummin' or 'nutmeg flower' is not only linguistically supported but attested by the widespread post-biblical custom of sprinkling the seeds over bread and cake and of flavoring dishes with them. The Arabic and Aramaic name is *kazḥa*. (The rendition of 'dill' for *ketzah* in the RSV is erroneous.)

The black cummin is the only one of 14 species that has been cultivated since ancient times. It is an annual herb, about 30 cm. tall, with abundant, finely incised leaves, its branches terminating in a showy lilac flower with five sepals, five petals, many stamens and an ovary of a few carpels. After pollination the ovary turns into a closed hairy capsule containing numerous black, angular seeds.

Coriander

Coriandrum sativum L.

Now the house of Israel called its name manna; it was like *coriander seed*, **white, and the taste of it was like wafers made with honey.**

Exodus 16:31

THE Bible tells us that the famous heavenly bread of the Israelites in the desert – the manna – was like the seeds of *gad*. To identify *gad* as 'coriander' is difficult because of contextual and linguistic discordances. The Septuagint translates *gad* as *korion*, which is a different plant. Similarly, the Arabic *gidda*, cognate with *gad*, refers to wormwood (*Artemisia*), not coriander. Most translators were probably guided by the Punic word for coriander, *goid*, which is also cognate with *gad*.

Coriander, moreover, is never found in the desert, and its brown grains cannot be compared with the white drops of manna, which should more appropriately be equated with any of a score of common desert plants with white round seeds or fruits, or with plants whose Arabic name is cognate with *gad*.

The coriander is an annual herb of the Carrot family, with deeply incised leaves and umbels of white flowers. Its fruits are globular, 1–3 mm. across, and are crowned by a rudimentary calyx. All parts of the plant have a strong odor. It is native to Israel and occurs as a weed among winter crops. Once widely cultivated as a condiment, its leaves are sometimes used to flavor soups, puddings, curries and wines. It also has some medicinal value.

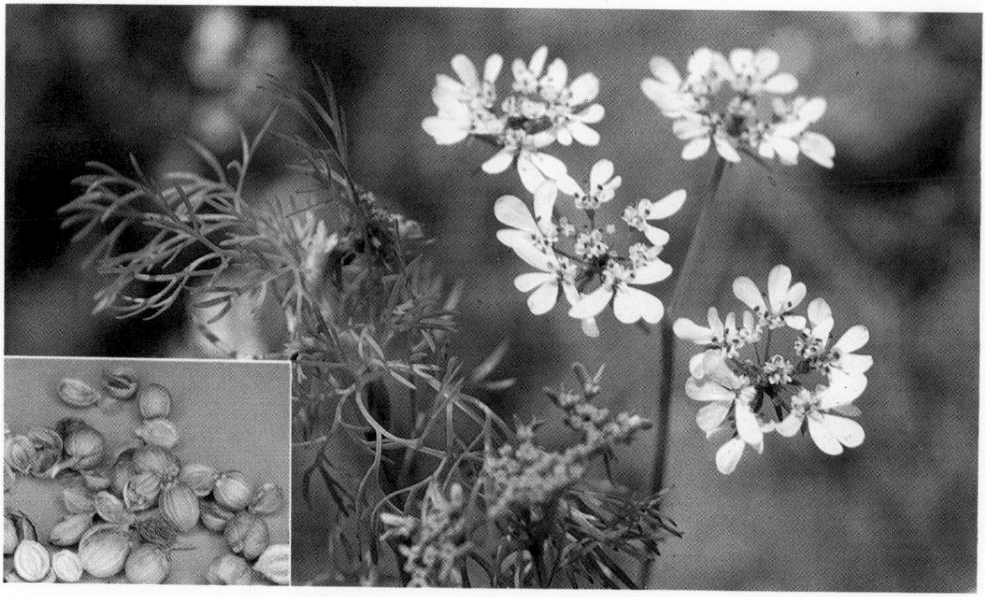

Black Mustard

Brassica nigra (L.) Koch

And he said, "With what can we compare the kingdom of God, or what parable shall we use for it? It is like a grain of *mustard seed*, which, when sown upon the ground, is the smallest of all the seeds on earth; yet when it is sown it grows up and becomes the greatest of all shrubs, and puts forth large branches, so that the birds of the air can make nests in its shade."

Mark 4:30–32

THE mustard of the New Testament is probably *Brassica nigra*, source of the important condiment black mustard, which has long been extensively cultivated and was in biblical times the source of mustard-seed oil and a medicament. Evidence for its identity is that it is the tallest plant in the local species of *Sinapis* and *Brassica*, often 2 m. and more in height; and since it is conspicuous in the vegetation around the Sea of Galilee and farther north, it suits the context of the parable, as does also the small size of its seeds (1 mm.).

The Greek *sinapis* is undoubtedly 'mustard'. Mustard is not mentioned in the Old Testament, but it is often referred to in the Mishnah.

The black mustard is an annual herb with large leaves clustered mainly at the base of the plant. Its central stem branches abundantly in its upper part and produces an enormous number of yellow flowers and small, many-seeded linear fruits, appressed to the branches.

3
Wild Herbs

THE Land of Israel has long been a home of livestock husbandry and its abundant non-arable mountain land was intensively used for grazing. No less than two hundred species of generally palatable grass can be found in this country, growing along with other herbs suitable for grazing. Even the biblical 'desert' is in some passages considered by commentators to mean 'grazing land' rather than 'wilderness'. Large areas of the Negev and the Judean Desert, in fact, sustain myriads of goats and sheep, and even when rainfall is sparse, grass and herbs are scattered everywhere: "Thou dost cause the grass to grow for the cattle, and plants for man to cultivate, that he may bring forth food from the earth" (Psalms 104:14).

Grass and herbs flourish in this country because it is situated at the limit of the woodland. Moreover, much of its woodland vegetation has been replaced through man's destruction by herbaceous steppes or semi-steppes which are rich in annual and perennial herbs and grasses. Since early prehistory, in fact, the flora of this country and its neighbors have accounted for the vegetable diet of the population.

During the wanderings of the Israelites in Sinai, the word *ḥatzir* primarily referred to 'leek', but later changed to 'grazing grass' or 'field herbs', and served as a symbol of mortality. Besides *ḥatzir*, the biblical *esev*, mentioned over thirty times, clearly relates also to herbs, as does *deshe*, apparently a general term for herbage and greenery. In the story of the world's creation the Bible uses the verb *tadshe*, 'to grow grass' (Genesis 1:11). The grass and herbs covering the earth roofs of small village houses were called 'the grass of the housetops', as appealing to the ancients as it is to us.

Pot-herbs, in biblical times, were scanty in the vegetable garden, and collected wild. The Bible's few references to these edible plants include such allusions as: "I have given you every plant yielding seed which is upon the face of all the earth" (Genesis 1:29); "and you shall eat the plants of the field" (Genesis 3:18).

Among pot-herbs is included a group of plants known as 'bitter herbs' (Hebrew: *merorim*), still gathered by villagers. This is a collective rather than a specific term for a whole group of plants – called in Arabic *murair* – and its cognates, mainly of the Composite family, whose foliage and soft young stems are gathered in rainy seasons for salad, although they are generally bitter.

Merorim (sing. *maror*) was at the time of the Exodus the name probably given to many edible plants in the desert, including some of the Mustard family. It was used primarily to flavor the tasteless unleavened bread (*matzoth*), but came to symbolize in Jewish tradition the 'bitter labor' of the Israelites' forefathers in Egypt; it is still eaten at the celebration of the Passover meal. Only a few of them are described here.

Syrian Hyssop

Origanum syriacum L.

Then Moses called all the elders of Israel, and said to them, "Select lambs for yourselves according to your families, and kill the passover lamb. Take a bunch of *hyssop* and dip it in the blood which is in the basin, and touch the lintel and the two doorposts with the blood which is in the basin.

Exodus 12:21–22

He spoke of trees, from the cedar that is in Lebanon to the *hyssop* that grows out of the wall.

I Kings 4:33

Purge me with *hyssop*, and I shall be clean; wash me, and I shall be whiter than snow.

Psalms 51:7

After this Jesus, knowing that all was now finished, said (to fulfil the scripture), "I thirst." A bowl full of vinegar stood there; so they put a sponge full of the vinegar on *hyssop* and held it to his mouth. When Jesus had received the vinegar, he said, "It is finished"; and he bowed his head and gave up his spirit.

John 19:28–30

THE word *ezov* refers in the Bible to a plant tied into bunches and used as a brush to sprinkle blood on the doorposts and lintels when the house was cleansed against leprosy (Leviticus 14:4), as well as for purposes of worship (Numbers 19:6). 'Hyssop' is now the conventional translation for *ezov*, but this was not always so, as their identity was inadequately attested. A particular source of error lies in the fact that the well-known European hyssop (*Hyssopus*) does not grow in Israel or the Sinai, while the Syrian hyssop *Origanum syriacum*, does grow abundantly there among the dwarf-shrubbery, usually on stony ground. The Arabs call it *zaatar* and use it in tea and in cooked and baked food. It is sold in the markets and is a popular Arab spice.

Because of its association with cleaning, the hyssop plant was thought to possess powers of spiritual purification (Psalms 51:7). At the same time, it was supposed to exemplify the stunted discredited plants that grow out of walls (I Kings 4:33), although it is actually a handsome plant, 50–80 cm. tall, and does not sprout on walls. Moreover it is rare in the Sinai, where Moses

ordered the people to take bunches of it, although there are frequent references to its use there.

The identity of the biblical *ezov* with *O. syriacum* is confirmed by a Samaritan custom whereby *Origanum* is traditionally used by Samaritans to sprinkle the blood of the Passover sacrifice. The hair on the stems is said to prevent coagulation of the blood, but this has not been proved. The above identification is thus still problematic.

The Syrian hyssop is a stout, many-stemmed, hairy gray shrub about 70 cm. tall, with ovate to elliptical leaves, opposite and entire. The white, rather small flowers are grouped in dense spikes on the upper part of the branches. The flowers, which appear in midsummer, are subtended by wooly bracts as long as the calyx, made up of a flattened hairy lip. The corolla, from which the four stamens are exserted, is two-lipped. The fruit is a minute nutlet enclosed in the calyx and is dispersed by the wind (see: 'Caperbush').

Caperbush

Capparis spinosa L.

The almond tree blossoms, the grasshopper drags itself along and *desire* fails; because man goes to his eternal home, and the mourners go about the streets.

Ecclesiastes 12:5

THE meaning of the passage quoted is in serious dispute, but the Hebrew word *avionah* ('desire' in the RSV) has been translated by many scholars as *Capparis* or 'caperbush.' In Talmudic literature, *avionah* generally means the fruit (and certainly the large flower buds) of the caper. It is astonishing that this common, useful, and beautiful plant, with its strikingly fresh leaves and large flowers, is mentioned only once in the Bible and then by a name hardly documentable. The Mishnah on the other hand, calls it *tzalaf*, which in the Bible is a proper name (Nehemiah 3:30), as is Zelopheḥad (appearing several times: in Numbers 26:33; Joshua 17:3; I Chronicles 7:15).

Tristram (1868), Balfour (1866) and other scholars think that the Hebrew name for 'caper' is *ezov*, because its Arabic name *lassaf* is in fact *el asaf*, which is cognate with *ezov*. They claim further that the caper is more common in the desert than *Origanum*, now generally believed to be the biblical *ezov* (see 'Syrian Hyssop').

The genus *Capparis* includes many tropical species in both the Old and the New Worlds. There are two tropical and two Mediterranean species in Israel. In all of them the flower buds and sometimes the fruits are pickled and eaten. In some countries, indeed, the plant is grown only for its buds for pickling.

The caperbush is an intricately-branched shrub growing on the ground and on stone walls, including the Western (Wailing) Wall in Jerusalem, as well as on rocks. Its rounded leaves have two spines (stipules) and its large white flowers consist of four sepals, four petals, several mauve stamens, and a single ovary on a long stalk. The flowers, which bloom in midsummer and are pollinated by hawk-moths, open in the evening and wilt the morning of the next day. After a few weeks the ovary becomes an oval, fleshy, many-seeded berry, which splits at maturity into valves and exposes the seeds to dispersal by the birds.

Mallow

Malva sylvestris L.;
M. nicaeensis All.

Hollyhock

Alcea setosa (Boiss.) Alef.

Can that which is tasteless be eaten without salt, or is there any taste in the slime of the *purslane*? My appetite refuses to touch them; they are as food that is loathsome to me.
Job 6:6–7

BIBLE scholars have good reason to consider the Hebrew *ḥalamuth* in the passage quoted as one or more species of the genera *Malva* and *Alcea*, both belonging to the *Malvaceae* family and common in Israel and its vicinity. This accords with the Mishnaic rendition of *ḥalamith* or *ḥalamuth* as a plant which was later translated into Latin as *malva* and into Arabic (by Maimonides) as *hitmiye* (*Alcea*). Plants of both genera are common pot-herbs, whose leaves are collected in early winter by peasants for soups and salads. Indirect support for *Malva* is the Arabic name *ḥubeize*, from *ḥubez*, 'bread' – probably because the edible fruits resemble small round loaves. If the original *ḥalamuth*, therefore, is corrected metathetically to *laḥamuth* or *laḥamith* it matches the Arabic name for this plant. This is linguistically and contextually fairly reasonable. Modern Hebrew renders *Malva* as *halamith*.

M. sylvestris is less common here than *M. nicaeensis*, which is a herb up to 40 cm. tall, well-branched and thickly covered with roundish leaves, 3–10 cm. in diameter. The flowers are pink and grow in small clusters which rise from the axils of the leaves. They open in the morning and close at night, and soon after pollination develop the fruit, which consists of several carpels around a central stalk, the whole looking like a pie cut in wedge-shaped pieces.

Mallow *Malva sylvestris*

Hollyhock *Alcea setosa*

Mallow *Malva nicaeensis*

Dwarf Chicory

Cichorium pumilum Jacq.

Reichardia

Reichardia tingitana (L.) Roth

They shall eat the flesh that night, roasted; with unleavened bread and *bitter herbs* they shall eat it.

Exodus 12:8

MANY plants, especially those belonging to the Mustard and Daisy families, are frequently collected and used as pot-herbs and salad plants. Among them are also a number of plants possibly consumed by the people of the Exodus in their Passover meals in the desert. The chicory and reichardia discussed here are only representatives of the group of 'bitter herbs', and may not have been the most important of the biblical *merorim*. Their Arabic names are *mureir* or its derivatives.

The dwarf chicory belongs to a special subgroup of the giant Composite family and is one of the nine Mediterranean species of the genus *Cichorium*, most of which grow on roadsides and in abandoned fields. The stem is normally short, but when growing ungrazed or under favorable conditions it attains a height of 1 m. or more. The rather large, oblong leaves, with their prominent mid-nerve and lobed margins, are used as pot-herbs and are also palatable to cattle. After ripening, the heads close and conceal the fruits until the rains come, which moisten the heads, force them open, and disperse the nutlets. This species is very closely related to the cultivated chicory used in salads and as an additive to or substitute for coffee.

The poppy-leaved reichardia is a desert plant with a thick rosette of rather large, entire or lobed leaves. It is sparsely branched and scarcely 20 cm. tall. The large flowering heads on their thick stalks are encircled by many large scales. They are strip-shaped and yellow and after pollination develop minute achenes, heavily tufted with white hairs.

Poppy-leaved Reichardia *Reichardia tingitana*

Dwarf Chicory *Cichorium pumilum*

Garden Rocket

Eruca sativa L.

One of them went out into the field to gather *herbs*, and found a wild vine and gathered from it his lap full of wild gourds, and came and cut them up into the pot of pottage, not knowing what they were. And they poured out for the men to eat.

II Kings 4:39–40

THE Hebrew *oroth* is mentioned as a plant only in the above passage. It was gathered near Gilgal in the Jordan Valley, where a plant called in Arabic *jarjir* (the garden rocket) is particularly common. The local villagers or Bedouin collect it as a pot-herb or wild salad. Since *oroth* also appears as *gargir* in the Talmud it can plausibly be identified with the rocket.

It is unlikely, however, that people collecting pot-herbs should have confused the edible rocket with the very different and poisonous wild gourd. Hence it seems that *oroth* is not a specific plant and that the Aramaic translation of *oroth* as 'vegetables' is correct, and so also is the rendition of the RSV. This assumption is supported by the biblical verb *aroh*, meaning 'to collect, pick, gather,' and also by the plural form in which the word appears.

The garden rocket is an annual of the Mustard family; its lower leaves are divided into large lobes and eaten as salad. The flowers are rather large, with strongly-nerved, cream-colored petals. It was formerly grown for its oil-bearing seeds that can also be used as a substitute for pepper.

4
Forest Trees & Shrubs

THE forests of the Land of Israel do not compare with those of more humid areas. Seldom have they been tall or imposing; those of the Bible consisted mostly of low trees and high shrubs which under certain circumstances could reach the stature of trees. One feature emphasized in the references to forests in the Bible was their harboring of wild beasts – boars, lions and bears: "The boar from the forest ravages it, and all that move in the field feed on it" (Psalms 80:13). These animals are almost entirely non-existent in the forests of Israel today, and this clearly indicates that over the centuries the forests have degraded and have hence become depopulated of their fauna.

The clearing of forests was always connected with flourishing agriculture and abundant forests were the result of its decline: "Then Joshua said to the house of Joseph, to Ephraim and Manasseh, 'You are a numerous people, and have great power; you shall not have one lot only, but the hill country shall be yours, for though it is a forest, you shall clear it and possess it to its farthest borders'" (Joshua 17:17–18). The "great power" is emphatically expressed here because the work of clearing forests in this country required then, and still does, very hard labor. In the stony and rocky ground the roots of the trees penetrate deep crevices which enable the tree to sprout and reappear even after being cut or burnt. Testimony to the fact that plants have from time to time reconquered derelict cultivated land is the occurrence of wine and oil presses, cemeteries, or even cultivated trees in the midst of dense forests.

It is now well known that the local forests not only supplied the raw materials for manufactures, industry and fuel in this country, but were also a source of timber for export to Egypt.

The Hebrew word for 'forest', *yaar*, is mentioned about sixty times in the Bible, as in Isaiah 44:23: "Sing, O heavens, for the Lord has done it; . . . O mountains, O forest, and every tree in it!" In certain instances the word *yaar* is coupled with a place name, obviously denoting localities renowned for their forests: the forest of Ḥereth (I Samuel 22:5); the forest of Ephraim (II Samuel 18:6); the forest of the Negeb (Ezekiel 20:47). Sometimes the names of various trees, the cedars of Lebanon or the oaks of Bashan, replace the general term of 'forest'. *Yaar* might denote 'wildness' too at times; such a phrase as "as an apple tree among the trees of the woods" (Song of Solomon 2:3) alludes to cultivated apple trees among wild trees rather than to apple trees growing wild in the woods.

Cedar

Cedrus libani Loud.

And Solomon sent word to Hiram the king of Tyre: "As you dealt with David my father and sent him *cedar* to build himself a house to dwell in, so deal with me ... Send me also cedar, cypress, and algum timber from Lebanon, for I know that your servants know how to cut timber in Lebanon."

II Chronicles 2:3, 8

I will put in the wilderness the *cedar*, the acacia, the myrtle, and the olive; I will set in the desert the cypress, the plane and the pine together.

Isaiah 41:19

IN the time of the Bible Lebanon and large expanses of the Cilician Taurus abounded with cedar forests, a number of which, though reduced in size, still stand today. The cedar is a mountain tree, snow-clad in winter, growing mainly on stony ground at an altitude of 1,500–1,900 metres. Its southern limit runs not very far from the northern boundaries of Israel, but is has never crossed the frontier.

It was highly esteemed by all peoples and by the royal houses of the entire Orient as "the glory of Lebanon" (Isaiah 35:2). From their earliest history the Egyptians imported cedar wood for buildings, ships, thrones, altars, etc., because of its superior quality, fragrance and durability. It symbolized strength, dignity and grandeur, and was considered the prince of trees; what the lion was to the animal world, the cedar was to the plant world. Egyptian and Assyrian royal reports extol the cedar wood from Lebanon and Amanus (II Kings 19:23), and the Ugarits have left poetic testimony to its supremacy. The negotiations between King Solomon and Hiram King of Tyre about wood for building the Temple and lesser houses are an example of timber transactions in the area. Both the First and the Second Temples in Jerusalem were constructed of cedar wood.

Erez, mentioned in the Bible over seventy times, is rightly translated in all the versions as 'cedar'. Most of the translations refer to the genus *Cedrus*, which, when coupled with 'Lebanon', is doubtless *C. libani* Loud., and otherwise may refer to *Pinus halepensis* Mill., a common local forest tree. There is, moreover, geographical evidence that the cedar, associated as in Numbers 19:6 with hyssop, "and the priest

Old sturdy cedar in the forests of Lebanon.

shall take cedarwood and hyssop and scarlet stuff, and cast them into the midst of the burning of the heifer'' (see also Leviticus 14:6), in connection with the cleansing of the leper and the house contaminated by leprosy, refers to trees similar to it in appearance, like certain species of tamarisk or Phoenician juniper.

The handsome and mighty cedar of Lebanon may attain 30 m. in height and two or more meters in diameter. It is an evergreen coniferous tree, reaching an age of two to three thousand years. As it ages, its pyramidal form acquires a flattish cone shape with thick widespreading horizontal branches, densely covered with clusters of short needle-like leaves, often bluish-green in color. Its male and female cones grow on separate branches; the adult female cone consists of many scales with seeds on their upper side. The cones are broad-ovoid, and split when mature into single scales that drop with their seeds.

Young cedars in the Jerusalem mountains.

Evergreen Cypress

Cupresus sempervirens L.

Cilician Fir

Abies cilicica (Ant. et Ky.) Carr.

Eastern Savin

Juniperus excelsa M.B.

And Hiram king of Tyre had supplied Solomon with cedar and *cypress* timber and gold, as much as he desired.

I Kings 9:11

O Tyre, you have said, "I am perfect in beauty." Your borders are in the heart of the seas; your builders made perfect your beauty. They made all your planks of *fir trees* from Senir.

Ezekiel 27:3–5

Open your doors, O Lebanon, that the fire may devour your cedars! Wail, O *cypress*, for the cedar has fallen, for the glorious trees are ruined!

Zechariah 11:1–2

THE biblical *berosh* (pl. *beroshim*) in the quoted passages, occurring more than thirty times in Scripture, denotes coniferous trees with small scale-like or short-linear (rather than needle-like) leaves, and refers in general to the evergreen or to the common (horizontal) cypress. The latter is now known to be native to Israel. It is rare in Galilee and Gilead, more abundant in the highlands of Edom, and was once common in the Judean mountains, as evidenced by pollen and by the frequent occurrence of the wood in the buildings and furniture found in archeological digs. A wealth of material has accumulated around the identification of *berosh*, which I consider a collective name for the three species in the heading.

Whenever *berosh* is coupled with 'Lebanon' or *erez*, it probably refers to *Abies cilicica*, the Cilician fir, which grows in Lebanon along with the cedar, forming a kind of mixed forest or the remnants of one. The great timber negotiations between King Solomon and Hiram of Tyre undoubtedly included this outstanding species of Lebanese tree, whose southernmost limit of distribution is today the village of Slenfe (at a latitude of about 34° north).

Indirect evidence that this fir is the Lebanese *berosh* is the Accadian word *burasu*, which designates *Abies*. According to Campbell-Thompson (1949), beams of *burasu* (fir) and *arinu* (cedar) were brought from the Amanus mountains by King Shalmanezer in the 9th century BC. Cedars and firs still occur there today, while the common cypress has so far not

Evergreen Cypress *Cupresus sempervirens*

been found in the region. The cypress was apparently never imported from Lebanon, and in any case, there were enough cypresses in the land to supply local building needs.

It must be noted that *Juniperus excelsa* (or *J. foetidissima*), one of the stately conifers of the Lebanon, very like the cedar and growing in the same environment, should also be included under the comprehensive name *berosh*, because the local Lebanese population calls it *brotha*, a name surely identical with the *berothim* of the Song of Solomon.

The Accadian *burasu* may also refer to *J. excelsa*, since according to Campbell-Thompson it was also imported from Eilam in the Zagros mountains, where *J. excelsa* is still found. There is a further reference to *J. excelsa* in Ezekiel's "fir trees of Senir" (27:5), for this tree still grows on Mt. Senir (Hermon).

The trees mentioned above have their minute flowers arranged in cones, the male ones located on the lower branches and the female on the upper ones. The seed-bearing cones are made up of woody scales, except for the eastern savin whose scales are fleshy.

Cilician Fir *Abies cilicica*

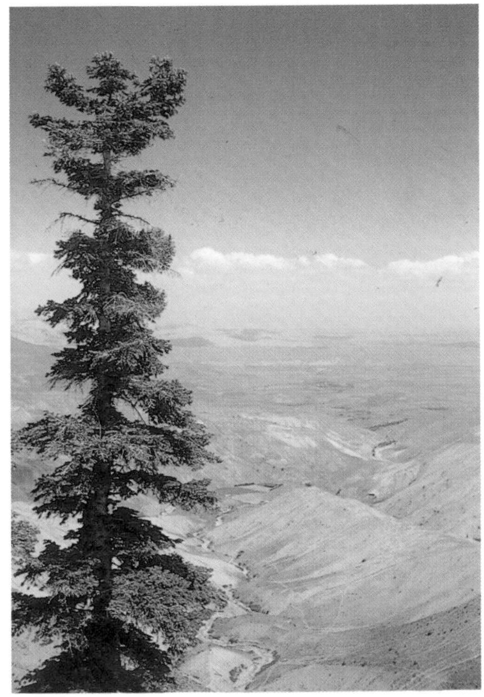

Eastern Savin *Juniperus excelsa*

Oak

Quercus ithaburensis Decne.;
Q. calliprinos Webb

And Deborah, Rebekah's nurse, died, and she was buried under an *oak* below Bethel; so the name of it was called Allon-bacuth.

Genesis 35:8

They sacrifice on the tops of the mountains, and make offerings upon the hills, under *oak*, poplar, and terebinth, because their shade is good. Hosea 4:13

Yet I destroyed the Amorite before them, whose height was like the height of the cedars, and who was as strong as the *oaks*.

Amos 2:9

THERE are three oak species in the thickets and forests of the Holy Land; two of them, the common evergreen oak and the Tabor oak, are the most impressive in their stature, age and dominance.

Both species are sometimes mighty trees, symbolic of power and longevity, pride and splendor. They were associated with worship, offerings and other ritual and religious customs; furnished burial sites for the honored dead; and were undoubtedly used in everyday life for buildings, ship oars, and other utensils.

The oak was not only worshiped (*allon* and *elon* [oak] are associated with the Hebrew word for 'god' – *el*), but also beloved, for quite a number of geographical localities in the Bible bear its name. Because of the Tabor oak's height and strength, it has been suggested that many of the devotional activities mentioned in Scripture relate to it rather than to the common oak.

The Hebrew *allon* (pl. *allonim*) or *elon*, with many citations in the Bible, should generally be translated 'oak', while *elah* should be rendered as 'terebinth tree'. This distinction has not always been strictly observed by the translators, including those of the RSV.

Single, old tall trees or stands of pure oaks can still be found in many places, supporting the assumption that the present maquis vegetation derives from long-ago primary forests – an assumption strengthened by the fact that pure oak stands, revered as 'sacred forests', grow here in a variety of soils. The oldest of them, according to tradition, is the oak of Abraham in Hebron. Like most trees of the maquis and forest, both species have vertical roots several meters deep, and horizontal roots that spread several meters near or below the surface.

Although at present the tree rarely forms forests, scattered stands and individuals indicate that Tabor oak forests once spread throughout the Coastal Plain (north of the Yarkon River), the Lower Galilee, the Dan Valley, the Ḥulah Plain and the Golan Heights. Judging from its local distribution, this species, unlike the common oak, does not seem to be characteristically Mediterranean. A species in the Zagros (Iranian) mountains is its close relative.

The Tabor oak is a stately deciduous tree, up to 25 m. tall and 20 m. in crown circumference. It is believed to attain an age of 300 to 500 years. The leaves are ovate to oblong, covered with a dense coat of hairs; their edges are dentate, the teeth ending in a short point. They sometimes do not drop until late winter and are occasionally retained throughout, at least in part, especially during mild winters. Since it requires warmer winters, the Tabor oak is limited to lower altitudes, plains, and valleys; it never climbs more than 500 m. up the mountains. It seems rather indifferent to soil, apparently feeling at home on sandy and basaltic soils, chalky *rendzina, terra rossa* and even deep alluvial ground. This tree flowers much earlier than the common oak, but in both types the male and female flowers, pollination, and the long time-lapse between pollination and fruit maturation are similar. The Tabor oak too displays a rich variety of acorn forms.

The Tabor oak is central in a series of Israeli arboreal plant communities, appearing in pure stands in the coastal region, but sharing a number of Mediterranean associates on the mountains, and semi-steppe associates in the eastern flanks of the mountains.

The common oak is properly a shrub, branching from the base; but under conditions not altogether clear, it occasionally becomes tall, with a trunk circumference of 1–3 m. Its leaves are ovate-oblong, relatively small, leathery, glabrous, with spiny-toothed margins. They begin to fall in the spring soon after new leaves have fully developed. The tree flowers in April, displaying hundreds of many-flowered male catkins hanging under the erect sparsely-flowered female spikes. The flowers of both sexes are inconspicuous but well adapted to wind pollination. The male florets consist of a green perianth of five to nine leaflets and five to ten stamens. The females are remote from one another, and are encircled by numerous minute overlapping scales which later become leathery or woody, cupule scales. When young, the ovary has two ovules in each cell, but only one of the six develops into a seed.

Tabor Oak *Quercus ithaburensis*

Terebinth

Pistacia atlantica Desf.;
P. palaestina Boiss.

So they gave to Jacob all the foreign gods that they had, and the rings that were in their ears; and Jacob hid them under the *oak* which was near Shechem.

Genesis 35:4

And Joshua wrote these words in the book of the law of God; and he took a great stone, and set it up there under the *oak* in the sanctuary of the Lord.

Joshua 24:26

THE terebinth's biblical name, *elah*, like that of the oak, stems from the Hebrew *el* (god) and is associated with might and sturdiness. These trees are among the most aged and widespread species, particularly in the Negev, Lower Galilee and the Dan Valley.

Like the oak, the terebinth was revered and deified by the ancient Hebrews and other peoples and terebinth stands have served as sites for worship and incense-burning and as burying places for the beloved or respected dead.

Several biblical stories are connected with the terebinth. An angel appeared before Gideon under a terebinth (Judges 6:11); Jacob buried Laban's idols under the terebinth at Shechem (Gen. 35:4); Saul and his sons were buried under another such tree (I Chronicles 10:12); David killed Goliath in the Valley of Elah – 'Terebinth' (I Samuel 17:2); and David's son Absalom died when his hair was caught among a terebinth's branches (II Samuel 18:9).

Atlantic Terebinth *Pistacia atlantica*

Four species of *Pistacia* (terebinth) are native to Israel and a fifth to Sinai and Edom, but only the two which head this entry fit the biblical context. Many translators and exegetes, unacquainted with the local flora, and embarrassed by the frequent occurrence in the Bible of *elah, elon, el, alah* and *allon*, have seriously misunderstood these names. While the primary sense might not always be appropriate, there are too many variations in the translations of different authors, and (as in the RSV) much inconsistency even within any given translation. Generally, *allon* and *elon* should be rendered 'oak', and *elah* and *alah* 'terebinth'. Even in their outer appearance the two trees cannot be confused.

In both species of terebinth the leaves are composed of two or more pairs of leaflets, and are shed in winter. The flowers are minute, green and thickly clustered, with male and female appearing on different trees. The fruits are small, fragrant drupes. The two species differ markedly from each other in structure, leaves and ecological requirements; the Palestine terebinth is typically Mediterranean, often occurring in company with the common oak tree, and the Atlantic terebinth, a dry-land tree with modest needs, grows mainly in the border areas between the evergreen woodland and the dwarf-shrub steppes. Since the latter achieves greater height and age than the former, it can be assumed that the *elah* of the Bible usually refers to the Atlantic terebinth.

Palestine Terebinth *Pistacia palaestina*

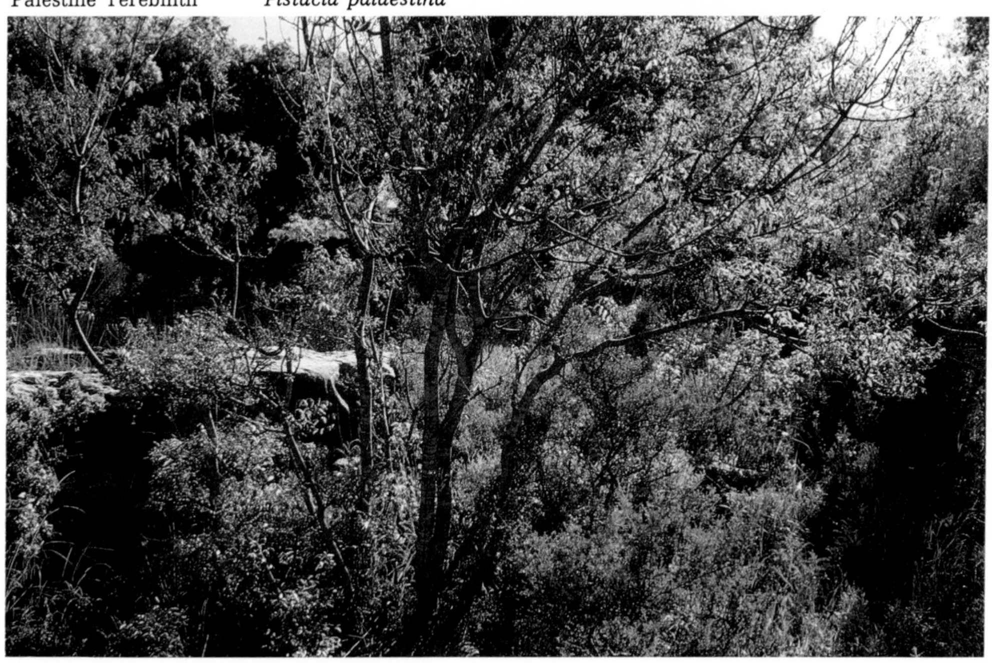

Laurestinus

Viburnum tinus L.

I will put in the wilderness the cedar, the acacia, the myrtle, and the olive; I will set in the desert the cypress, the *plane* and the pine together.

Isaiah 41:19

The glory of Lebanon shall come to you, the cypress, the *plane*, and the pine, to beautify the place of my sanctuary; and I will make the place of my feet glorious.

Isaiah 60:13

THE scholarly efforts to identify linguistically or contextually the Hebrew *tidhar* with any plant have thus far failed. In the two quoted passages, *tidhar* and the other trees are symbols of revival. The only way to overcome the difficulty is to accept the reliable Aramaic translation of the *Targum Yonathan*, which renders *tidhar* as *mornian*, which is cognate with the Arabic *murran* – the only Arabic name for *Viburnum tinus*. No other suggestion has the slightest linguistic support.

A handsome low tree growing in the forest of Carmel, the laurestinus may aptly be described as the 'glory of Carmel'. It is widely cultivated as an ornamental tree.

The laurestinus is an evergreen, 3–5 m. tall, with opposite ovate to oblong leaves and large umbels of white flowers. It blooms in early spring and produces one-seeded blue-black berries.

Stone Pine

Pinus pinea L.

He cuts down cedars; or he chooses a *holm tree* or an oak and lets it grow strong among the trees of the forest; he plants a cedar and the rain nourishes it.

Isaiah 44:14

THE tree named *tirzah* appears only in the quoted passage. In the RSV it is translated 'holm tree', which in fact has never grown in the Holy Land; other translations name other trees, but without contextual or linguistic justification. Etymologically, the word's radical *rz* suggests kinship with *erez* (cedar). This may have led Saadia Gaon, translator of the Bible into its first Arabic version (tenth century), to render *tirzah* as 'stone pine'; and indeed in many languages, Arabic among them, the names of various conifers include the radical *rz* or *arz*. An allusion to this is found in the Talmudic statement (*Rosh ha-Shanah* 23a) that there are ten kinds of *arazim* (cedars). Indirect evidence for *tirzah* as the stone pine is offered by Tomson (1860), who says that this tree was common in the Coastal Plain of Palestine during the last century and formed extensive forests there. Such forests also occur on the Aegean coast and in the Lebanon (Feinbrun, 1959). The groves of stone pine or their remnants at Yarka on the Coastal Plain of Galilee and on Mt. Carmel may be what is left of extensive old planted or spontaneous groves, the seeds (nuts) of whose trees are said to have been exported in quantity.

The stone pine is a handsome parasol-shaped tree, up to 30 m. tall. The stem has a grayish-brown bark; the twigs are grayish-green when young and turn brown with age. Leaves appear in pairs, 10–15 cm. long, rather thick and acute. The cones are a shining brown, 8–14 cm. long. The seeds are 15–20 mm. long and about 7 mm. broad. They are wingless and fall down with the disarticulating cone scales. They are edible and are known as pignolia nuts in the market.

Aleppo Pine

Pinus halepensis Mill.

In the inner sanctuary he made two cherubim of *olivewood*, each ten cubits high ... For the entrance to the inner sanctuary he made doors of olivewood; the lintel and the doorposts formed a pentagon.

I Kings 6:23, 31

Go out to the hills and bring branches of olive, *wild olive*, myrtle, palm, and other leafy trees to make booths, as it is written.

Nehemiah 8:15

PINE forests were once widespread in the Holy Land, and could not possibly have been ignored by the biblical writers. The Hebrew word now used for 'pine' (*oren*) has a different meaning in the Bible (see 'Laurel'); but *etz shemen*, which occurs five times in the Bible, sometimes side by side with the olive tree, should be rendered 'pine tree', and not as erroneously translated in the RSV: 'olive wood', or 'wild olive'. One of the reasons for this identification is that the Jewish villages of North Kurdistan, where *P. brutia*, a species closely related to *P. halepensis*, forms natural forests, have – probably since the Babylonian exile – preserved the name *etz shemen* for the pine. Further indirect evidence is available in Talmudic and exegetical literature.

The Aleppo pine is much less abundant now than it was in biblical times, but in spite of severe abuse through the ages it still accounts for some conspicuous forest stands in the country, notably on chalky-marly rocks and grayish-white rendzina soils. Since it attains a height of 20 m. and an age of 100–150 years, the 'pride of the Carmel' celebrated in the Bible must have been the pine forest growing there. The many vestiges of it in all the Mediterranean parts of Israel strengthen the assumption of its former abundance.

Stately and quick-growing, the Aleppo pine is a tree which makes light demands. Its horizontally spreading lower branches die away when overshadowed by the upper ones, and its evergreen foliage is two-needled. Like other pines, its flowers are enclosed in cones, male on the lower branches, female on the upper. The yellow, dust-like pollen is scattered by the wind, thus causing pollination, which occurs fifteen months before seed-setting. The long-winged seeds are hidden in the scales of the oblong cones, which open and release them at the end of the second year. Most of the 85 species of the genus *Pinus* are American, but the Aleppo pine is strictly Mediterranean.

Leafless Tamarisk

Tamarix aphylla (L.) Karst.

Abraham planted a *tamarisk tree* in Beer-sheba, and called there on the name of the Lord, the Everlasting God.

Genesis 21:33

And they took their bones and buried them under the *tamarisk tree* in Jabesh, and fasted seven days.

I Samuel 31:13

STATELY tamarisk trees are scattered throughout the sandy areas of the Negev, where they were planted by the desert Bedouin for their shade and their soft branches, which the flocks eat. For centuries the villages of the Coastal Plain have propagated this tree by cuttings. It is, however, indigenous in the hot wadies of the Aravah Valley.

In the quoted passages the Hebrew *eshel* is certainly the tamarisk. It is cognate with the Arabic *atl* or *ethl*, which refer either to *Tamarix aphylla* or to another species of the genus. It is noteworthy that the word *eshel*, which originally indicated a definite species, became in post-biblical literature a general term for 'trees'. In the Bible itself, *eshel* in I Samuel 31:13 was replaced in the parallel I Chronicles 10:12 by *elah*. It is surprising that this common tree, of which twelve species are native to Israel (generally confined to deserts, marshy places, and swamps), should be mentioned far less in the Bible than the alien cedar (*erez*). Presumably because of the outward similarity between the two, the name 'cedar' was also applied to the tamarisk, especially in connection with the cleansing of lepers and their houses (Leviticus 14:4).

Much more common is the Nile tamarisk (*T. nilotica*), which grows in nearly every deep wadi of the desert, near water, in marshes and on sand.

The leafless tamarisk is a richly-branched evergreen tree up to 10 m. tall and up to 1 m. in diameter, with an oval crown. Its twigs, intensely green or grayish-green, are leafless, but their green joints function as photosynthesizing and transpiratory organs. The small, spiked white flowers bloom in autumn and quickly produce fruits which are capsules with many minute seeds, each with a tuft of hairs. Very wasteful of water, this hot-desert tree excretes salt through special glands in its leaves.

Leafless Tamarisk *Tamarix aphylla*

Nile Tamarisk *Tamarix nilotica*

Common Acacia

Acacia raddiana Savi

And you shall make upright frames for the tabernacle of *acacia wood.*

Exodus 26:15

And Joshua the son of Nun sent two men secretly from *Shittim* **as spies, saying, "Go, view the land, especially Jericho."**

Joshua 2:1

THE common acacia is the most correct identification of the *shittah* whose wood was used for constructing the Tabernacle. None of the other four species of acacia native to this country, namely *A. laeta, A. tortilis, A. negevensis* and *A. albida*, could have been so suitable for building and so compatible with the text as is the common acacia (*A. raddiana*). *A. laeta* and *A. albida* are altogether absent in Sinai, where the Israelites were wandering, while the other two are rare in Sinai or unsuitable for construction.

Of the twenty-four references in the Bible to *shittim*, nineteen are to the acacia tree and five to places associated with it. Proof that *shittim* means 'acacia' is supplied by the Arabic *sunt*, a linguistic equivalent of the Hebrew *shittah. Sunt* designates certain species of *Acacia* in Egypt, Arabia and southern Israel.

The phrase in Isaiah 41:19, "I will put in the wilderness the cedar, the acacia [*shittah*], the myrtle, and the olive," raises the question why the *shittah* trees should be brought to a place that abounds with them, and illustrates the difficulty of identifying the many plants the prophet Isaiah mentions.

The common acacia attains a height of 5–8 m. and is branched above. The long, white, sharp spines of the twigs are the stipules of the leaves, which are bipinnately divided into small, oblong to elliptical, glabrous leaflets. The flowers, which have globular heads, are minute and borne on long stalks. The main flowering season is spring, the second season is late summer. The many-seeded fruits are glabrous, twisted pods, which fall from the tree and are consumed by various animals.

Phoenician Juniper

Juniperus phoenicia L.

From *Aroer*, which is on the edge of the valley of the Arnon.

Deuteronomy 2:36

Cursed is the man who trusts in man and makes flesh his arm, whose heart turns away from the Lord. He is like a *shrub* in the desert, and shall not see any good come.

Jeremiah 17:5–6

THE Phoenician juniper is common in the mountains of northern Sinai and the red sandstone of Edom but in neither place is it a true desert plant, lonely and scattered in the far south, like the carob tree; nor does it occur in the wilderness of Israel, as the text requires. A second species of *Juniperus* native to Israel is a forest tree in the Upper Galilee, which is also inappropriate.

It is now strongly believed, however, that these two isolated stands of *Juniperus phoenicea* were bridged in the geological past by scattered growths all across the Negev, and that single stands and perhaps single individuals survived during biblical times in lonely and disparate parts of the desert. These isolated trees were eventually destroyed.

The identification of the biblical *arar* with *Juniperus* is based solely on the Arabic name given to this and other species of *Juniperus* in several Arabic-speaking countries.

The Phoenician juniper is a tree or shrub, usually less than 5 m. tall, which attains an age of several hundred years. It has a thick trunk and is heavily-branched above; the branches bear minute, scale-like leathery leaflets, which are closely appressed to the twigs in opposite pairs or in whorls. Their lower face is marked by a linear gland. The flowers are unisexual, the males in erect catkins, the females consisting of a few scales, each with a single ovary. The seed-bearing cones are globular, tawny red, berry-like and fleshy, with three to six seeds.

Styrax

Styrax officinalis L.

Then Jacob took fresh rods of *poplar* and almond and plane, and peeled white streaks in them, exposing the white of the rods.

Genesis 30:37

They sacrifice on the tops of the mountains, and make offerings upon the hills, under oak, *poplar*, and terebinth, because their shade is good.

Hosea 4:13

THE Hebrew *livneh* occurs only twice in the Bible. In Hosea it is definitely styrax (*S. officinalis*), coupled as it is with the oak and the terebinth. Both have grown since biblical times in Israel's evergreen forests or maquis, often together with styrax. The Arabic *libna* and *abhar* (white, bright) support this identification. The *livneh* of Genesis 30:37, however, should be rendered *Populus alba* (white poplar); an example of the assigning of a single name to two or more plants which is not uncommon in the Bible (see 'White Poplar'). Styrax should not be equated with storax, for it yields no gum, and the disputes about extracting storax from it are due to misunderstanding. Styrax is, therefore, a misnomer.

The styrax is a deciduous tree about 3–6 m. tall, with a richly-branching trunk and orbicular to oval leaves about 5 cm. long, green in the upper face and white-hairy beneath. The whitish color of the leaves, visible from a distance, is responsible for the name *livneh* (white). The tree has its leaf-break in March and starts to bloom in April, its showy white flowers strongly resembling those of the orange tree. They grow in small clusters, each flower with a short calyx and a 3–5 cm. white, bell-like corolla. The fruit is a one-seeded, hard, wooly green drupe, which turns yellow when ripe and is especially striking in autumn after leaf-shed. The large, poisonous seeds are frequently used by fishermen to stun the fish in order to catch them more easily.

Common Myrtle

Myrtus communis L.

Go out to the hills and bring branches of olive, wild olive, *myrtle*, palm, and other leafy trees to make booths, as it is written.

Nehemiah 8:15

I will put in the wilderness the cedar, the acacia, the *myrtle*, and the olive; I will set in the desert the cypress, the plane and the pine together.

Isaiah 41:19

THE Hebrew and the Aramaic names for myrtle are *hadas*; the Arabic, *as* and *riḥan*; the Accadian, *asu*. It is one of the 'four species' the Israelites were ordered to use on the first day of Tabernacles.

The myrtle was popular with the biblical and post-biblical population of the Holy Land and its name was given both to men (Assa) and to women (Hadassah - as in Esther 2:7). Its aromatic branches had many uses. They figured in betrothal rites and were even used sometimes as remedies, because the leaves have oil-secreting glands located in cavities within the palisade tissue.

In ancient Greece, the myrtle, significant in ritual, art and poetry, was dedicated to Aphrodite. Some authors believe that the generic name derives from the Greek *myron*, meaning 'myrrh', owing to its odor and high sweet-scented oil content. It is important in gardening even today, both as an ornament (because of its deep evergreen color) and as hedging, on account of its dense branches.

The common myrtle is a native plant growing not only in damp plains like the banks of the Jordan River and the Dan Valley, but also in the Golan, in Upper Galilee and, rarely, on Mt. Carmel. An all-Mediterranean species, it belongs to the *Myrtaceae* family, which comprises about 3,000 species dispersed among 100 genera. The genus *Myrtus* includes about 100 mainly tropical species, and the one dealt with here is unique in departing from the main area of the family.

It is an evergreen shrub up to 2 m. tall, with dense upright branches bearing opposite or whorled, deep green, leaves, ovate-oblong 3–5 cm. long. It blossoms in summer and its flowers consist of a globular calyx, from which a white five-lobed corolla and many white stamens are exserted. Its fruit is a blackish-blue berry.

Laurel

Laurus nobilis L.

He cuts down cedars; or he chooses a holm tree or an oak and lets it grow strong among the trees of the forest; he plants a *cedar* and the rain nourishes it.

Isaiah 44:14

ALTHOUGH it is not generally thought to be mentioned in the Bible, the laurel, often lauded for its fragrance, its oil content, and its berries, useful as a condiment and used as a medicine, could not have been ignored by the biblical writers, especially in the context of praise of the Carmel, where it abounds. There is in fact strong linguistic support for recognizing the laurel in the Hebrew *oren*, which the RSV renders as 'cedar' (in modern Hebrew, *oren* = pine). The Aramaic *Targum Yonathan* gives *aranye*, and the Arabic name is *ar*. Moreover, post-biblical literature and commentators use the name *ar* or its derivatives for 'laurel', and the Accadian name *eru* is rendered as *Laurus* by Campbell-Thompson (1949).

The tree was particularly esteemed by the ancient Greeks, whose heroes were adorned with laurel garlands.

The laurel is a dioecious evergreen forest tree, up to 8 m. high, which grows on stony ground on Mt. Carmel and in the Galilee. Its deep green leaves are somewhat leathery and contain volatile oil. The male flowers have four petals and many stamens, partly provided with nectariferous glands; the females have a few stamens and a pistil which, after pollination, develops into a black-blue drupe as large as an olive and is dispersed by birds. It is commonly used today as an ornamental tree in gardens, and its leaves serve as a condiment in different foods. It is also known as 'sweet bay'.

Ivy

Hedera helix L.

And when the feast of Dionysus came, they were compelled to walk in the procession in honour of Dionysus, wearing wreaths of *ivy*.
II Maccabees 6:7

THE ivy, now rare in Israel and found only in Upper Galilee and Samaria, may once have been much more widely distributed. It is common in the forests of temperate countries and is a popular ornamental hedge plant.

The ivy is an evergreen perennial climbing shrub with a thick, woody, densely-branching stem. It climbs by means of short rootlets, forming a toothbrush-like body. The leaves are borne on long stalks; their blades are dark green, with a cordate or rounded base and three to five ovate-triangular entire lobes. The small, yellowish-green flowers, arranged in umbels, have minute calyxes and petals. The fruit is black and globular.

Apple of Sodom (Mudar)

Calotropis procera (Ait.) Ait. f.

The country of Sodom borders upon it [Lake Asphaltitis]. It was of old a most happy land, both for the fruits it bore and the riches of its cities, although it be now all burnt up. It is related how, for the impiety of its inhabitants, it was burnt by lightning; in consequence of which there are still the remainders of that divine fire, and the traces or shadows of the five cities are still to be seen, as well as the ashes growing in their *fruits*, which fruits have a colour as if they were fit to be eaten, but if you pluck them with your hands they dissolve into smoke and ashes.

Josephus, Jewish Wars, Book IV, 8:4

THIS peculiar plant, totally different from any other, requires hot oases and is common in the areas of the Dead Sea and the lower Jordan Valley, spreading widely from the Sudanese region to northern India. Wherever it is found it is usually called by its Arabic name, *osher*. The apple of Sodom symbolizes the evil and condemned Sodom and Gomorrah; its accursed fruit is fleshless and puffy and full of hairs. The juice is poisonous. In Africa it is used to poison arrows and wells.

The passage supplies the sole reference in biblical or post-biblical literature to the apple of Sodom, but other plants - *Citrullus colocynthis*, *Solanum incanum* - have also been so named by some, although unjustifiably. The apple of Sodom is a symbolic conception rather than a denotative term.

The apple of Sodom is a small tree, 3-5 m. tall; the stems are corky, with peeling bark and branches full of milky latex, a violent local irritant. Its thick, mostly ovate leaves are sometimes 20 cm. long. Its flowers, in umbel-like clusters, have a corolla about 2 cm. in diameter and five whitish lobes with dark purple tips. The fruit develops quickly into twin green apple-like bodies, often 7-10 cm. across. The flat seeds have a tuft of hairs which allows the wind to scatter them. The stems are used for ropes and fishnets and the fleece for filling pillows and mattresses.

Citron

Citrus medica L.

And you shall take on the first day the fruit of *goodly trees*, branches of palm trees, and boughs of leafy trees, and willows of the brook; and you shall rejoice before the Lord your God seven days.

Leviticus 23:40

WHAT is the Hebrew *etz hadar*, the biblical 'goodly trees'? Translators and exegetes insist that it is a citrus species, *Citrus medica*, the fruit of which is the Hebrew *ethrog*. Goor (1968) and Moldenke (1952), on a thorough discussion of the question, agree that *etz hadar* is *C. medica*, which was introduced from India into some countries of the Near East at a very ancient date, and that it grew in Israel at the time of the Bible. Others are of the opinion that *etz hadar* was not a specific tree. It is mentioned only once, as one of the 'four species' for the Feast of Tabernacles (Leviticus 23:40), and does not appear at all in the passage in Nehemiah: "Go out to the hills and bring branches of olive, wild olive [more correctly, Aleppo pine], myrtle, palm, and other leafy trees to make booths as it is written" (8:15). This passage, however, does not refer to the 'four species' but to the making of booths.

It is, however, surprising that no mention is made in Nehemiah of the goodly trees in connection with the observance of the Feast of Tabernacles, if one accepts the opinion of those who credit the exiles who returned from Babylon, of whom Nehemiah was one of the leaders, with having introduced the *ethrog* into Israel for the first time.

The citron tree is small, bearing short spines and evergreen dentate leaves. The flowers are white inside and purplish outside. The fruit is ovate or oblong, its color bright yellow. The fruit's skin is highly aromatic, its flesh is very acid.

Ebony

Diospyros ebenum Koenig

The men of Rhodes traded with you; many coastlands were your own special markets, they brought you in payment ivory tusks and ***ebony*****.**

Ezekiel 27:15

EBONY is one of the woods which must have been imported as a luxury from remote places over the ancient land or sea routes. *Ḥovenim* in Hebrew and *hbu* in Egyptian is ebony, the heartwood of a tall evergreen tree native to India and Ceylon. Many species of the genus *Diospyros* supply this costly wood, which is soft and white when young, and hard and black inside at maturity. It is used in cabinet-making, turnery, and the manufacture of ornaments and instruments. In associating it with ivory, also a luxury item, the prophet alludes to the fact that the two were used together, ivory being inlaid in the ebony for a stunning contrast.

Ezekiel only sketchily records the commercial routes and the countries with which Israel traded. We are not sure whether ebony and ivory were brought direct from India, but we do know that both Asian and African merchandise were shipped to Dedan, a Phoenician commercial center on the Arabian coast. Nor is the identity of the imported articles named in the Bible always clear, an instance of which is the dispute about the identity of costly timber like ebony.

The ebony is a tall tree with evergreen leaves and unisexual flowers, whose corolla is bell-shaped or tubular. The fruit is a fleshy berry about 2 cm. in diameter. It is the inner part of the trunk that is black and known as 'black ebony', so prized in commerce.

Red Saunders

Pterocarpus santolinus L. f.

Moreover the fleet of Hiram, which brought gold from Ophir, brought from Ophir a very great amount of *almug wood* **and precious stones. And the king made of the almug wood supports for the house of the Lord, and for the king's house, lyres also and harps for the singers; no such almug wood has come or been seen, to this day.** I Kings 10:11–12

Send me also cedar, cypress, and *algum timber* **from Lebanon, for I know that your servants know how to cut timber in Lebanon.** II Chronicles 2:8

THE first Book of Kings tells us that the precious timber of the *almug* tree was used in constructing the House of the Lord and for making the lyres and harps played by the Levites in the Temple. Its origin is clearly attested by the description of a commercial exchange between King Solomon and Hiram of Tyre. It was brought from far away, probably via the reputed 'silk route' leading from the Far East to the Mediterranean countries.

As to the identification of *almug* with the red saunders, there is no direct linguistic evidence, but the recorded past trade in this tree and the continuing desirability of its timber admirably suit the context. A further difficulty in identifying the tree in question arises from the different names given to it in the Bible - both *almug* and *algum*. The context shows, however, that these must be names for the same tree, the letters *m* and *g* having been transposed.

In both cases the tree is the red *almug*, a tropical tree which cannot be grown on Mt. Lebanon, where also there are no instances of trees of precious timber other than those previously identified, and surely none out of which musical instruments have been made. In order to reconcile the apparent conflict between the passages as to the wood's provenance, the word order in II Chronicles 2:8 should be changed to read: "Send me also cedar, cypress from Lebanon and algum timber", so that it is clear that the origin of *algum* is not in Lebanon.

The red saunders, a member of the large Bean family, is a tree with trifoliate leaves and ovate leaflets, hairy beneath and smooth above. Its yellow flowers are grouped in axillary spikes and its fruit is a two-seeded pod. It is native to India, developing best in the mountains of Coromandel and Ceylon, but is cultivated in southern India and the Philippines as well.

Future archeological investigations on the site of the Temple Mount will certainly show whether or not *almug/algum* was red saunders. Until then, however, the RSV has done well to transliterate the original Hebrew.

5
Plants by Rivers & Marshes

ALTHOUGH Israel is on the rim of the desert, it is relatively rich in water plants, which appear in the Jordan Valley, the Coastal Plain, along riverbanks, springs and brooks. This lushness is partly due to the land's situation between the temperate and the tropical plant zones and to its location on the north-south bird-migration track.

The number of species in wet habitats exceeds two hundred. In Scripture, however, barely ten are mentioned, despite the admiration for water plants which uses them as symbols for goodness and righteousness: "He is like a tree planted by streams of water" (Psalms 1:3).

Words like *agam* (lake) or *bitzah* (marsh) clearly imply places of swampy vegetation. *Ahu* (meadow) specifically denotes damp swampy land used for grazing.

Wet meadows occur in low places or riverbanks inundated in winter and covered in summer with grass, such as are found along the banks of the Nile and in or near swamps and banks in the Holy Land. They provide grass and other palatable herbs and pasture after the herbs of the mountains have dried up.

Because of the enormous variety it is difficult to identify certain swamp plants, but willow, poplar, oriental plane, hairy elm, oleander, papyrus and reed are among those whose identification is unquestionable.

Hairy Elm

Ulmus canescens Melv.

He cuts down cedars; or he chooses a holm tree or an oak and lets it grow strong among the trees of the forest; he plants a cedar and the *rain* nourishes it.

Isaiah 44:14

THE common translation of the Hebrew words *ve-geshem yegadel* as 'and the rain nourishes it' (which also appears in the RSV) is thematically unfounded and illogical. Contextually, *geshem* must also be a kind of tree – one of the five species contained in the quoted passage.

Neshem, Arabic for the hairy elm (*Ulmus*), might be substituted for *geshem*. The letter *n* in Hebrew can easily be mistaken for the similar *g*.

The hairy elm is a deciduous tree, up to 8 m. tall. The leaves are rather large, ovate to oblong, with dentate margins and a long apex, gray-hairy beneath and asymmetrical. The minute flowers are grouped in catkins and appear before the leaves. The fruit is a compressed broadly-winged nutlet dispersed by the wind.

The 18 species of the genus *Ulmus* grow in humid and temperate regions. They are used as softwood in carpentry. The relevant species is probably a relic of a rainier period, since it survives in this country only on banks of water-courses in Galilee and Samaria.

Oriental Plane

Platanus orientalis L.

Then Jacob took fresh rods of poplar and almond and *plane*, and peeled white streaks in them, exposing the white of the rods.

Genesis 30:37

I grew tall like a palm tree in En-gedi, and like rose plants in Jericho; like a beautiful olive tree in the field, and like a *plane tree* I grew tall. Ecclesiasticus 24:14

The cedars in the garden of God could not rival it, nor the fir trees equal its boughs; the *plane trees* were as nothing compared with its branches.

Ezekiel 31:8

THERE is no reason to doubt the identity of *armon* with the oriental plane tree. The word is rendered as *dilba* in Aramaic, a name preserved by the Arabs for the plane tree. It is suggested that *armon* is derived from the Hebrew *erom*, which means 'naked', because the tree's bark peels off easily, leaving the trunk naked.

The fact that the name Wadi Dilb was given to several rivers, including those that no longer support plane trees, suggests that the tree was distributed more widely in the past.

The oriental plane tree is fairly common in northern Israel and is especially conspicuous in the riverine forest. Aged specimens, 20 m. tall and 3 or more m. in circumference, are found by permanent rivers. Generally deciduous, the leaves are 3–5 lobed and covered with sharp and readily removable hairs which are harmful to the skin and eyes, a fact noted by Dioscorides and Galen.

The flowers are unisexual, males and females growing on the same tree, in separate spherical, almost sessile heads on pendant stalks. The male flowers have a minute green perianth and three to eight stamens, and the females a small pistil. Pollination is effected by the wind, which also disperses the small nutlets thus produced.

Euphrates Poplar

Populus euphratica Oliv.

He set it like a *willow* twig, and it sprouted and became a low spreading vine, and its branches turned toward him, and its roots remained where it stood.

Ezekiel 17:5–6

By the waters of Babylon, there we sat down and wept, when we remembered Zion. On the *willows* there we hung up our lyres. For there our captors required of us songs, and our tormentors, mirth, saying, "Sing us one of the songs of Zion!"

Psalms 137:1–3

THE Euphrates poplar is particularly characteristic of the bank (or flood) forest of the Jordan. Tolerant of a high degree of salt in the soil, this species of poplar, along with the wild date palm, grows in many of the springs of brackish water in the desert (see 'Willow').

The dispute in the Talmud over *tzaftzafah* and the much-cited biblical *aravah*, as to the halakhic question of the 'four species' to be taken at the Feast of Tabernacles (of which the willow or poplar is one), has been sustained by later scholars. The "willows" of the Babylonian rivers (Psalms 137:2) are clearly the *Populus euphratica* dominant in riverine Euphrates vegetation. They are commonly called *gharab* by the Arabs (a name equivalent to the Hebrew *aravah*). But the *tzaftzafah* of Ezekiel may be either a poplar or a willow, here again because the Arabic name for the latter is *safsaf*. The controversy is intensified by the names given to the two species by Arabs in different countries: all species of *Salix* (willow) are called *safsaf* in Egyptian Arabic; whereas the Euphrates poplar, commonly called *hawr* (white), are called in Iraq *gharab* and in North African Arabic *safsaf el abiad* or simply *safsaf*.

The reason for this confusion probably lies in the fact the the Euphrates poplar displays two kinds of leaves: those of the younger shoots and branches, being oblong, are similar to those of the willow, while the leaves of the older shoots are ovate to rhombic and resemble those of the poplar.

Willow

Salix alba L.;
S. acmophylla Boiss.

And you shall take on the first day the fruit of goodly trees, branches of palm trees, and boughs of leafy trees, and *willows of the brook*; **and you shall rejoice before the Lord your God seven days.**

Leviticus 23:40

I will pour my Spirit upon your descendants, and my blessing on your offspring. They shall spring up like grass amid waters, like *willows* **by flowing streams.**

Isaiah 44:3–4

THE identification of the biblical *aravah* with the willow is unquestionable, except for Psalms 137:2: "On the willows there we hung up our lyres", which must refer to the Euphrates poplar. Willow and Euphrates poplar are confused, probably because part of the foliage of the latter is similar to that of the willow. This illuminates the Talmudic saying that after the destruction of the Second Temple the *aravah* became *tzaftzafah* and vice versa.

Willow boughs are among the 'four species' which the Hebrews were commanded to take at the Feast of Tabernacles.

The two native species of willow are rather common along the banks of permanent streams and near fresh-water springs, in the Coastal Plain, on the mountains and in the upper Jordan Valley. The differences between them are often blurred by hybridization, but *S. alba* is in general a northern species demanding a cooler climate than *S. acmophylla*, which is more heat-tolerant. In the forest along the Jordan River, willows dominate in the north where the water is fresh, and towards the south give way to the Euphrates poplar, which is tolerant of salt water (see: 'Euphrates Poplar').

The willow is a deciduous tree with oblong acute leaves shed at the end of summer. The flowers are arranged in catkins, males and females on different trees. The minute greenish flowers appear in early winter, while the many-seeded fruits mature in early summer.

Common Willow
Salix acmophylla

White Poplar

Populus alba L.

Then Jacob took fresh rods of *poplar* and almond and plane, and peeled white streaks in them, exposing the white of the rods.
Genesis 30:37

THE Hebrew name *livneh* as it appears in the quoted passage is a homonym, used both for the white poplar and for the styrax. The context in Genesis 30:37 forbids 'styrax' as a rendering because the scene is in a region where no Mediterranean tree (including styrax) ever grew, but where the poplar might then have flourished on the riverbanks; as it does today in the Dan reserve of northern Israel and elsewhere (see 'Styrax').

The white poplar owes its name to its whitish-gray bark and to the white wooly lower face of its leaves, which are 3–5 lobed. It is native to Middle Eastern countries, including Syria and Lebanon, and thrives along riverbanks and in damp places, where its whiteness stands out in the landscape against the surrounding verdure. It was cultivated for its soft, workable timber, useful in making various agricultural and domestic tools, and for its straight trunk, excellent for roofing the houses in villages throughout the Middle East. Whether it was native to northern Israel is uncertain, but it was grown widely until the middle of this century and is still used not only for timber and as an ornamental, but as a tonic and febrifuge, because of the salicid and glucosid populin in its bark.

The white poplar is a deciduous, dioecious tree with ovate or rhombic leaves. The minute flowers, growing in loose, pendant catkins, appear before the leaves, each with a cup-shaped disk at its base and borne in the axil of a bract. The male flower has four or more stamens, the female a two-celled ovary with two or more stigmas. After pollination by the wind, the ovary becomes a capsule whose numerous small seeds are surrounded at the base by a tuft of long silky hairs which allow the seeds to be dispersed.

There are 30 species of the genus *Populus* throughout the temperate countries, many of them used as ornamentals, others planted commercially for timber. They are easily propagated by means of cuttings, and grow rapidly.

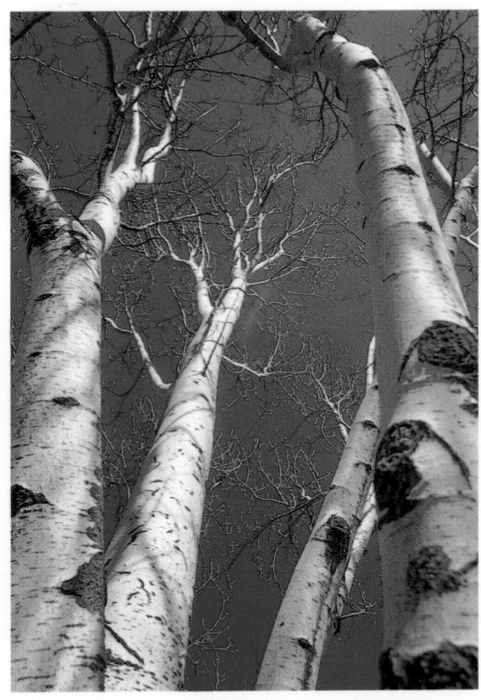

Oleander

Nerium oleander L.

So I went, as he directed me, into the field which is called *Ardat*; and there I sat among the flowers.

II Esdras 9:26

THE oleander is common on the riverbanks in Israel, especially where the ground is stony. It constitutes fairly broad belts of the riparian vegetation. It has been introduced into the garden for ornamental purposes and a number of varieties have been developed. All parts of the plant, including its beautiful foliage and flowers, contain a poison, already known to the ancients, and used in medicine.

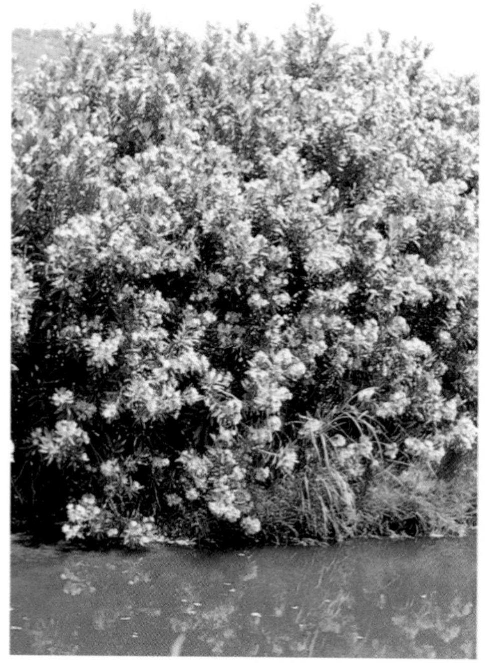

The place name mentioned in this passage of the Apocrypha seems to be cognate with *ardaf*, the Hebrew name for the oleander (*harduf* in modern Hebrew). In the Armenian translation of Esdras 'Ardat' was rendered as 'Ardab'. Since *b* and *t* are interchangeable, this lends support to the identification, which is made yet more plausible contextually.

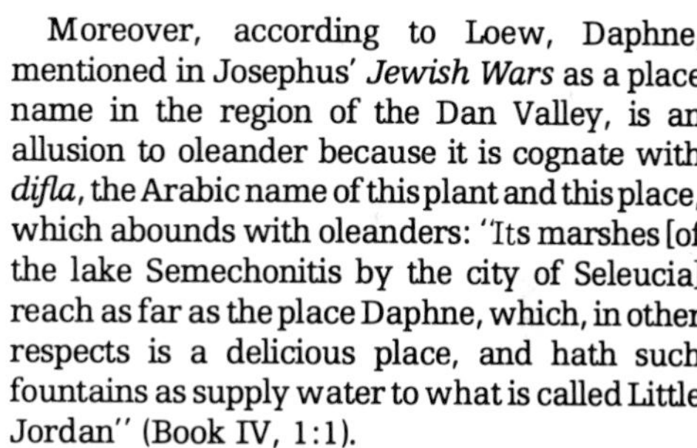

Moreover, according to Loew, Daphne, mentioned in Josephus' *Jewish Wars* as a place name in the region of the Dan Valley, is an allusion to oleander because it is cognate with *difla*, the Arabic name of this plant and this place, which abounds with oleanders: "Its marshes [of the lake Semechonitis by the city of Seleucia] reach as far as the place Daphne, which, in other respects is a delicious place, and hath such fountains as supply water to what is called Little Jordan" (Book IV, 1:1).

The genus *Nerium* comprises three species of which the most common is *N. oleander*, whose stem reaches a height of 2–4 m. It is an evergreen shrub with a well-developed branching top-root, heavily branched and leaved, the oblong to elliptical leaves growing in opposite pairs or in whorls of three. Both leaves and stems contain a reputedly poisonous milky resin. The pink-to-white flowers, which start to bloom early in summer, are funnel-shaped, wide open, sweet-smelling and about 5 cm. in diameter. The oleander fruit is a long double pod, each of whose many small seeds has a tuft of hair. The pods dehisce at the end of the summer and disperse their seeds in the wind.

Reed

Phragmites australis (Cav.) Trin.

The Lord will smite Israel, as a *reed* is shaken in the water.

I Kings 14:15

And plaiting a crown of thorns they put it on his head, and put a *reed* in his right hand.

Matthew 27:29

THE Hebrew *kaneh* is a reed that grows in swamps and marshes. It is sometimes used to symbolize weakness and fragility owing to its hollowness: "Behold you are relying now on Egypt, that broken reed of a staff" (II Kings 18:21); but usually it denotes plants of a swampy habitat and riverbanks.

The identity of *kaneh* (English 'cane') with 'reed' has linguistic and contextual attestation and is further supported by the use of the term for fencing, the shaft of the lamp stand (Exodus 25:31), measures of length (Ezekiel 40:5), and reed pens (3 John 13).

The history of the word helps to explain its usage. Of Sumerian origin, it entered into Semitic languages with the meaning of 'reed' or 'cane', and later 'measuring rod', both of which senses passed into Greek. Metaphorically, it came to be used for a rule or standard of excellence. It was the Church Fathers of the fourth century who first applied 'canon' to the sacred Scriptures.

In Israel there are four species of reed with long rootstocks and tall stems, hollow and jointed, entirely covered with large leaves, each ending in tassels of flowers. Of the four, the most common and conspicuous is *Phragmites australis*, which is referred to in the above passages, even though a collective concept of 'reeds' also exists.

During the biblical period, the reed provided one of the materials extensively used in everyday life, and was therefore also grown in the gardens. It was utilized for field hedges, mats, flutes, scales, pens and walking canes and for house construction.

Lake Rush

Scirpus lacustris L.

So the Lord cut off from Israel head and tail, palm branch and *reed* in one day.

Isaiah 9:14

Is such the fast that I choose, a day for a man to humble himself? Is it to bow down his head like a *rush*, and to spread sackcloth and ashes under him?

Isaiah 58:5

THE quoted verses render the Hebrew *agmon* as 'rush' and 'reed'. *Agmon* is derived from *agam*, which always means 'pool', 'lake' or 'vegetated swamp', but also a swamp- or water-plant. In the quoted passages *agmon* seems to be a general term for water-plants of a particular appearance, like 'rush' in English. It has been rendered by some *Scirpus*, though without adequate reason. All other specific plant names proposed for *agmon* must be rejected. On linguistic and contextual grounds, the collective term 'rush' remains the most plausible.

Among the six local species of *Scirpus*, the lake rush (*S. lacustris*) is the most striking. It fits the phrase in Isaiah 58:5 in that the mature spikelets (heads) of the plant are indeed 'bowed down'; but other species of the genus are equally possible.

The lake rush, rather common in marshes, is a perennial herb with a creeping rootstock and round green leafless stalks up to 1 m. tall. The flowers are minute, green, and clustered in spikelets borne on long rays forming a compound umbel.

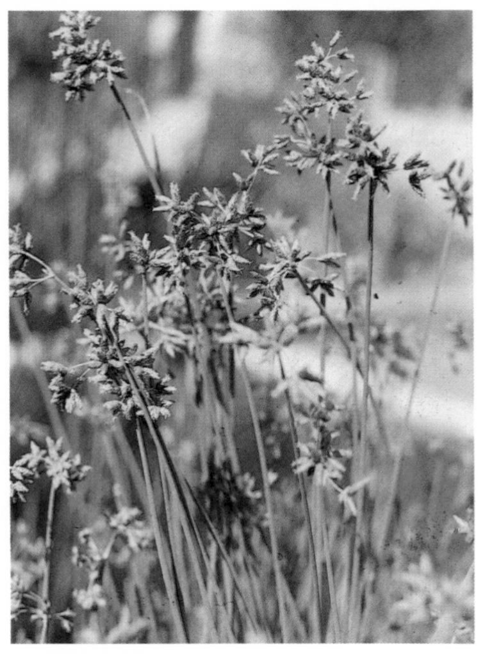

Like the reed, the lake rush was used for constructing walls and partitions for the home. Its other uses were similar to those of the reed.

Cattail

Typha sp.

And when she could hide him no longer she took for him a basket made of bulrushes, and daubed it with bitumen and pitch; and she put the child in it and placed it among the *reeds* at the river's brink. And his sister stood at a distance, to know what would be done to him. Now the daughter of Pharaoh came down to bathe at the river, and her maidens walked beside the river; she saw the basket among the *reeds* and sent her maid to fetch it.

Exodus 2:3

And its canals will become foul, and the branches of Egypt's Nile will diminish and dry up, reeds and *rushes* will rot away.

Isaiah 19:6

The waters closed in over me, the deep was round about me; *weeds* were wrapped about my head.

Jonah 2:5

THE Hebrew *suf* may have been used as a collective rather than a specific name for water plants. In Jonah, for lack of a more accurate word, it denotes sea weeds. But in the quotations from Exodus and Isaiah *suf* can be translated specifically as *Typha*, especially when, as in Isaiah, it is associated with *kaneh* (*Phragmites*) and is thus appropriate to the reeds and cattails which are outstanding in the local hydrophytic vegetation. Further evidence for identifying *suf* with *Typha* is its striking dominance in the ditches and tributaries of the Nile in lower Egypt (where it was reputedly called *tupai*), as in the descriptions in Exodus (2:3–5) and Isaiah (19:6). A variety of millet from Ethiopia, which resembles the cattail with its long leaves, is locally called *tef*, probably cognate with *Typha* and the Hebrew *suf*.

Of the two species of cattail, the more common is *Typha australis*, conspicuous in some plant communities in the Mediterranean region of Israel and tolerant of brackish springs and brooks in the desert. It is a perennial herb 3–4 m. tall, whose stem contracts into a long thick rootstock which spreads across the swamps or along riverbanks. It has erect strip-shaped leaves and a long stick-like stalk ending in a thick spike of flowers, the females below the males. The fruits are minute grains, tufted with hair. The leaves are used for basketwork and matmaking.

Papyrus

Cyperus papyrus L.

And when she could hide him no longer she took for him a basket made of *bulrushes*, and daubed it with bitumen and pitch.

Exodus 2:3

Can *papyrus* grow where there is no marsh? Can reeds flourish where there is no water?

Job 8:11

Ah, land of whirring wings which is beyond the rivers of Ethiopia; which sends ambassadors by the Nile, in vessels of *papyrus* upon the waters!

Isaiah 18:1–2

THE Hebrew word *gomeh*, variously rendered in the quoted passages, must contextually (and according to the translations) be a swamp plant. In view of the different uses mentioned, *Cyperus papyrus* is the only possibility. The Septuagint for Job 8:11 and the Vulgate for Isaiah 18:2 strengthen the argument. The word *gemi* in post-biblical literature probably derives from *gomeh* and refers to papyrus - because of its impressive appearance and its multiple uses in making boxes, mats, ropes, boats and especially paper. Barrels, shoes, huts and clothing were also made from papyrus for the poor.

As early as the 18th Dynasty, the Egyptians used papyrus to manufacture paper from the long and thick stalks, green outside and full of white pith. The stalks were pared and the pith was cut into long strips, glued together with a special adhesive, and then pressed and dried.

Israel is the northern limit of the papyrus distribution. This tropical plant is found on some coastal riverbanks, but has its main distribution center in the upper Jordan Valley.

The papyrus is a member of the Sedge family, which comprises 3,700 species and 70 genera. Some 50 species, both temperate and tropical, meet in this country's various plant communities. *C. papyrus* is a tropical, perennial plant, with a thick, horizontal rootstock from which vertical roots penetrate into the muddy ground and many stems shoot up. The stems, covered with short scale-like leaves at the base, are triangular and may attain a diameter of 10 cm. and height of 2–6 m. They are leafless and terminate in a large, umbel-like inflorescence with thousands of flower spikelets. The soft pith consists of widely-spaced thin-walled cells.

6
Plants of the Wilderness

WITH the desert areas of the Land of Israel covering roughly half the country, it is hardly surprising to find in the Bible several designations for 'desert', attesting to the variety of the desert land and its flora.

The common Hebrew word for 'desert' or 'wilderness' is *midbar*, mentioned in the Bible over three hundred times, although other names like *shmamah, tziah* and *yeshimon* also denote 'desert'. When *midbar* occurs as a place name – *midbar Yehudah* (Judean Desert), *midbar Sinai*, or *midbar Beer Sheva* – it refers to specific geographic areas. As it is used in Scripture, it encompasses the entire range from semi-arid land (e.g., *midbar Tekoa*) where there is enough perennial vegetation for grazing, to sterile plantless wastes, where even scattered nomadic life is impossible, and for which *tziah* and *yeshimon* (completely arid and desolate wasteland) seem indeed more appropriate.

Apart from its physical and geographical connotations, the term *midbar* is frequently used in the Bible allegorically and spiritually: "Thus says the Lord, I remember the devotion of your youth, your love as a bride, how you followed me in the wilderness" (Jeremiah 2:2). Several passages evoke a religious longing for the desert as an antidote to the evil, corruption, and injustice of civilization. The desert epitomizes solitude, purity and holiness, never failing throughout history to attract persecuted kings, prophets and hermits seeking a peaceful seclusion: "O that I had in the desert a way-farers' lodging place, that I might leave my people and go away from them!" (Jeremiah 9:2). However desolate, the desert also inspires consolation and hope, as a place which in the days of redemption will rejoice and blossom, be settled and planted.

Opinion differs as to what distinguishes desert from semi-desert, steppe, semi-steppe and the like. There are no clearly defined lines, but true deserts have one common characteristic – they cannot sustain human life because scanty precipitation permits little or no plant growth. Even in a true desert, however, plants can grow in depressions and dry stream-beds, where tiny quantities of rain-water may collect and water runs in from elevated surroundings. Such is a part of the Zin desert, whose gullies were made by sporadic but powerful floods which erode the soil and eventually create a deep and bowl-shaped valley. On the bottom of the valley, the permanent vegetation is conspicuous for arboreal broomshrubs, tamarisks and other trees and shrubs dealt with in the present section. In this wadi and elsewhere one sees an incipient oasis, where poplars, wild date palms and, more rarely, clumps of acacia trees flourish.

Other sites, such as depressions and mountain slopes, also harbor quite a number of desert shrubs; and it is surprising that none of these plants, which could certainly not have been overlooked, find any mention in the Bible. The author believes that some of them do in fact appear there – not as plants, but as proper names and place names.

Senna Bush

Cassia senna L.

And the angel of the Lord appeared to him in a flame of fire out of the midst of a bush; and he looked, and lo, the *bush* was burning, yet it was not consumed. And Moses said, "I will turn aside and see this great sight, why the bush is not burnt." When the Lord saw that he turned aside to see, God called to him out of the bush, "Moses, Moses!" And he said, "Here am I." Exodus 3:2–4

Now when forty years had passed, an angel appeared to him in the wilderness of Mount Sinai, in a flame of fire in a *bush*.

Acts 7:30

WHETHER or not God's revelation to Moses was supernatural, the plant in question, specifically named *sneh*, might well have been a real plant in the local flora. As there is no hint in the text that the *sneh* was a thorny bush, and there are no plants in Sinai or anywhere else that are not consumed when burnt, *sneh* may be identified linguistically only.

Only one species has a similar Arabic name – *sene* (*Cassia senna*); but this identification has been rejected by most students of the Bible, who believe that *sneh* should be rendered 'bramble' (*Rubus sanguineus*). This is in accordance with the post-biblical literature, especially the exegetical, which assumes that *sneh* is a spiny bush. As a matter of fact, the rendition of *sneh* as *Rubus* is based only on the Aramaic translation of *sneh* as *sania*, which can be a term for a certain species of *Rubus*.

Sania seems to be a mere Aramaization of *sneh*, for the translator was altogether ignorant of the Sinaitic plant growing hundreds of miles away from his home. And although *sania* can be a species of *Rubus*, the fact that no native *Rubus* occurs in Sinai or Egypt or even in southern Israel argues strongly against its identity with *sneh*. The bramble in the garden of the monastery of Santa Caterina in Sinai is a cultivated one, planted by the monks to strengthen the belief that the 'burning bush' has grown there since the revelation, so completely is *sneh* equated with brambles in the minds of scholars and Bible lovers.

As botanists, Moldenke and Tristram repudiate bramble in favor of *Acacia nilotica*, called *sunt* in Arabic. But given the fact that *A. nilotica* does not grow and probably never has grown in Sinai, this identification is less sound than *Cassia senna*. The assumption of Fonck that the *sneh* could be the hawthorn that grows on the Sinai mountains is much more plausible, perhaps, because its crimson fruits do recall a flame. But here also there is no linguistic support.

Other scholars (like Smith) suggest that the burning bush might have been an acacia bush infested by the crimson-flowered mistletoe known as *Loranthus acaciae*. This too is as imaginary as the bramble. Another plant that could fit is perhaps the shrub named *Colutea istria*, which grows on Mt. Sinai and is densely clad with yellow flowers in spring; but for this as well no linguistic support has been found.

It follows from the above that the most plausible identification for *sneh* is *Cassia senna*, named *sene* in all Arabic-speaking countries.

The senna bush is a shrub up to 1 m. high. The stems and branches are richly beset with pinnate leaves, made up of three to seven oblong, acute leaflets. In the axils of the upper leaves the plant develops racemes of large yellow flowers, which yield straight or slightly curved, many-seeded pods.

A tropical plant requiring warmth, it grows in stony wadis both in the Sinai and in southern Israel. It is known medically as a stimulant and purgative, under the name *folia sennae*.

Some scholars consider the hawthorn bush (*Crataegus sinaica*), seen here at the foot of Mt. Moses in Sinai (left), to be the biblical senna bush. A more plausible identification of the senna bush, however, is the *Cassia senna* (below).

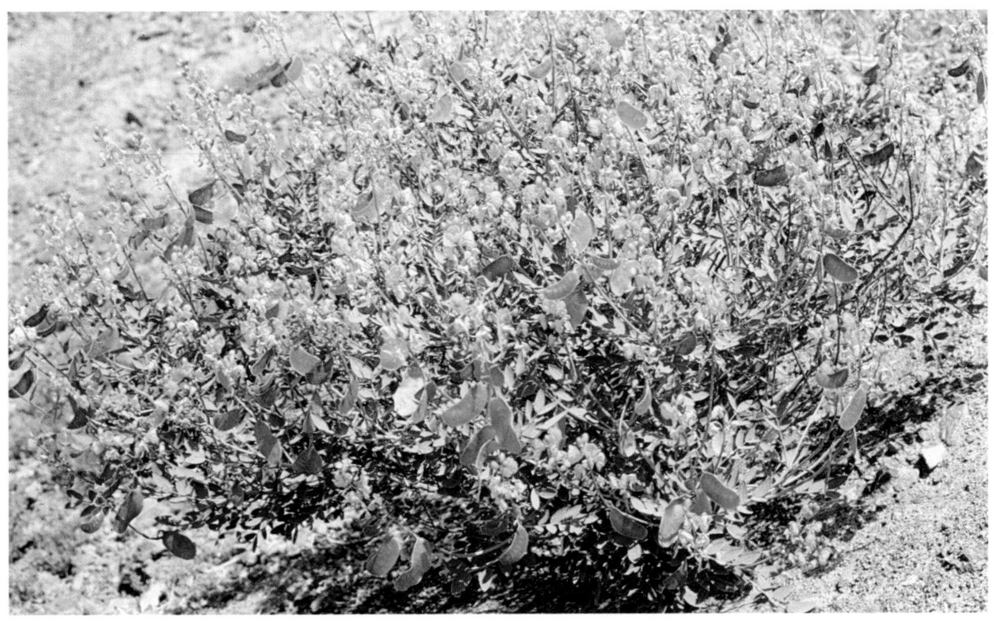

Manna

Then the Lord said to Moses, "Behold, I will rain *bread* from heaven for you; and the people shall go out and gather a day's portion every day, that I may prove them, whether they will walk in my law or not."

Exodus 16:4

Now the house of Israel called its name *manna*; it was like coriander seed, white, and the taste of it was like wafers made with honey.

Exodus 16:31

So they said to him, "Then what sign do you do, that we may see, and believe you? What work do you perform? Our fathers ate the *manna* in the wilderness; as it is written, 'He gave them bread from heaven to eat.'"

John 6:30–31

WHAT was the heavenly bread?

It is appropriate to consider here the question of the biblical manna, although it belongs to the biblical realm of the miraculous, for miracles can also be deeply rooted in reality. The miracle of the meat provided to the Israelites in the wilderness has been satisfactorily explained by the fact that the coveys of quail flying (then as today) across the Mediterranean arrived in the Sinai so exhausted that they were easily caught. But the miracle of the manna is less easy to fathom. All efforts to remove it from a supernatural to a realistic plane have been frustrated and must return to its name *man*, which means 'What?', or *man-ha*, 'What is that?'

An attempt to identify it with the lichen of a certain species of *Lecanora*, never found in the Sinai, was followed by a hypothesis about another lichen - collema - whose clumps are slimy at night and dry in the morning. These suggestions have not the slightest substantiality.

Flueckiger (1891) was among the first to suggest that manna was a sweet exudation produced by small, scaly insects feeding on the tamarisk tree, among others. The expedition of Bodenheimer and Theodor in 1927 found that the insects in question were *Trabulina mannifera* or *Najacoccus serpentina*. They exude a sweet liquid which hardens quickly, drops to the ground and is collected by the Bedouin as a substitute for sugar or honey.

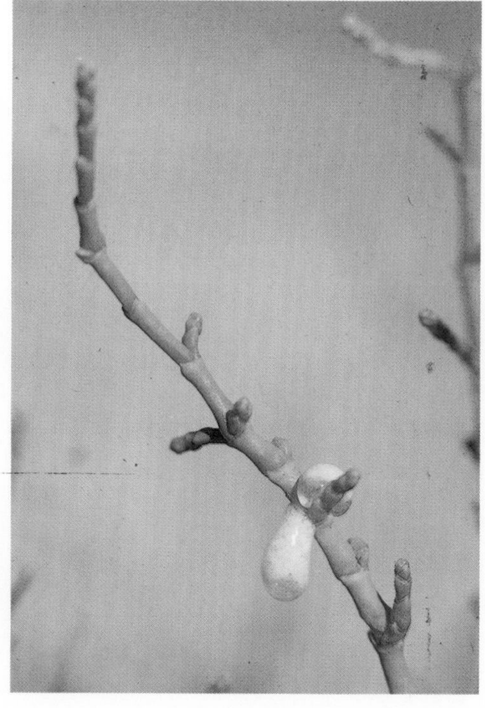

For a long time this was considered the scientific explanation for the miraculous 'bread from heaven'; but since the activity of the insects is seasonally limited, the number of tamarisks in the Sinai small, and that of the Sinai wanderers large, the story of the manna, though realistically based, still remains mysterious and legendary despite the fact that this exudation has been observed also in a few other plants such as *Anabasis setifera, Capparis cortilaginea, Gomphocarpus sinaicus* and, most particularly, *Hammada salicornica.* This last is a plant extremely widespread in southern Sinai. A. Danin (1972) describes how its sweet exudations are collected by the Bedouin and used as a conserve in cakes. But all these sources together could not provide much more than a tidbit for the hungry people wandering in the desert.

The biblical manna was believed to be the sweet exudation produced by small scaly insects feeding on the branches of the Nile tamarisk (*Tamarix nilotica*, below). Some scholars maintain that the sweet liquid on the branches of the white hammada (*Hammada salicornica*), extremely widespread in southern Sinai, is the biblical manna. The Bedouins call this sweet exudation *man rimth* and use it as a sweetener (left).

White Broom

Retama raetam (Forssk.) Webb

But he himself went a day's journey into the wilderness, and sat down under a ***broom tree*****; and he asked that he might die, saying, "It is enough; now, O Lord, take away my life; for I am no better than my fathers."**

I Kings 19:4

Through want and hard hunger they gnaw the dry and desolate ground; they pick mallow and the leaves of bushes, and to warm themselves the roots of the ***broom*****.**

Job 30:3–4

THE white broom is the Hebrew *rothem*, a tall shrub common in the Sahara Desert and the deserts of Israel and Arabia. A special variety with fleshy pods grows in the coastal sand of Israel.

In the desert the white broom is bound mainly to sandy soil and ephemeral water courses, and in eastern Samaria to stony hillsides. It may provide enough shade in the scorching treeless desert. Its roots, excellent cooking and heating fuel, are exceedingly long and allow the plant to reach ground water sources which sustain it even in the driest months and through consecutive rainless years.

The white broom has a short trunk branching from the base into rigid, erect, wand-like twigs. In winter it develops a few hairy leaves which fall after a few weeks, photosynthesis being taken over by the numerous green or silver-gray grooved leafless branches. White flowers cover the branches in spring and make the bush look like a snowball. They are typically papilionaceous and pollinated by bees. The fruits are one- or two-seeded pods which do not open when mature, but fall to the ground.

Shrubby Orache

Atriplex halimus L.

They pick *mallow* **and the leaves of bushes, and to warm themselves the roots of the broom.**

Job 30:4

THE passage from Job is not easy to understand. A reasonable substitute might read: "They pick the leaves of the orache and the wormwood..." The rendition of *maluaḥ* as 'orache' – and not 'mallow', as in the RSV – leans on the fact that Job is referring to the desert, where orache is common. Certain *Atriplex* species, furthermore, are called *mulaḥ* in Arabic, and the leaves are in times of famine eaten both by shepherds and by their flocks.

The shrubby orache is among the commonest desert plants, growing in salines, on dry riverbanks, roadsides and in oases as a weed. It is 1–2 m. tall and branches from the base. Stem and branches have ovate, silver-gray leaves whose surfaces are covered with fine vesicular hairs. The minute flowers grow in spike-like inflorescences, the male florets beside the female ones. The fruits are minute nutlets enclosed in two leathery scales.

Shaggy Sparrow-wort

Passerina hirsuta L.

And from the wilderness they went on to ***Mattanah*****, and from Mattanah to Nahaliel.**
Numbers 21:18

IN the Aramaic version of the Pentateuch, Mattanah in the quoted passage is translated as *Matnan*. This is the name of a locality in the desert, but it might also be identical with the Arabic *mitnan*, the name for *Passerina hirsuta*. Such indirect identification, which permits this important species to be included in the flora of the Bible, is supported by the fact that *matnan* or *mitnan* frequents dry wadis and other desert habitats and is so called in modern Hebrew. Possibly related are the proper names Ethnan (I Chronicles 4:7), Mattenai (Nehemiah 12:19) and Matan (Jeremiah 38:1). This supposition leans on the fact that many plant names are recorded in the Bible as proper names which have equivalents or cognates preserved in the Arabic language.

The shaggy sparrow-wort is a dioecious shrub, 1 m. tall, evergreen, many-branched, and densely clad with minute scale-like leaves, green beneath and wooly white above. From its tough stems and branches the local Bedouin prepare very rough rods. The plant produces minute yellow flowers and inconspicuous nutlets or fruits. It often appears in steppe and desert plant communities.

Jointed Anabasis

Anabasis articulata (Forssk.) Moq.

The sons of Gad: Ziphion, Haggi, *Shuni*, **Ezbon, Eri, Arodi, and Areli.**

Genesis 46:16

THE Arabic *ushnan* or *shenan* and *agram* for jointed anabasis are cognate with the biblical proper names Shuni (or Ashna) and Hagarmi (I Chronicles 4:19). The author believes that there must have been Hebrew names for a species predominant through hundreds of miles of the Judean Desert, the Negev, Edom, and elsewhere, and that these names, while not finding a place among the flora of the Bible, have survived as proper names in Hebrew and as plant names in Arabic.

The jointed anabasis is an intricately-branched dwarf-shrub with a leafless stem and branches consisting of cylindrical, very fleshy joints, green at first but becoming woody and dry after a year or two. Small green flowers growing from the axils of the upper joints appear in early winter and often produce small fruits enclosed in the green perianth. The fruiting perianth has white or pink membranous wings, which adorn the desert when winter begins, but are carried away by the wind. The 25 species of the genus *Anabasis* spread across the Sahara, northern Arabia, and the deserts of Middle Asia. Some contain, among other substances, the medicinal alkaloid anabasine.

Bean Caper

Zygophyllum dumosum Boiss.

And they set out from Marah, and came to *Elim*; at Elim there were twelve springs of water and seventy palm trees, and they encamped there. And they set out from Elim, and encamped by the Red Sea.

Numbers 33:9–10

THE bean caper flourishes over hundreds of square miles of the deserts of Israel and certain regions of the Sinai, so that the Israelites wandering in the desert could not possibly have failed to notice it. Since it is not mentioned directly in the Bible, I suggest that Elim, which appears several times as a Sinai place name, is in fact its Hebrew name, cognate with the Arabic *illam* (*Zygophyllum dumosum*).

Zygophyllum is one of those miraculous desert plants which can live through several consecutive rainless years, suffering heavy bodily losses by sacrificing lateral branches to the drought and yet preserving living cells in some branches. When the rains come, it can produce new branches and thus restore itself. This relatively low shrub is very long-lived; specimens have been found with more than 300 annual growth-rings on their trunks, to which must be added many drought years during which no such rings were produced.

The bean caper is an evergreen woody shrub, 1 m. tall, with a shallow but extensively branching root-system, a very short main stem and numerous lateral branches. The small succulent leaves have a cylindrical petiole and two oblong leaflets which fall at the start of the dry period. The white flowers, appearing in early spring, are centered on the upper part of the branch and consist of five conspicuous sepals and petals. The fruits are winged, dehiscent, many-seeded capsules.

White Saxaul

Haloxylon persicum Bge.

Lamech said to his wives: "*Adah* and Zillah, hear my voice; you wives of Lamech, hearken to what I say."

Genesis 4:23

BESIDES the seven references to Adah as one of Lamech's wives, the Bible mentions other such proper names as Ido, Adaiah, and Adiel. *Ada* in Arabic is 'saxaul', a plant abundant in the sandy deserts of northern Arabia, Edom, the Aravah Valley and Sinai. Adada, a place in the northern Negev, may be related to the same plant and, in fact, Ada is still the name given by the Arabs to an oasis in the Aravah Valley (En Adian, modern Yotvatha) where saxaul is extremely common.

The white saxaul, superficially recalling the white broom, belongs to the Goosefoot family, richly represented in deserts. It is leafless, the fleshy green joints of its stems and branches functioning as leaves in photosynthesis. It flowers in spring and its minute fruits are enclosed in a green perianth with membranous wings. It is especially common in the Middle and Central Asian deserts and provides shade and cooking and heating fuel for desert travelers, and good food for their caravan camels.

Sea Blite

Suaeda spp.

Ashhur, **the father of Tekoa, had two wives, Helah and Naarah.**

I Chronicles 4:5

Shamsherai, *Shehariah*, **Athaliah.**

I Chronicles 8:26

THE proper names in the passages quoted presumably stem from the Hebrew *shaḥor*, meaning 'black'. The Arabic name for many species of the genus *Suaeda* is *suweda*, or *suaid* ('black'); the Danish botanist Fôrsskål latinized the name into the genus *Suaeda*. Israel boasts about ten species of *Suaeda*, nearly all flourishing in the desert, especially in those with saline ground. They are too many and too striking to have been overlooked, but although saline deserts are mentioned three times in the Bible as *mleḥah* (Jeremiah 17:6; Job 39:6; Psalms 107:34), not a single name is allotted to the plants that grow there. Since *Suaeda* species are possibly the most characteristic of saline vegetation, the people's recognition of their existence and that of other salt plants, as well as their knowledge of their names, can be inferred from the personal names cited above.

The plants are shrubs, mainly perennial, with heavily-branching stems and small cylindrical or semi-cylindrical, very fleshy leaves. The flowers are green and inconspicuous, with five stamens and a small ovary; the fruit is a one-seeded nutlet enclosed in a little calyx.

One of the most striking species is *S. monoica* Forssk., of arboreal stature and extending over large tracts of the southern Aravah Valley and the Dead Sea salines.

Hammada

Hammada salicornica (Moq.) Iljin ;
H. scoparia (Pomel) Iljin

Though you wash yourself with *lye* and use much soap, the stain of your guilt is still before me, says the Lord God.

Jeremiah 2:22

BIBLICAL soap – *borit* or *bor* – was prepared by mixing the ashes of certain plants with olive oil. The white and black species of the hammada and several other genera of the Goosefoot family have long served as soap-producing potash plants. One still finds hammada and anabasis on sale in the markets of the larger cities of the Orient for making soap.

H. salicornica is the Arabic *rimth*. Although this name is not mentioned in Scripture, several proper names – Jarmuth (Joshua 21:29), Jeremoth (Ezra 10:26; I Chronicles 25:22), Remeth (Joshua 19:21), and the like – are cognate with it. The plant's frequent occurrence in the Aravah Valley, the eastern Negev, Sinai, Arabia, and many other countries, in all of which it is known as *rimth*, strengthens the assumption that the people of the Bible must have been familiar with it and that the proper names cited were derived from it.

The white hammada is a member of the Goosefoot family, most of which are succulents and some of which are leafless shrubs, like the plant we are concerned with here. In Israel it often grows alongside acacia trees, with which it develops conspicuous savannah-like plant communities. It is a shrub up to 80 cm. tall, with a leafless stem of fleshy green joints. Its flowers, which appear early in winter, are inconspicuous and wind-pollinated. The fruit is one-seeded and spreads by means of the white-winged calyx in which it is enclosed.

The black hammada is a close relative, growing throughout much of the Negev and further west to North Africa. Its darkness is in striking contrast to the brightness of the loess soil on which it grows.

White Hammada *Hammada salicornica*

7
Thorns & Thistles

MORE than seventy species of spiny plants grow among the flora of Israel and more than twenty are mentioned in Scripture. No other group of plant names in the Bible is so frequently misidentified and arbitrarily translated.

It is most unlikely that the people of the Bible, any more than people anywhere, had specific names for their thistles, which even today are individually unknown to the average person. It seems that even the original writers or prophets could not identify the many names which they themselves used, among them some legendary and metaphorical, handed down through generations. Many names assigned in the Bible to thorns were therefore probably synonyms, or loose collective names, or conceptually obsolete vestiges of archaic phraseology. Those occurring in pairs, for instance *shamir va-shayith, kotz ve-dardar,* are hendiadys and simply strengthen the concept of thorniness. And even if the names had a clear identity they could not be reliably translated into the languages of countries which have few or none of the same plants – that is, all the European countries.

Scholarly efforts to match the twenty biblical names for thorns with twenty plants out of the seventy have ended in error and failure. Only those etymologically or geobotanically based, or paralleled by other Semitic languages, offer plausible clues, and there are few such.

Thus it appears that no thorn name in any version of the Bible is reliably translated, and to avoid incorrect identifications, future versions should in all instances use 'thorn' or 'thistle' as applied to the entire group of spiny plants, or retain the original Hebrew. (Other general English terms are 'bramble', 'brier' and 'weed'.) The names in this category must therefore be treated collectively. The few that are described in the present section are outstanding by virtue of their frequent occurrence, their striking appearance, their special uses or their identity with Arabic names. Some are mentioned only because they often, although unjustifiably, appear in various translations.

Christ Thorn

Ziziphus spina-christi (L.) Desf.

Then all the trees said to the *bramble*, "Come you, and reign over us." And the bramble said to the trees, "If in good faith you are anointing me king over you, then come and take refuge in my shade; but if not, let fire come out of the bramble and devour the cedars of Lebanon."
Judges 9:14–15

Then the soldiers of the governor took Jesus into the praetorium, and they gathered the whole battalion before him. And they stripped him and put a scarlet robe upon him, and plaiting a crown of *thorns* they put it on his head, and put a reed in his right hand. And kneeling before him they mocked him, saying, "Hail, King of the Jews!"
Matthew 27:27–29

So Jesus came out, wearing the *crown of thorns* and the purple robe. Pilate said to them, "Behold the man!" John 19:5

THE humble king of the trees in the 'parable of the trees' – *atad* in Hebrew – appears once as a plant name, once collectively for 'thorns', and once as a place name. There is no linguistic evidence for its identity. The most reasonable suggestion is to identify *atad* with *Ziziphus spina-christi* (or *Ziziphus lotus*), as these plants are fairly common in the northern part of Israel, especially on the eastern slopes of the adjacent plains of Samaria, where Jotham related his 'parable of the trees' to the people.

Moreover, *Ziziphus* is in accord with the requirement in the parable for a tree which gives fruits inferior in quality to those of the fig and the olive, and for which the words "take refuge in my shade" make sense. *Atadim* are included with fruit trees such as the pistachio and terebinth in Talmudic literature, indicating that the *atad* was certainly considered a tree or shrub bearing edible fruit. The mature fruits of the *Ziziphus* (*dum* in Arabic) are in fact edible and are sometimes marketed.

The question so frequently and lengthily discussed as to whether the 'crown of thorns' mentioned in Matthew, Mark and John, was made of *Ziziphus* can be answered as follows: there are at least a dozen different spiny plant species in Jerusalem. Of these, the thorny burnet (*Sarcopoterium spinosum*), a dwarf-shrub, is extremely common, and might therefore with much more reason be regarded as the plant in

Lotus Thorn *Ziziphus lotus*

question (see 'Thorny Burnet'). Christian tradition, however, looks upon the *Ziziphus* as the 'crown of thorns', and for those who insist upon having a Christ thorn growing in Jerusalem, there are still a few Christ thorn trees on the eastern slopes of Mt. Moriah (the Temple Mount).

The Christ thorn is a stately evergreen up to 10 m. tall, which develops a large, oval, intricately-branching crown. Its ovate, prominently nerved and dentate leaves are from 3–5 cm. long and about 2 cm. wide, with two spiny stipules, one straight, the other hooked. It flowers most of the year, but most extensively during the summer. The flowers are bisexual and yellowish-green, and their yellow fleshy drupes, the size of cherries (though less tasty), are eaten and even marketed. The plant is fairly common in Samaria and in southern Israel, and also very common in the upper Jordan Valley, especially on fine-grained and alluvial soils.

The lotus thorn, 1.5 m. tall, and similar to the Christ thorn though shrubby, sheds its leaves in winter and yields smaller, blander fruit. It is very common in the upper Jordan Valley and Samaria, and, like the Christ thorn, needs warmth without requiring the deep soils of the plain.

Christ Thorn *Ziziphus spina-christi*

Thorny Burnet

Sarcopoterium spinosum (L.) Spach

Therefore I will hedge up her way with *thorns*; and I will build a wall against her, so that she cannot find her paths.

Hosea 2:6

For as the crackling of *thorns* under a pot, so is the laughter of the fools; this also is vanity.

Ecclesiastes 7:6

THE thorny burnet fits best the Hebrew *sir* (occurring only in the plural *sirim*) of the above-mentioned quotation. The local peasants have a longstanding custom of hedging their courts and gardens with intricately-branched and spiny dwarf-shrubs, and of these the burnet is the most suitable, while it is also used as fuel for cooking and for lime kilns.

It should be noted that the Arabic *sir* or *thir* designates a series of dwarf-shrub species such as *Noea mucronata, Gymnocarpus decander* and *Traganum nudatum*, which are generally used for fuel. In modern Hebrew, this type of vegetation dominated by the thorny burnet is *bathah*, 'waste' (garigue), a name adopted from Isaiah: "I will make it a waste; it shall not be pruned or hoed, and briers and thorns shall grow up" (5:6).

Sir as thorny burnet was first identified by Post (1896) and Loew (1924) and accepted by Hareuveni (1933) – with reason, since it does not contradict the context of the quoted verses or of other relevant ones.

The thorny burnet is important in many plant communities that characterize the Mediterranean landscape. Since it abounds in Jerusalem, it might have been the plant from whose spiny branches the Roman soldiers plaited the 'crown of thorns' (Matthew 27:27–30; Mark 15:17; John 19:5).

The thorny burnet is a dwarf-shrub, up to 50 cm. tall. Its stem is much-branched and its leaves are divided into several pairs of toothed leaflets; they are used by peasants as a pot-herb. The upper part of the branches forks into spiny branchlets, which die annually after having produced flowers and fruits. The minute green flowers are unisexual, the female above and the male beneath. They appear in spring and produce small globular fruits with a pericarp and two or three seeds.

Bramble

Rubus sanguineus Friv

But if you do not drive out the inhabitants of the land from before you, then those of them whom you let remain shall be as pricks in your eyes and *thorns* in your sides, and they shall trouble you in the land where you dwell.

Numbers 33:55

***Thorns* and snares are in the way of the perverse; he who guards himself will keep far from them.**

Proverbs 22:5

For each tree is known by its own fruit. For figs are not gathered from thorns, nor are grapes picked from a *bramble bush*.

Luke 6:44

TZINIM or *tzininim*, rendered 'thorns' in the quoted passages, is cognate with *sinim, sina, sinaia* and other variations of that root (excluding *sneh* – see 'Senna Bush'), frequently found in post-biblical (Talmudic and Mishnaic) literature, and possibly identical with the true bramble (*Rubus sanguineus*).

The bramble is a prickly, evergreen, erect or twining, very intricately-branching bush, with hooked prickles all over the stem and branches. The leaves have three to five leaflets, and the flowers, grouped at the branch tips, have five pink-to-white, 6–9 mm. long petals each. The fruit is a small compound edible blackish berry of many one-seeded fleshy drupelets, ripening at the end of summer. It is a common species in middle and northern parts of Israel, often clustered in impenetrable thorny thickets along riverbanks and swamps.

Syrian Thistle

Notobasis syriaca (L.) Coss.

Holy Thistle

Silybum marianum (L.) Gaertn

Globe Thistle

Echinops viscosus DC.

And Gideon said, "Well then, when the Lord has given Zebah and Zalmunna into my hand, I will flail your flesh with the *thorns* of the wilderness and with briers."

Judges 8:7

And he took the elders of the city and he took thorns of the wilderness and *briers* and with them taught the men of Succoth.

Judges 8:16

THERE is no concrete evidence that the three thorny species of the Composite family listed in this entry are the *barkanim* of Gideon, but they are preferable to other thorns because they are tall plants which were probably used as whips, and are the most plentiful of all the thorns in Ophra, where Gideon the judge was "beating out wheat in the wine press" (Judges 6:11)

The Syrian thistle and the holy thistle are annuals with large leaves appressed to the ground during the winter. In spring they are the first thistles to produce tall stems covered with smaller spiny leaves. Their upper part branches, each branch ending in a large head of pink or white flowers which is encircled with numerous leathery, very spiny, simple or branched small leaves. At the end of spring, the plants produce small nutlets (fruits), each with a tuft of long white hairs by means of which they are dispersed.

The globe thistle (*E. viscosus*) is a perennial plant with stout, tall, spiny stems which appear in early summer and produce globular, spiny heads of purplish-blue to lilac flowers and small fruits which often have sharp spines. They grow among dwarf-shrubs and are common in Samaria and other parts of Israel.

The holy thistle is also known as 'Mary's thistle'.

Syrian Thistle *Notobasis syriaca*

Holy Thistle *Silybum marianum*

Globe Thistle *Echinops viscosus*

Spanish Thistle

Centaurea iberica Spreng.

And to Adam he said, "Because you have listened to the voice of your wife, and have eaten of the tree of which I commanded you, 'You shall not eat of it,' cursed is the ground because of you; in toil you shall eat of it all the days of your life; thorns and *thistles* it shall bring forth to you."

Genesis 3:17–18

The high places of Aven, the sin of Israel, shall be destroyed. Thorn and *thistle* shall grow up on their altars.

Hosea 10:8

Beware of false prophets, who come to you in sheep's clothing but inwardly are ravenous wolves. You will know them by their fruits. Are grapes gathered from thorns, or figs from *thistles*?

Matthew 7:15–16

THE word *dardar*, twice mentioned in the Bible, may refer to certain species of the genus *Centaurea* distinguishable from other thorns and thistles by their whorl-like leaves, which lie flat on the ground throughout the winter.

The most common local species, called *dardur* by the Arabs, is *C. iberica*, a much-branching annual plant which frequents roadsides and neglected places. Throughout the winter and in early spring, the pinnately lobed leaves are appressed to the ground in dense whorls, forming a large rosette. At this time the villagers gather the leaves for pot-herbs, also called *mureir*. This term is identical with the Hebrew *merorim*, a collective name for a series of herbs similarly used.

With the advent of the dry period, the stem, fifty or more cm. tall, grows rapidly out of the rosette and develops laterally spreading branches and scores of small flower heads crowned with long sharp spines, so that the whole plant becomes almost untouchable. Each head comprises many minute florets with a yellow corolla and pink stamens. Pollination is effected mainly by bees. The small fruits have a tuft of bristles which allows them to be dispersed.

Both the Hebrew *dardar* and the Arabic *dardur* mean 'whorls', which reflects the appearance of the plant. In both passages quoted *dardar* is coupled with *kotz*. As a rule, when such pairing occurs it does not indicate two separate things but serves as an intensifier (here, of thorniness). However, *dardar* may once have been a specific plant, and later lost that sense for a more general one. A further weakness in the identification is that this species of *Centaurea* nowhere occurs as a weed in the fields and does not fit the context of the passage in Genesis 3:18. However, this species might contextually fit the citation in Matthew (7:16).

Golden Thistle

Scolymus maculatus L.;
S. hispanicus L.

If I have eaten its yield without payment, and caused the death of its owners; let *thorns* grow instead of wheat, and foul weeds instead of barley.

Job 31:39–40

I am a rose of Sharon, a lily of the valleys. As a lily among *brambles*, so is my love among maidens.

Song of Solomon 2:1–2

Thorns shall grow over its strongholds, nettles and *thistles* in its fortresses.

Isaiah 34:13

THE quoted verses have been chosen from nine which contain the biblical name *ḥoaḥ* (pl. *ḥoḥim*). Contextually *ḥoaḥ* seems to be a thorny plant occurring as a weed in wheat fields (*S. maculatus*) and as a ruderal in ruins and neglected places (*S. hispanicus*), but it is probably also a general name for thorns, as the other references (such as II Kings 14:9; Proverbs 26:9; Song of Solomon 2:2) indicate. The Accadian *hahin* is generally rendered 'thorns'.

The golden thistle is a widespread, tall annual, with a stout, rigid, whitish stem, branching above. Its leaves spread all along the stem, are leathery and divided into very spiny lobes. It has composed heads of yellow flowers and the seeds are minute nutlets.

The New Testament mentions thorns which grow in grain fields (see, e.g., Matthew 13:7), and which might therefore be identified as golden thistles.

This noxious weed, sprouting in borders and abandoned or fallow fields, is found especially in the alluvial soils all over the lower altitudes of the country.

S. hispanicus differs from *S. maculatus* by reason of its stems, which branch abundantly from the base. It is usually found in neglected places and along the road, but less frequently than *S. maculatus*.

Golden Thistle *Scolymus maculatus*

Darnel

Lolium temulentum L.

Syrian Scabious

Cephalaria syriaca (L.) Schrad.

The kingdom of heaven may be compared to a man who sowed good seed in his field; but while men were sleeping, his enemy came and sowed *weeds* among the wheat, and went away.

Matthew 13:24–25

DARNELS and scabious are both noxious weeds that grow only among crops, and damage them. Since the grains of the tare or darnel are similar in size and shape to those of wheat, the two can be sieved together to produce a mixture which spoils the ground meal.

The darnel is a more specific weed and accords with the Hebrew *zun* and the Arabic *ziwan* (*Lolium*). Also known as 'tare', it is a member of the Grass family and resembles a wheat-like grass. A weed in whose grains lives a poisonous fungus, it grows exclusively in grain fields throughout the Middle East. Its grains have been found in a 4,000 year-old Egyptian tomb.

The Syrian scabious belongs to the Teasel family and resembles wheat only by virtue of its grains. Called *zuwan aswad* or *taradan shalam* by the Arabs, it is no less noxious than the darnel and, though not related to the wheat plant, has adopted many of its traits. Thus its grains are similar to those of certain wheat varieties, and since they are reaped, threshed and sieved together they continue to be sown together year after year, producing bitter flour and bitter bread. Sometimes the weed overwhelms the wheat, so that the farmer is forced to harvest it instead of the sown plant.

This is a classic example of the conversion of a weed into a crop, which is what happened, for instance, to rye and oats.

The darnel is a grass up to 70 cm. tall. It branches from its base into secondary culms each terminating in a compact spike 6–12 cm. long, made up of appressed spikelets, each bearing a few flowers producing grains not unlike those of wheat.

The Syrian scabious is a shaggy annual herb with angled stems up to 80 cm. tall, branching above into spreading branches, each terminating with a head-like group of blue flowers made of a 4-lobed corolla. The fruit is a black grain not unlike a wheat grain.

Darnel *Lolium temulentum*

Nettle

Urtica urens L.;
U. pilulifera L.

Instead of the thorn shall come up the cypress; instead of the *brier* shall come up the myrtle; and it shall be to the Lord for a memorial, for an everlasting sign which shall not be cut off.
Isaiah 15:13

And you, son of man, be not afraid of them, nor be afraid of their words, though *briers* and thorns are with you and you sit upon scorpions.
Ezekiel 2:6

Moab shall become like Sodom, and the Ammonites like Gomorrah, a land possessed by *nettles* and salt pits, and a waste for ever.
Zephaniah 2:9

ALL four species of nettle in this country are ruderal, which means that they grow in abandoned places and need excessive organic matter. Their capacity to sting makes them useful for metaphors, and it is unlikely that the Bible should have ignored them.

The writer believes that all the three different Hebrew names quoted – *sirpad* (rendered 'brier' in Isaiah 55:13), *seravim* (rendered 'briers' in Ezekiel 2:6) and *ḥarul* (rendered 'nettles' in Zephaniah 2:9) – are synonyms, the roots *s-r-f* and *ḥ-a-r* both meaning 'scorching' or 'burning'. The nettle is the only plant which irritates the skin so severely that it may cause inflammation. The Arabic name for one of its species is *ḥorreig* in Israel and *sorbei* in Egypt. Linguistically and contextually, then, the rendition of 'nettles' for all three words seems quite plausible.

The nettle is an erect annual herb, 1 m. tall, with a four-angled stem and large, opposite, ovate, dentate leaves profusely covered with stinging hairs. Its flowers are unisexual, green in color. The fruits are minute nutlets enclosed in the green sepals.

The nettle grows everywhere in the country's settled regions and sometimes in the desert.

Roman Nettle *Urtica pilulifera*

Tournefort's Gundelia

Gundelia tournefortii L.

O my God, make them like *whirling* **dust, like chaff before the wind.**

Psalms 83:13

The nations roar like the roaring of many waters, but he will rebuke them, and they will flee far away, chased like chaff on the mountains before the wind and *whirling* **dust before the storm.**

Isaiah 17:13

GUNDELIA, primarily a steppe-plant, is called by travelers to Asia the steppe-monster, because several of them often stick together and roll through the vast, empty steppes like grotesque balloon-men.

The Hebrew *galgal* is not properly the name of a plant, but does probably indicate this tumbleweed, a heavily-branched herb that detaches itself from the root of the mother plant and tumbles about, releasing and scattering its seeds.

Gundelia is one of 30 different species of tumbleweed in the local flora. It is taken here as an example because it is the most noticeable of them all, and because its large, leathery, wing-like leaves are very strong and make it a most effective roller. It is called *akuvith* in post-biblical Hebrew literature, and in Arabic *akub* or *k'aub. Akov*, possibly derived from the plant, occurs several times in the Bible as a proper name.

The gundelia, an unusual and biologically interesting plant, is a perennial thistle of the Composite family; its position within the family is rather uncertain because of its flower heads. The plant is 30–50 cm. tall, with a thick stem divaricately branched at the base. Its ovate to oblong, very spiny, lobed to pinnatifid leaves, attaining a length of 20 cm. or more, are soft when young and consumed as pot-herbs, but become stiff and leathery when adult. Each of the branches terminates in a flowering head, 5–8 cm. across, trifoldly composed. The innermost headlets consist of 6–7 florets of which only the central one is fertile, producing a large angled nut crowned with a few spiny appendages; all the others are sterile. The young fleshy heads are made by peasants into a delicious dish. The nuts contain a high degree of fat and are edible and tasty.

Gray Nightshade

Solanum incanum L.

The way of a sluggard is overgrown with *thorns*, but the path of the upright is a level highway.

Proverbs 15:19

The best of them is like a *brier*, the most upright of them a thorn hedge. The day of their watchmen, of their punishment, has come; now their confusion is at hand. Put no trust in a neighbour, have no confidence in a friend; guard the doors of your mouth from her who lies in your bosom.

Micah 7:4–5

THE Hebrew *ḥedek* occurs only in the two quoted passages, and in both is associated with a thorny hedge. Such hedges are common in this country, and effectively protect fruit and vegetable gardens against animals and theft. The context and etymology of *ḥedek* also point to a rather thorny plant.

The Arabic *hadaq*, however, specifically refers to the gray nightshade (*Solanum incanum*), which although sometimes used as a thorny hedge is somewhat rare. This does not however weaken the interpretation of *ḥedek* as a name for thorns because biblical plant names, originally specific, often became conceptual or collective (e.g., *eshel* for both 'tamarisk' and 'tree', *shoshan* for both 'lily' and 'flower').

The gray nightshade is a tropical plant, limited in Israel to the lower Jordan Valley and the Dead Sea region. It is a grayish, hairy, spiny, abundantly-branching shrub, with large ovate leaves. Its sizable lilac flowers are wide open and pollinated by bees, and its fruits – large yellow berries – contain numerous seeds which the birds disperse. It ranges from southern Africa to northwestern India.

Syrian Acanthus

Acanthus syriacus Boiss.

And they made an ivy growing out of the stone swathed with *acanthus*.

Letter of Aristeas 70

ACANTHUS is mentioned only in the quoted passage of the Pseudepigrapha, which describes the table of the Showbread in the Temple, whose leg-ends were made of precious stones and carved in the shape of various plants.

Although this name denoted thorny or spiny plants generally, here it seems to specify Syrian acanthus, which is notable for its rosette of large, spiny-lobed leaves that are known to have been models for decorative stonework, especially on the capitals of columns. It has long spikes of colorful, two-lipped large flowers, with spiny bracts and spiny upper sepals.

Spiny Zilla

Zilla spinosa (L.) Prantl

Lamech said to his wives: "Adah and *Zillah*, hear my voice." Genesis 4:23

And for the house of Israel there shall be no more a *brier* to prick or a thorn to hurt them among all their neighbors who have treated them with contempt. Then they will know that I am the Lord God. Ezekiel 28:24

ZILLA, or *Silla*, the Arabic name for a very spiny and very conspicuous plant, was latinized by P. Forsskål (1732–1763) as *Zilla spinosa*. It seems not too risky to suggest that Zillah, wife of Lamech, was named for this plant, so characteristic of the desert in the Land of Nod. On the other hand, *silon* (Ezekiel 28:24) seems to be a general word for 'thorn'.

The spiny zilla is a perennial herb of the Mustard family, up to 1 m. tall and 1 m. wide, with intricately-forked branches tapering into strong sharp spines. The leaves are large at the base of the stems, growing smaller toward the apex. The good-sized pink flowers have four sepals and four pink-to-purple petals, and the fruit is a sharp-pointed woody nutlet, about 6–8 mm. long. It has two seeds and never dehisces. When mature, the whole plant is pulled out of its bed and goes bouncing through the desert.

Boxthorn

Lycium europaeum L.

Now the Philistines gathered their armies for battle; and they were gathered at Socoh, which belongs to Judah, and encamped between Socoh and *Azekah*, in Ephesdammim.

I Samuel 17:1

AZEKAH, a place in Judea at the foot of the western mountains, is mentioned seven times in the Bible. The name is cognate with the Arabic *ausseg* (boxthorn), identical with *Lycium.*

Giving plant names to places is common in the Bible. The names for pomegranate, olive, date palm, acacia, oak, pistachio, willow, and many others frequently appear as the names of localities, either individually or coupled with another word. It can thus be assumed that other plants have served in a similar capacity. Azekah may therefore be regarded as bearing the name of the boxthorn shrubs with which it abounds.

The boxthorn is a thorny shrub branching diffusely in the upper part, with small oblong leaves shed at the onset of summer. The flowers are solitary and axillary, and the minute calyx is often 5-toothed. The long tubular corolla is pink to blue in color, and the fruit is a small edible berry dispersed by birds.

8
Flowers of the Field

WANDERING in springtime in Israel's valleys and mountains, or even in its deserts, one is moved by the beauty of the hundreds of flowers. Most of the many flowering species of the Land must have had specific names in biblical times, as they have today. But since the Bible is not a book of natural history it often assigns collective names to groups of species which are not easily distinguished by laymen. The words *peraḥ*, *tzitz*, *nitzah* all mean 'flower' in the Bible. One group – the first of the spring flowers – is formed by the conspicuously beautiful anemones, tulips, poppies and crowfoots, all collectively named *nitzanim* in the Song of Solomon 2:12: "The flowers [*nitzanim*] appear on the earth, the time of singing has come, and the voice of the turtledove is heard in our land." The word possibly derives from the verb *hanetz*, 'to come into blossom', often encountered in Scripture.

This group of plants with red flowers is called *nissan* by the Iraqi people, which suggests that the Hebrew spring month *Nissan* was named for or refers to the spring blooming of the *nitzanim*.

Daisies and daisy-like plants are striking too in their abundance and brightness, though humble in size and shape. They are probably also included in the collective term 'flowers of the field' (*tzitz ha-sadeh*), used as a symbol of short-living creatures: "All flesh is grass, and all its beauty is like the flower of the field. The grass withers, the flower fades ... but the word of our God will stand for ever" (Isaiah 40:6, 8; I Peter 1:24–25). 'Grass' (*esev*), coupled with flowers in this verse and others in the Bible, obviously also connotes flowers of some sort: "like the flower of the grass he will pass away" (James 1:10); see also the "grass of the field" (Matthew 6:30).

Another group of flowers is called the 'lilies of the field': "Consider the lilies of the field, how they grow; they neither toil nor spin; yet I tell you, even Solomon in all his glory was not arrayed like one of these. But if God so clothes the grass of the field, which today is alive and tomorrow is thrown into the oven, will he not much more clothe you, O men of little faith?" (Matthew 6:28–30). No true lilies in fact grow in the fields, so the term should not be taken to indicate real lilies but simply 'pretty wild flowers'. Only a few of the many flowers which significantly brighten the Israeli landscape will be described in this section, while some attention will also be given to the true lily, which grows in the mountains.

Although flowers were not commonly used in religious rites, they served for decoration and were appreciated for their scent: "My beloved is to me a cluster of henna blossoms" (Song of Solomon 1:14).

Crown Anemone

Anemone coronaria L.

And why are you anxious about clothing? Consider the *lilies of the field*, how they grow; they neither toil nor spin; yet I tell you, even Solomon in all his glory was not arrayed like one of these. But if God so clothes the grass of the field, which today is alive and tomorrow is thrown into the oven, will he not much more clothe you, O men of little faith?

Matthew 6:28–30

IN early spring thousands of crown anemones in scarlet (sometimes also in purple, pink, blue and white) dot every field, bush, wasteland and sandy hill in all the Mediterranean areas of the Land, and penetrate into the desert. On account of its loveliness and charm, this is the favorite flower of spring.

The crown anemone is a member of the *Ranunculaceae* family, which comprises 35 genera and about 2,000 species. The salient features of its structure include reduction of the stem to an underground corm-like rhizome in which reserve substances are stored and from which the aerial parts, the leaves and flowers, are built up, so that every year the green plant exploits a part of its rhizome to form a new one.

The flower of the crown anemone is considered a perigon because there is no differentiation between calyx and corolla. There can be five to thirteen petals but there are usually six, predominantly scarlet with a white patch near the base. Other colors – purple, pink, blue and white – which have been shown to be genetically determined, are rarer.

The flowers open in the morning and close at night. Though they do not secrete nectar they attract a number of insects, which feed on the abundant pollen produced by the numerous stamens. Recent observations have shown that cross-pollination is predominant here. After pollination the fruit, which produces hundreds of seedlets dispersed by the wind, develops quickly.

Traditionally this flower is sometimes regarded as the "lily of the field" of Matthew (6:28) and Luke (12:27).

Flowers of the field in the mountains of Jerusalem.

Common Poppy

Papaver rhoeas L.

Dog Chamomile

Anthemis sp.

All flesh is grass, and all its beauty is like the ***flower of the field...*** **The grass withers, the flower fades; but the word of our God will stand for ever.** Isaiah 40:6, 8

All flesh is like grass and all its glory like the ***flower of the grass*****. The grass withers, and the flower falls, but the word of the Lord abides forever.** I Peter 1:24–25

Common Poppy

THIS plant, one of the most common poppies in the fields of Israel, has a short-living flower of only two to three days. Because its life and beauty fade away so quickly this flower might contextually fit the "flower of the field" in Isaiah (40:6) and the "flower of the grass" in I Peter (1:24).

The common poppy is an annual with bluish-green leaves, 30–50 cm. tall, with several long stems terminating with flowers. The leaves are hairy and rather large, the lower divided in oblong lobes, the upper pinnatisect and clasping the stem. The large crimson flower sheds its two-leaved calyx when it opens. The corolla is made up of four broad-ovate petals, extremely crumpled in bud, with a blackish spot at base; they fall readily after pollination. The stamens are numerous, and the oblong pistil at the center has no styles but several hairy stigmas, arranged in a roof-like cover. The flower closes in the evening and opens in the morning. Insects visiting to collect pollen (no nectar here!) bring about pollination. The fruit is an obconical or pear-shaped capsule, with as many pores as stigmas, hoisted beneath the roof-like cover.

Common Poppy *Papaver rhoeas*

Dog Chamomile

THE yellow-white, fairly large flower-heads of this species catch the eye, assuring it of a primary place among the 'flowers of the field'. No individual name is given to the species in the Bible, but there must have been a Hebrew designation to match the Arabic *ribyaan* or *ikhawan*.

The genus *Anthemis*, which is not unlike the chamomile in appearance, is a member of the Composite (or Daisy) family and includes some 150 species, most of them in the East Mediterranean and adjacent countries. Some of the more than 20 species throughout Israel can also be found in steppes and deserts.

The flowers are mostly annuals, up to 20 cm. tall, generally many-branched and densely covered with dissected leaves. Each branch and branchlet terminates in a head with hundreds of florets, the yellow central tubular ones possessing both five stamens united by their anthers and a pistil with a long style ending in two bent stigmas. The peripheral flowers are white and strip-shaped, and are mainly pistil-bearing.

The contrasting colors of the heads attract many insects, which pollinate the flowers by collecting the pollen and sipping the nectar. When in bloom, the head turns the peripheral flowers down in the evening and spreads them out in the morning. The very small achenes (nutlets) are often crowned with a membranous appendage which may facilitate fruit dispersal.

Dog Chamomile *Anthemis sp.*

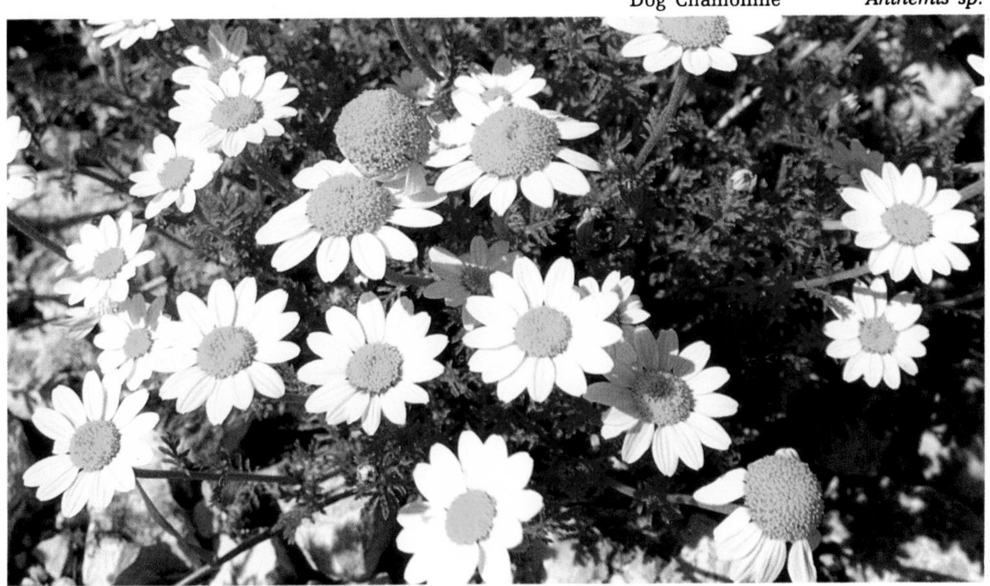

Scarlet Crowfoot

Ranunculus asiaticus L.

Crown Daisy

Chrysanthemum coronarium L.

Scarlet Crowfoot

THIS is the most beautiful crowfoot in Israel and the only species that penetrates deep into the arid zones. Because of the abundance of its large red flowers, it is outstanding in the local flora, and can also be regarded as one of 'the flowers of the field'.

The scarlet crowfoot usually blooms after the anemone, and, unlike it, lacks an underground tuber-like rhizome to store food. Instead, it produces thick storage roots, side by side with fibrous absorption roots. These change annually, which means that the food reserves are removed each year to build up aerial shoots, which, in their turn, produce new roots. The true stem of the plant is very short, producing both flower buds and foliage. The lower leaves are dentate or shallowly lobed, and the remainder dissected into toothed lobes. The scape branches above and each branch terminates in a single crimson or, more rarely, yellow flower, 5–7 cm. across, usually with five sepals and five petals, each with a deep nectariferous pit. The elongated receptacle in the heart of the flower has numerous stamens below and numerous carpels above, with a style and a stigma at the apex of each. The mature fruit is made up of numerous one-seeded, flat winged carpels that separate one by one from the receptacle and are carried off by the wind. Apart from reproducing by carpels, the short stem can send out thin horizontal stolons capable of producing additional shoots.

Crown Daisy

THE flower's name derives from the Greek *chrysos*, 'golden', and *anthemon*, 'flower', and it

Scarlet Crowfoot *Ranunculus asiaticus*

was used by the early Greeks to designate most golden-yellow flowers. It is common in Israel and its requirements are modest, allowing it to grow in wastes, along roadsides and otherwise neglected sites. This flower might also be regarded as one of 'the flowers of the field', and perhaps well fits the spirit of the verse in James: "Let the lowly brother boast in his exaltation, and the rich in his humiliation, because like the flower of the grass he will pass away" (1:9–10).

The genus *Chrysanthemum* is believed to comprise 200 species, of which only a few have been introduced into the garden as ornaments. But so various are they and so important is their role in garden flora that only specialists can know them fully. Scores of books have been written on them and there are magazines devoted exclusively to the taxonomy of the hundreds of garden varieties, which are reliably said to be derived from two wild species of East Asian origin.

The common chrysanthemum is an annual plant, 40–80 cm. tall, with branching and leafy stems. Its leaves are bipinnately parted into a dense mass of segments. The yellow flower-heads are 4–5 cm. across with over 100 disk-florets, their corollas terminating in five triangular teeth, and 15–20 ray florets. The head is surrounded by a number of unequal bracts. Within the corolla are five stamens with free filaments and united anthers forming the staminal tube around the style, which terminates in two stigmas. After all the florets have been pollinated by insects, the ray florets bend over and press themselves against the head.

Crown Daisy *Chrysanthemum coronarium*

White Lily

Lilium candidum L.

Now the capitals that were upon the tops of the pillars in the vestibule were of *lily*-work, four cubits. I Kings 7:19, 26

I am a *rose* of Sharon, a *lily* of the valleys. As a lily among brambles, so is my love among maidens.

Song of Solomon 2:1–2

I will be as the dew to Israel; he shall blossom as the *lily*, he shall strike root as the poplar.

Hosea 14:5

The desert shall rejoice and blossom; like the *crocus* it shall blossom abundantly, and rejoice with joy and singing.

Isaiah 35:1–2

THE white lily adorned the capitals of columns in many ancient civilizations, in Egypt, Assyria, and the land of the Minoans, and in Solomon's Temple in Jerusalem. It was a symbol of beauty, and often of fertility and fruitfulness as well. In the Christian era it became a symbol of spiritual purity, holiness and resurrection, and as such was planted in church courtyards. Called the 'Madonna lily', the flower frequently appears in old church paintings showing Mary holding it in her hand.

The biblical Hebrew term *shoshan* (*shushan*) is certainly the white (true) lily, despite the massive literature and the furious debate among linguists as to its identification. The white lily grows in Galilee and on Mt. Carmel, and was once much more common in the Holy Land.

Ḥavatzeleth, translated by the RSV as 'rose' in the Song of Solomon 2:1 and 'crocus' in Isaiah 35:1, should also be rendered 'lily', in accordance with the parallel "blossom as the lily" (Hosea 14:5), and "like the crocus [*ḥavatzeleth*] it shall blossom". *Ḥavatzeleth* appears only in the two quoted passages and is clearly synonymous with the true lily.

The white lily is a bulbous herb, 1–1.5 m. tall, its bulb consisting of many fleshy scales, with green blades only on the inner ones. The stem is leafy throughout and terminates in a cluster of large white horizontally-oriented flowers, which live four or five days and are open day and night, but are more heavily scented by night. Their night-scent and white color, contrasting with the darkness, attract hawk-moths, the pollinating agents. The lily sets normal, viable, flattish seeds in large capsules, which dehisce when mature.

The spiritual qualities anciently attributed to the white lily were given official religious recognition by a papal edict issued in the 17th century, which referred to this flower in connection with the artistic representation of the Annunciation. Indeed, the striking whiteness and graceful form of the *Lilium candidum* appear in many Renaissance paintings of the Madonna, among them works by Botticelli and Titian.

Sea Daffodil

Pancratium maritimum L.

Narcissus

Narcissus tazetta L.

THE sea daffodil and the narcissus are considered by some to be the biblical lily (*shoshan*), but without justification.

Sea Daffodil

THE sea daffodil is aptly regarded as the herald of rain in Israel. Its snow-white flowers bloom long before the appearance of the leaves.

A common bulbiferous seashore plant of the mainly tropical Amaryllis family, the sea daffodil radiates out to certain temperate zones. Some of the approximately fifteen species of the genus *Pancratium*, including the one dealt with here, have been introduced into the garden because of their lovely large white flowers. The name comes from the Greek *pan*, 'all', and *krotion*, 'power', in reference to its overall healing powers. The Arabs call it *susan al bahr*, 'lily of the sea-shore'.

It belongs to a group which flowers late in summer and develops leaves a month or more afterwards. Whether this separation of the two phases has any ecological advantage is not clear.

Since the plant grows on unstable sand fields and dunes, where the bulb is in danger of exposure, it produces contractile roots which drag it back to its optimal depth.

The fleshy flowering scape terminates in an umbel-like inflorescence of four to ten large white funnel-shaped flowers, often 8 cm. long. They open in the late afternoon and, like the daffodil, have an extra inner crown which is regarded as the united stipules of the six stamens. Pollination is performed mainly by hawk-moths, attracted by the intense aroma at night and the white flower color in the dark. An individual flower lives only for a night and a few hours in the morning. Soon after flowering large fruit capsules are produced. They contain many blackish seeds, which are provided with a spongy cover enabling them to float a long time on the sea-water surface and disperse the seeds from coast to coast.

Narcissus

THE narcissus, sometimes like the sea daffodil believed to be the biblical lily, but without reason, is a member of the Amaryllis family, which includes 65 genera and 800 species, the

Narcissus *Narcissus tazetta*

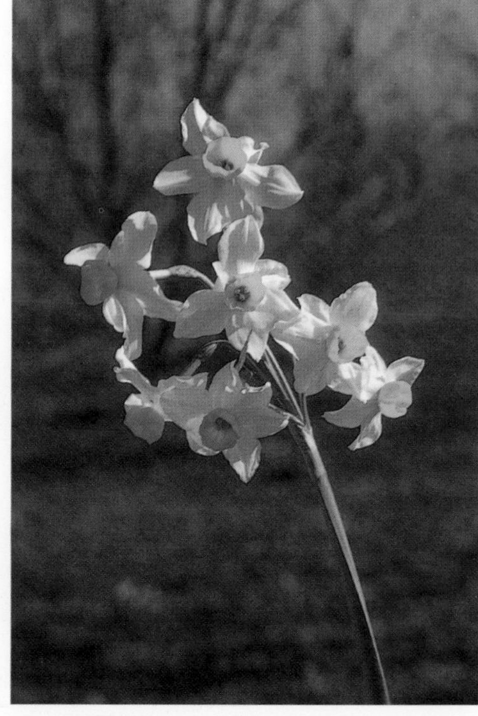

vast majority limited to the southern hemisphere.

Two species of narcissus are native to Israel, and the narcissus of the heading is common not only in the damp soil of the alluvial plains but also in the hills and among shrubs and rocks, even in the northern Negev. It flowers in November and goes dormant in February.

The flowers, which open successively and spread horizontally, consist of four parts: the thickened inferior ovary, the green flower tube above it, the spreading white six-petal lobes and the erect lemon-yellow crown, considered to be stipules of the six stamens. The style barely exserts from the flower. The horizontal or pendant position of the flower protects pollen and nectar from rain.

Attracted by the contrasting colors and by the pleasant scent, which intensifies at night, long-tongued insects, greedy for the pollen and nectar, visit the flowers. The fruit, a short capsule on a weak stalk, falls when it is ripe and releases seeds, probably to be dispersed by ants.

Sea Daffodil *Pancratium maritimum*

Mountain Tulip

Tulipa montana Lindl.

The *flowers* appear on the earth, the time of singing has come, and the voice of the turtledove is heard in our land.

Song of Solomon 2:12

THE tulip with its diversity of color is probably one of the Hebrew *nitzanim*, a group of flowers mentioned once in the Song of Solomon 2:12. *Nitzanim* is identical with the Arabic *nissan*, commonly designating in Arabic-speaking countries (notably Iraq) a whole group of plants with handsome red flowers. These species do not bloom coincidentally but sequentially, beginning with the crown anemone and ending with the common poppy, a fact which must have been recognized in biblical times as it is in ours.

In Israel, the mountain tulip is the prevailing species of the genus *Tulipa*, believed to comprise about 100 species. Because of their beauty and variety of color, they became garden plants very early in history and the center of their cultivation has for centuries been the Netherlands. The local species has, after meticulous breeding, become horticulturally important as an ornamental plant.

The mountain tulip is a bulbiferous herb with a few lanceolate-linear leaves centered mainly at the base of the 20–40 cm. long stem, which terminates in a large crimson flower whose six oblong leaves close in the evening and open in the morning. The flower lives for a week or so and thereafter large fruit capsules with many flattened seeds are produced. The capsules split into three valves and release their seeds.

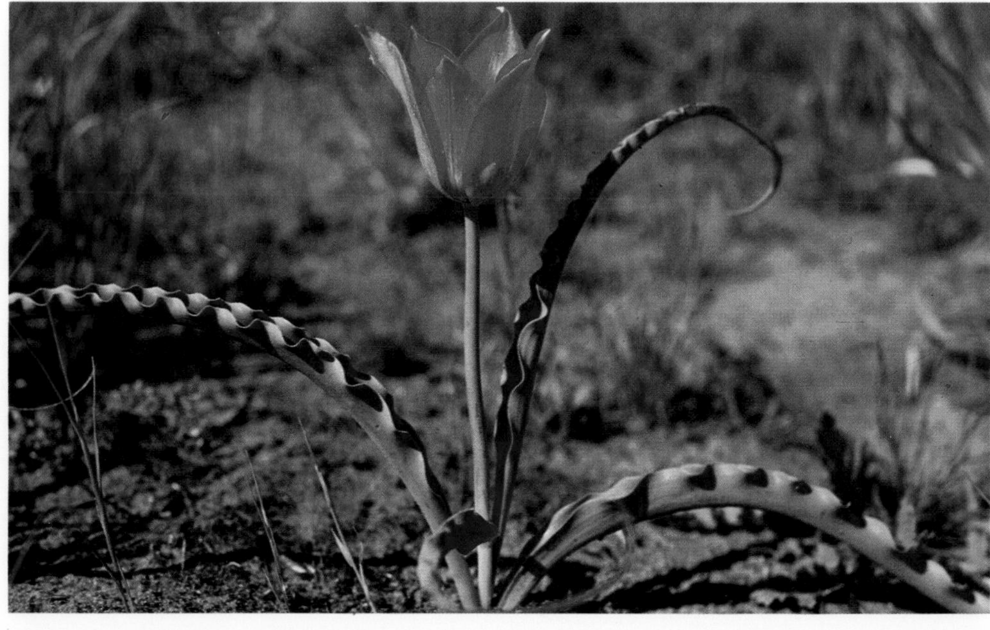

Phoenician Rose

Rosa phoenicia L.

I grew tall like a palm tree in En-gedi, and like *rose plants* **in Jericho.**

Ecclesiasticus 24:14

IN biblical times a cultivated variety of rose, originating in a nearby country, was grown in the garden for cosmetic and ornamental purposes. Orientals have always had a high regard for perfumes, and rosewater was one of the earliest of these. Although the date of the earliest rose cultivation is not fully documented, we are more or less sure that it began in Mediterranean countries to which several species are native.

The Hebrew *vered*, which can be identified with the rose, is mentioned only in post-biblical literature - several times in the Talmud: "No gardens and orchards should be established in Jerusalem, with the exception of *rose* gardens that have existed there since the Early Prophets" (*Baba Kama* 82b); "The bridegroom wears a crown of roses" (*Meggilath Taanith* 327).

Four species of the genus *Rosa* are native to Israel, two of them small alpine shrubs, one on Mt. Hermon, the other on Mt. Sinai. Of the others, *R. canina* is also common in many temperate countries, whereas *R. phoenicia* is a plant growing on riverbanks and brooks in East Mediterranean countries only.

These roses are shrubs with many intricately-branched, thorny stems and leaves consisting of two or three pairs of toothed leaflets. The large white flowers grow in clusters. The fruits are edible and mature in late summer.

9
Drugs & Spices Incense & Perfume

ALTHOUGH healing by plants is not explicitly mentioned in the Bible, herbal remedies were numerous and specific. That the Bible never prescribes cures by incantations or magic – with the single exception of the serpent bite – is surprising in view of the wide incidence of such rites at the time; but the Law forbade them on the grounds of idolatry. The ultimate healer was God, and prayer was therefore the remedy most often prescribed: "The Lord sustains him on his sickbed; in his illness thou healest all his infirmities" (Psalms 41:3).

About a hundred local plants are still used medicinally today, with varying results, by the peasants and Bedouin. Those mentioned in the Bible, without reference to their healing power, include poison hemlock, castor bean, cassia, laurel, olive, and wild gourd, and others like hyssop, caper, garlic, cummin, and saffron. Thompson (1949) presents a list of medicinal plants destined as *materia medica* for the royal families of Assyria, but his documents imply that such plants were also commonly used by ordinary people for healing. Because this defied the belief in God's exclusive healing power, they were not mentioned in Scripture. Some of them appear in Egyptian literature as well. Mallow, for instance, was (and still is) officially recognized in the pharmacopoeia of various countries. Although less widely used than formerly, some other plants like myrrh, frankincense, balm, laurel, myrtle, tragacanth, storax, and ginger grass are still employed in the pharmaceutical industry.

Man has always been in need of spices to improve the taste and flavor of his daily food. The production of cosmetics and incenses flourished in Assyria and Sumeria, for the sensuous pleasure arising from perfume was equally sought after. Indeed, odoriferous plants are known to have been cultivated as early as 3000 BC. The hanging gardens of Babylon were heavily scented. Song and poetry celebrated perfume for its delicate fragrance and the aphrodisiac qualities it was believed to possess. Perhaps this is why spices and perfumes were eventually made use of in religious rites, for healing, holy ointments, magic, purification and embalming.

The Bible, especially the Song of Solomon, abounds with descriptions of perfumes: "I arose to open to my beloved, and my hands dripped with myrrh, my fingers with liquid myrrh, upon the handles of the bolt" (Song of Solomon 5:5). Such costly perfume oil was used for anointing kings – Saul and David being thus anointed by Samuel – and for the High Priest in the Temple. The New Testament frequently mentions the practice of anointing the body with perfume oil (see Mark 16:1; Luke 23:56; and John 19:39–40).

The identification of this group of plants – some of which were imported to the Land of Israel, though others grew here formerly (but are now extinct) – has caused many controversies among scholars. Some of these problems are discussed in this chapter.

White Wormwood

Artemisia herba-alba Asso

Therefore thus says the Lord of hosts concerning the prophets: "Behold, I will feed them with *wormwood*, and give them poisoned water to drink." Jeremiah 23:15

O you who turn justice to *wormwood*, and cast down righteousness to the earth.

Amos 5:7

THE Hebrew word *laanah*, appearing eight times in the Bible, has occasioned much dispute because there is no linguistic or obvious contextual evidence that *laanah* is a bitter plant. Yet its identification with wormwood is strongly supported by many commentators, who base their conclusions on ancient translations such as the Septuagint and the Vulgate. Because it is frequently coupled with *rosh* (poison hemlock), some scholars believe that the two words are synonymous, like other name-pairs in the Bible.

The Greek word *apsinthos* for the biblical *laanah* was applied to the local *Artemisia herba-alba* because this species of wormwood covers vast stretches of desert in Israel, but there is no real evidence for the identity of *laanah* and *Artemisia*.

Although the whole plant is strongly aromatic and rather bitter, it is eaten by desert goats and the dried leaves are used to prepare a tea drunk by the Bedouin of the Sinai and the Negev. Wormwood is also widely used as a healing beverage against intestinal worms, a fact reflected in its name.

The white wormwood is a dwarf-shrub 40 cm. tall, heavily branched from the base, with gray, densely haired, much-dissected leaves shed at the end of the rainy season and replaced by small, scale-like summer leaves. The stems and branches develop small flowers in autumn, which like those of other members of the Composite family are arranged in heads, each comprising two to four florets. After pollination they produce minute fruits with a tuft of hairs that facilitates dispersal.

Wild Gourd

Citrullus colocynthis (L.) Schrad.

One of them went out into the field to gather herbs, and found a wild vine and gathered from it his lap full of wild *gourds*, and came and cut them up into the pot of pottage, not knowing what they were. But while they were eating of the pottage, they cried out, "O man of God, there is death in the pot!"

II Kings 4:39–40

THE wild gourd (or colocynth) grows in the southern part of the Coastal Plain and the Jordan Valley, where, near Gilgal, Elisha and the sons of the prophets were gathered. "Wild vine" suitably describes its stems, leaves and tendrils, and the words, "there is death in the pot!" are a further indication that the colocynth is the plant in question, as its fruit is a deadly poison. Thus it is both contextually and linguistically correct to render 'wild gourds' for the Hebrew *pakuoth-sadeh*; some of the classical translations, furthermore, render *colocynthis*.

Sinai and the western Negev supply peeled colocynth in quantity to the world medical market. The seeds are edible and when ground provide a kind of rude bread for the Bedouin in years of famine.

The wild gourd is a perennial hot-desert herb with a thick root high in water content, and a very short stem branching from the base into long trailing shoots bearing ovate, palmately lobed leaves and branched tendrils. Its yellow flowers, scattered through the leaves, are not unlike those of the watermelon. The fruit is globose, yellow when ripe, as large as an apple, with a hard, smooth, often dark-nerved shell, a spongy pulp, and white or brown seeds. It is widely used medicinally, especially for stomach pains. The pulp is a drastic hydragogue cathartic, sometimes fatal in large doses.

Poison Hemlock

Conium maculatum L.

Their grapes are grapes of *poison*, their clusters are bitter; their wine is the poison of serpents, and the cruel venom of asps.

Deuteronomy 32:32–33

Remember my affliction and my bitterness, the wormwood and the *gall*! My soul continually thinks of it and is bowed down within me.

Lamentations 3:19–20

And when they came to a place called Golgotha (which means the place of a skull), they offered him wine to drink, mingled with *gall*; but when he tasted it, he would not drink it.

Matthew 27:33–34

THE Hebrew word *rosh* is variously translated, even within the same version. Some scholars have identified it as poison hemlock. There is no linguistic support for this rendition, although it is conventional in modern Hebrew. In context it seems to denote a bitter and poisonous drink or food: "They gave me poison [*rosh*] for food, and for my thirst they gave me vinegar to drink" (Psalms 69:21). Its frequent association with *laanah* (wormwood) suggests either a specific plant or a synonym.

It may not be far-fetched to assume that *Conium*, common in Greece, was the poison-drink of Socrates. The poison, conine, is especially abundant in the fruit.

The poison hemlock belongs to the Carrot family. It is an annual or perennial herb, 1 m. or more tall, with a branching stem and dense, pinnately dissected leaves. The branched inflorescence is arranged in umbels of small white flowers and the fruit consists of two small, ribbed carpels. It flowers in spring near houses and in neglected sites.

This plant has also been identified with *Hyoscyamus* (see: 'Henbane') because *sakaran* (poisoning) is the Arabic name for *Hyoscyamus muticus* and also for *Conium*. It is also possible that *rosh* originally referred to a specific plant but came gradually to mean all kinds of poison.

Henbane

Hyoscyamus aureus L.;
H. muticus L.

The boundary goes out to the shoulder of the hill north of Ekron, then the boundary bends round to *Shikkeron*, and passes along to Mount Baalah, and goes out to Jabneel.
Joshua 15:11

WHILE the natural habitats of some of the henbane species are crevices of rocks and old city walls, this species grows in the desert of Israel and in Sinai.

It can be identified with the Hebrew *shikrona*, as was indeed done by Josephus (*Antiquities*, Book III, 7:6), who identified the plant *saccharus* with *Hyoscyamus*, in a description which fits henbane. The identity of this name with henbane is thus supported both by the Greek word and by the biblical place-name Shikrona in Judea (Joshua 15:11), where *Hyoscyamus aureus* is abundant.

There are five species of henbane in Israel, the most common of which is *H. aureus*, which grows in rock crevices and on old city walls, as in Jerusalem. It is a perennial herb, 30–50 cm. tall, very viscid and much branched from the base; the dentate or lobed leaves are covered with glandular hairs. The thick clusters of flowers turn spiky after blooming. They are large and more or less two-lipped, with a dark purple spot on the upper lip. The stamens and style are exserted. The fruit is a capsule divided into two carpels and opened by a lid but hidden within the hardened 5-footed calyx.

Because they contain the alkaloid hyoscyamine, most henbane species, some of which are poisonous, are used medicinally. The most poisonous is *H. muticus* L., widely used in medicine also as a narcotic.

Henbane *Hyoscyamus aureus*

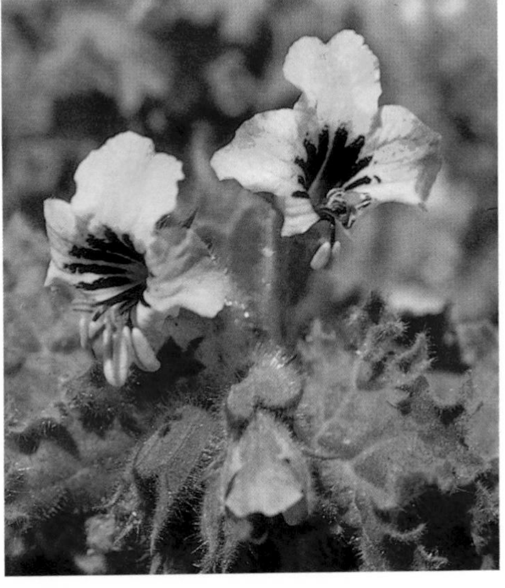

Mandrake

Mandragora autumnalis L.

In the days of wheat harvest Reuben went and found *mandrakes* in the field and brought them to his mother Leah. Then Rachel said to Leah, "Give me, I pray, some of your son's mandrakes." But she said to her, "Is it a small matter that you have taken away my husband? Would you take away my son's mandrakes also?" Genesis 30:14–15

The *mandrakes* give forth fragrance, and over our doors are all choice fruits, new as well as old, which I have laid up for you, O my beloved. Song of Solomon 7:13

My brother Reuben brought *mandrakes* from the field ... and there were apples sweet scented growing above the water beds in the land of Aram.
Testaments of Issachar 1:3–5

THE magical powers of the mandrake have been the subject of a mass of literature. We are concerned here with the Hebrew *dudaim*, translated 'mandrakes' in the quoted passages. *Dudaim* in Genesis 30:14–15 can certainly not be *Mandragora*, which has never grown in Mesopotamia, where Jacob, Leah and Rachel lived. In the passage from the Pseudepigrapha, furthermore, the *dudaim* are described as apples, found not in the field but on riverbanks. In the Song of Solomon it seems nonsensical to list mandrakes with "all choice fruits". The only evidence for equating *dudaim* with *Mandragora* is the Aramaic translation of Genesis and the Mishnaic rendition *yavruḥim*, still used by the Arabs of some Mediterranean countries for *Mandragora*. *Dudaim* was also translated as *Mandragora* by the Greeks. It is not certain, however, if the translation is justified.

Mandrakes were used as aphrodisiacs in post-biblical times and are mentioned in later literature, especially in medieval treatises, for the great value of their roots. The Greeks, in whose country the mandrake is common and valued for its aphrodisiac powers, called it 'love apple' and considered it effective as a love-potion when soaked in wine. They also believed that it helped a barren woman to conceive. The Arabs called it 'the devil's candle' because they thought it shines in the dark, as Josephus Flavius also relates in his *Jewish Wars* (Book VII, 6:3). Primitive people still prize mandrakes and endow them with mystery, especially in regard to their strange roots, which are sometimes disturbingly human in shape.

Recent experiments have shown that the mandrake contains both sedatives and aphrodisiacs. Because the sedatives are in larger quantity, the small number of stimulating hormones may not really produce an aphrodisiac effect.

The mandrake, a member of the Nightshade family, is a Mediterranean genus. It is a stemless perennial herb with thick, bizarrely branched roots and large, ovate or oblong, very wrinkled leaves growing in a rosette. In winter it bears bluish, bell-shaped flowers on long stalks. The fragrant, plum-like, yellowish-red fruits ripen in spring and sometimes remain in the field until early summer. They are edible, but are said to be narcotic and purgative.

Henna

Lawsonia inermis L.

My beloved is to me a cluster of *henna* blossoms in the vineyard of En-Gedi.
Song of Solomon 1:14

HENNA is mentioned only in the Song of Solomon, which abounds with proverbial but not always realistic phrases. It is believed that henna, then as now, grew as an individual tree or in groups in courtyards for domestic use, but was not, as the Song of Solomon implies, a garden tree.

It was grown mainly for its dye, which is prepared by crushing the dried leaves into a powder and mixing it with water to make a paste for application to various parts of the body, notably the nails and hair. Henna also dyes clothes permanently and is an ingredient of perfume, and its dense fragrant whitish flowers were offered in bouquets in Indian temples.

The Egyptians were among the first to use henna as a cosmetic, and they wrapped their mummies in henna-colored clothes. Henna powder is still sold in the bazaars of all the great Arab cities. Distilled from its flowers is a fragrant essential oil called *mehendi*, used as a perfume and in religious feasts. A decoction of the bark serves the Arabs medicinally.

The Hebrew *kopher* as 'henna' is supported philologically and contextually. The dye itself was called *puker* by the ancient Egyptians, *kupr* or *kufer* by the Copts, and *kufra* in Aramaic and Accadian, by which name it is known in post-biblical literature.

Lawsonia inermis, a member of the Willow-herb family, is the only species in the genus. Its natural distribution area extends from tropical northeast Africa to Arabia, Persia, and northwest India. Brought very early into cultivation, its original home is unknown.

The henna 'tree' is a tree-like shrub up to 4 m. tall, branching heavily above, with ovate, opposite, entire leaves. It is impressive in spring when its bunches of small whitish fragrant flowers appear. Its fruits are many-seeded, small globular capsules torn at maturity. Although it is still found in Jericho and other villages in the Jordan Valley and on the Coastal Plain, it has altogether disappeared from En Gedi.

Dyers Madder

Rubia tinctorum L.

After Abimelech there arose to deliver Israel Tola the son of *Puah*, son of Dodo, a man of Issachar; and he lived at Shamir in the hill country of Ephraim.

Judges 10:1

IN biblical times, the madder was chiefly valued for its roots, containing a red dye known as alizarin, widely used for dyeing clothes and leather goods. For this purpose it was cultivated in all the Near Eastern countries, either in separate plots or in olive groves.

The Hebrew name for madder is *puah, puvah* or *fuah*. In the Bible it is mentioned only as a proper name in Genesis 46:13, Judges 10:1 and I Chronicles 7:1. Its Arabic name is *fuwwa*.

In post-biblical literature it is mentioned not only as a useful dyeing plant, but also as possessing virtuous properties, probably because the red color is endowed with many folkloristic attributes; the thread of scarlet, for instance, recurring in the lore of many peoples. It has also long been used for curing jaundice, and as such is mentioned by Pliny in his *Naturalis Historia* (24, 27, 95) and by Dioscorides in *Materia Medica* (3.150). However, since the introduction of synthetic dye into industry, the cultivation of the madder has been largely reduced.

The madder is a perennial herb with a long herbaceous climbing and scabrous stem. Its oblong-lanceolate leaves are arranged in whorls of 2–6. The minute flowers are yellowish-green and the fruits are red globular berries.

Storax

Liquidambar orientalis Miller

Then they sat down to eat; and looking up they saw a caravan of Ishmaelites coming from Gilead, with their camels bearing gum, *balm*, and myrrh, on their way to carry it down to Egypt.

Genesis 37:25

Is there no *balm* in Gilead? Is there no physician there? Why then has the health of the daughter of my people not been restored?

Jeremiah 8:22

THE identification of biblical *tzori*, appearing six times in the Bible, three times in association with Gilead, is highly controversial. The variety of opinion cannot be recorded here. However, there is no doubt that *tzori* is a gum or resin obtained by wounding the bark of a particular tree (named *kataf* in post-biblical Hebrew literature). The word *nataf*, mentioned only once in the Bible (Exodus 30:34) as one of the ingredients of the holy oil and rendered 'stacte' in the RSV and the Septuagint, is a synonym of *tzori* which is *Liquidambar orientalis*.

The reference to Gilead as a storax-gum center in Jeremiah and in Genesis and the distribution and climatic requirements as reflected in the distribution of *Liquidambar orientalis* in southwest Turkey (and reportedly in Lebanon) both give credence to the assumption that the tree grew in Gilead, northeast of Israel in biblical times; but like other nearly extinct northern plants has since disappeared.

The genus *Liquidambar* consists of four species, two native to the Sino-Japanese region, one to North and Central America, and one (*L. orientalis*) to southwest Anatolia and probably Lebanon. This species has recently been shown to be specifically identical with the *L. styraciflua*.

The storax grows 6–10 m. tall. Its leaves fall in winter, its flowers form globular yellowish heads and its fruits are beaked capsules. There are stands of such trees in southwestern Anatolia, which yield gum known commercially as Levant storax, valuable medicinally. The gum, obtained by wounding the trunk, is a grayish-brown sticky mass, becoming semi-liquid to solid, with about a thirty percent content of total balsamic acids.

The present writer accepts the suggestion of Lagarde (1886) that the Greek name *storax* derives from the Hebrew *tzori*.

Castor Bean

Ricinus communis L.

And the Lord God appointed a *plant*, and made it come up over Jonah, that it might be a shade over his head, to save him from his discomfort. So Jonah was exceedingly glad because of the plant. But when dawn came up the next day, God appointed a worm which attacked the plant, so that it withered.

Jonah 4:6–7

THE Hebrew *kikayon* appears in the Bible only in this passage. It is rendered differently in various translations: in the Septuagint as *kolucunti*, in the Vulgate as *hedera* and in the Authorized Version as 'gourd'. None of these fits the context better than the castor bean, a rapidly-growing annual or perennial herb attaining a height of 4 m. or more. Its erect stem produces so many large palmate leaves that the plant may shade a traveler from the burning sun. All the other plants suggested are creeping or straggling.

Egyptian medicinal documents mention *kaka* as a plant, which according to Herodotus was grown abundantly in Egypt for *kiki* oil, used for lighting. The Talmud sometimes refers to *kikayon* as a plant yielding the castor oil long known in medicine.

The castor bean is in the main a tropical plant of unknown origin. It is frequently said to come from tropical Africa, and has indeed been found in 6,000-year-old Egyptian tombs, which attests to its very early growth in Egypt. It is native to Israel, where it occurs in neglected places and also in some desert wadis. Stately 'forests' of castor bean have been observed in the delta of the Arnon River in Jordan.

At the end of its stem and branches are unisexual flowers on a spike-like axis, the females below the males. The fruits are 2–3 celled capsules, 1–3 cm. long, each cell with a large single seed whose endosperm consists of as much as sixty percent of the oil so much utilized in medicine, as well as a deadly toxic substance known as ricinine. Its main use, presently, is as a lubricant for aircraft and in plastics.

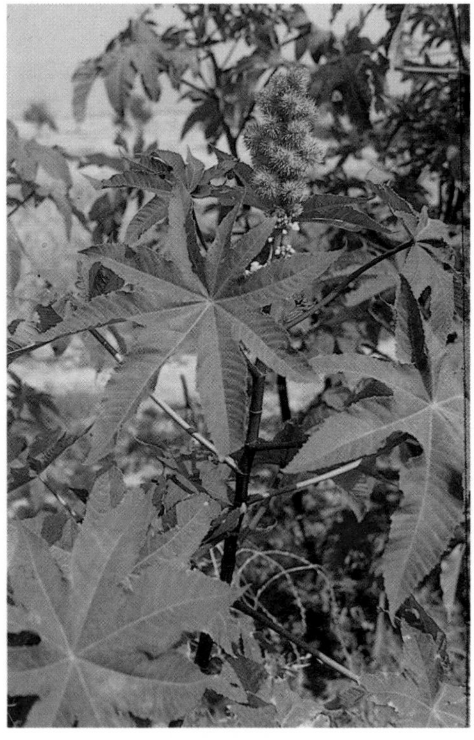

Ladanum

Cistus incanus L.

Then they sat down to eat; and looking up they saw a caravan of Ishmaelites coming from Gilead, with their camels bearing gum, balm, and *myrrh*, on their way to carry it down to Egypt.

Genesis 37:25

A little balm and a little honey, gum, *myrrh*, pistachio nuts, and almonds.

Genesis 43:11

ALL drugs and delicacies listed in Genesis seem to be native to biblical Gilead (Transjordan), where myrrh, a tropical shrub, cannot be grown. It cannot therefore be a correct translation for *lot*, as in the RSV text. Most scholars have translated *lot* as 'ladanum' – *Cistus creticus* (or more precisely, *C. incanus*) – with which it accords in usage and linguistics.

Ladanum or labdanum is a resinous substance obtained from some species of *Cistus* (*Cistaceae* family), whose juicy exudate on the leaves and branches is collected with rake-like instruments with leather thongs instead of teeth, which are drawn over the plant and to which the sticky juice adheres. It can also be obtained by boiling the branches in water or, as on the island of Cyprus, by combing the beards of the goats which graze on the *Cistus* leaves.

Common labdanum is marketed in contorted or spiral pieces and has a balsamic odor and a bitter taste. From its resin comes a gold-colored essential oil with the penetrating odor of ambergris. Labdanum, which as a stimulant and expectorant was formerly prescribed for catarrh and dysentery, is now chiefly used in the perfume industry and as incense in Eastern churches, where its heavy odor can easily be discerned.

Ladanum is probably the North African *latai*, cognate with the Assyrian *ladanu*, the name of the gum exuded by *Cistus*. The Aramaic translation of *lot* in Genesis, furthermore, is *letem*, clearly identical with the Talmudic *lotem*, which in use and context fits *Cistus incanus*, widespread in Gilead and elsewhere.

Ladanum is a shrub up to 70 cm. tall, with hairy and viscid leaves; when it blooms, in spring, its large pink flowers brighten the surrounding dull vegetation. Its fruits are capsules with minute seeds. It is a dominant in many dwarf-shrub communities, thriving mainly on the calcareous-marly soils (rendzinas) of the Mediterranean area (see 'Myrrh').

Tragacanth

Astragalus gummifer Labill.;
A. bethlehemiticus Boiss.

Then they sat down to eat; and looking up they saw a caravan of Ishmaelites coming from Gilead, with their camels bearing *gum*, balm, and myrrh, on their way to carry it down to Egypt.

Genesis 37:25

A little balm and a little honey, *gum*, myrrh, pistachio nuts, and almonds.

Genesis 43:11

THE biblical *nekhoth* which was carried with other fruits and drugs from Gilead may well have been tragacanth gum, obtained from a local species of *Astragalus* or from *A. gummifer* on Mt. Hermon. Furthermore, the close connection of Gilead with the articles listed in the passages above suggests that this area might have been a commercial or production center for drugs and delicacies.

The RSV rendition of 'gum' for the Hebrew *nekhoth*, twice mentioned in the Bible, is too general; it should be translated specifically as 'tragacanth', a dried gum exuded from certain spiny and shrubby species of *Astragalus* occurring in several countries of the Middle East, including Israel. The amount of scholarly dispute about the word *nekhoth* makes it worthwhile to offer a few arguments in support of so specific an identification. *Nakaa*, or *nakaath*, is the Arabic name for the tragacanth gum, which has been widely known and used since ancient times in medicine, industry and the manufacture of confections. Trade in tragacanth, once widespread, continues to flourish.

The tragacanth gum is obtained by incisions made in the root of the shrub a few centimetres underground and left open for a day or less to allow the small flakes of gum to ooze out. The flakes are usually collected by shepherds for local and foreign markets.

The genus *Astragalus*, which belongs to the Bean family, comprises about 1,800 species, many of them producing the tragacanth gum. In the Middle East there are 30 or more species growing in alpine and sub-alpine altitudes which supply this gum. Notable among them are *A. gummifer* and *A. adscendens*. Among the other gummiferous species, the Bethlehem tragacanth growing in Judea and Gilead also produces this gum.

The plants concerned here are spiny shrubs 30–50 cm. tall. They branch densely from the base and bear pinnate leaves with several pairs of leaflets borne on a spiny axis. The flowers are crowded in axillary heads. The minute fruits are densely wooly and are dispersed by the wind.

Hermon Tragacanth *Astragalus gummifer*

Ginger Grass

Cymbopogon martinii Stapf;
C. spp.

Take the finest spices: of liquid myrrh five hundred shekels, and of sweet-smelling cinnamon half as much, that is, two hundred and fifty, and of *aromatic cane* two hundred and fifty.

Exodus 30:23

To what purpose does frankincense come to me from Sheba, or *sweet cane* from a distant land? Your burnt offerings are not acceptable.

Jeremiah 6:20

Wine from Uzal they exchanged for your wares; wrought iron, cassia, and *calamus* were bartered for your merchandise. Dedan traded with you in saddlecloths for riding. Arabia and all the princes of Kedar were your favored dealers.

Ezekiel 27:19–21

AROMATIC grasses were in daily use in the ancient world for perfume, cosmetics, flavoring and medicine, and were imported into the Near East from India or its vicinity.

The age-old usage of these plants is attested by the fact that when the tombs of the Pharaohs of the 20th and 21st dynasties were opened in Egypt in 1881 - some 3,000 years after burial - the pleasant odor of *C. schoenanthus*, among others, was still perceptible (Schweinfurth, 1884).

The Hebrew words *kaneh hatov, knei-bosem* and sometimes *kaneh* by itself are believed to designate herbaceous perennial aromatic grasses. It is hopeless to speculate about which of the three or four possible species was intended. It is even doubtful whether the biblical authors had in mind any particular species of the genus *Cymbopogon*, although one of them does grow wild in Israel.

Chief among the sweet grasses are *Cymbopogon martinii* (the palmerosa oil grass), *C. schoenanthus Spreng*. (camel grass), and *C. citratus* (DC.) Stapf (lemon grass), which like most species of this genus yield aromatic oils chemically distinct from one another. The oil is produced by steam distillation of the aerial parts of the plant.

Some of the aromatic grasses are still cultivated today in India and elsewhere for their essential oils.

Ginger grass is also known as 'sweet calamus'.

Cymbopogon citratus

Frankincense

Boswellia sacra Flueckiger

Take sweet spices, stacte, and onycha, and galbanum, sweet spices with pure *frankincense* ... and make an incense blended as by the perfumer, seasoned with salt, pure and holy.

Exodus 30:34–35

When they saw the star, they rejoiced exceedingly with great joy; and going into the house they saw the child with Mary his mother, and they fell down and worshiped him. Then, opening their treasures, they offered him gifts, gold and *frankincense* and myrrh. Matthew 2:10–11

Now while he was serving as priest before God when his division was on duty, according to the custom of the priesthood, it fell to him by lot to enter the temple of the Lord and burn *incense*. And the whole multitude of the people were praying outside at the hour of incense.

Luke 1:8–10

NUMBERED among the Temple treasures (Nehemiah 13:5), frankincense was an important ingredient of incense and also of perfume. The resins from the two species listed above – and probably of others of the 24 species of the genus *Boswellia*, occurring in Arabia and East Africa – are exudations like those of balm and myrrh, commonly traded throughout the ancient world. With other costly commodities, frankincense was imported into the Land of Israel by the Phoenicians via the famous spice route across southern Arabia and some of the littoral stations of East Africa, a caravan highway also used for imports from India and farther east.

Today, frankincense is frequently used as incense in the ceremonies of the Roman Catholic Church. It is also widely used in medicine.

The Hebrew name for frankincense is *levonah*. The identification of *Boswellia* with *levonah* is well-founded and linguistic support is furnished by the Arabic name *luban*.

The species of *Boswellia* under discussion are medium-sized shrubs with pinnate leaves and small greenish or whitish flowers. The resin, exuded naturally from the leaves and twigs, can be increased greatly in amount by incising the stems. The drops are shiny, yellowish or reddish, highly aromatic and bitter.

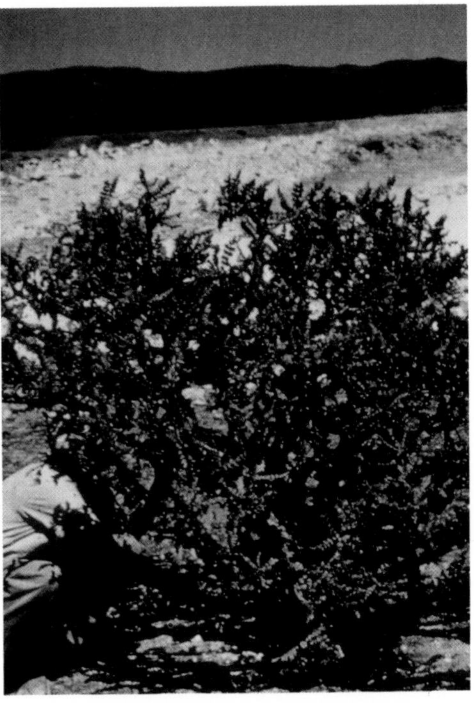

Balm

Commiphora gileadensis (L.) Engl.

I come to my garden, my sister, my bride, I gather my myrrh with my *spice*, I eat my honeycomb with my honey, I drink my wine with my milk.

Song of Solomon 5:1

THE balm (balsam) tree of Judea was praised by ancient writers and travelers like Josephus, Pliny, Tacitus and Dioscorides, and during the war with the Romans the Jews tried in vain to destroy Judea's near-monopoly of balm groves. At approximately that time, the plant was successfully introduced into Egypt. The accounts of travelers during the early centuries of this era show that remains of the balm plantations survived the destruction of Judea.

Recent excavations at the ancient site of En Gedi have unearthed the tools, vessels and furnaces of ancient workshops for production of the balm commercially.

Balm resin was known in trade long before it was recorded in the Bible. It was a very profitable commerce exclusively controlled by the Arabs, who were so secretive about its origin and manufacture that they invented horrifying tales about it, claiming, for example, that the trees were guarded by winged serpents.

It is the opinion of some scholars that the balm tree of En Gedi and Jericho, famous for its quality, was brought in seedling form by the Queen of Sheba and given to King Solomon along with other gifts. This is botanically plausible, since it has been proved that the Egyptian queen Hatchepsut successfully introduced living myrrh plants from Punt (Somalia) into Egypt in 1,600 BC. However, it is also reasonable to suppose that a species of balm might have grown wild in En Gedi along with other wild tropical trees, and was taken from its wild state into cultivation *in situ*. If so, this wild plant, like others, has since disappeared.

The uses of balm were threefold: as an ingredient of the holy oil, as a healing agent for wounds and an antidote to snake bites, and as an ingredient of perfume, for which the pungent resin was squeezed into an oil or paste.

Since many tropical trees and shrubs grow under the tropical conditions of the Rift Valley (Aravah Valley, the Dead Sea and nearby portions of the Jordan Valley), the species concerned may once have been among them. As a matter of fact it grows today in Hedjas (southwest Arabia) under conditions not unlike those of the Jordan Valley. The balm shrub mistakenly called in Latin 'Balm of Gilead' may therefore have been cultivated from native stocks and bred by the peasants of Jericho and En Gedi into the superior varieties from which the Israeli balm derived its reputation. It is in any case the most probable assumption and more plausible than the legend that the balm shrub was brought by the Queen of Sheba as a gift from Arabia to King Solomon. Indeed, some of the tropical shrubs which grow in conjunction with the balm tree in Arabia still thrive near En Gedi and Jericho.

The words *basam, bosem,* and *besem* appear more than forty times in the Bible and the Apocrypha in various forms and inflections, usually in connection with healing, balms and incenses. The same biblical name is applied specifically to the balm or balsam tree, as in the verse quoted in the heading, where it is translated 'spice'.

It is called in Arabic *balasam* or *balsham*. Its derivative *parsam*, the Talmudic *aparsimon* and its Greek derivative *opobalsamum*, was later given as an epithet to *Commiphora*. Following the rules of nomenclature its name was replaced by *Commiphora gileadensis* ; although the plant never grew in Gilead. Rendering this species of *Commiphora* as biblical *basam* seems to be reasonable and geobotanically more plausible than the other ill-documented translations.

The balm tree is a shrub or small tree which grows in hot deserts or semi-deserts. Its leaves have 3–5 leaflets which are shed in the dry period. Its small clusters of white flowers produce fruits which are small drupes containing a fragrant yellow seed. It is native to southwest Arabia and Somaliland, where it grows in the thorn-bush formations under arid tropical conditions, often in the company of such shrubs and trees as *Balanites aegyptica* and species of *Maerua, Ziziphus*, and the like.

There are about 100 species of *Commiphora*, formerly known as *Balsamodendron*, some of which are notably resiniferous, or gum-exuding. The resinous, fragrant balm exudes spontaneously or is obtained artificially by incision from the stems and branches, in droplets that accumulate in clumps. Their initial bright green color later turns brown and when solidified they drop to the ground, from which they are collected.

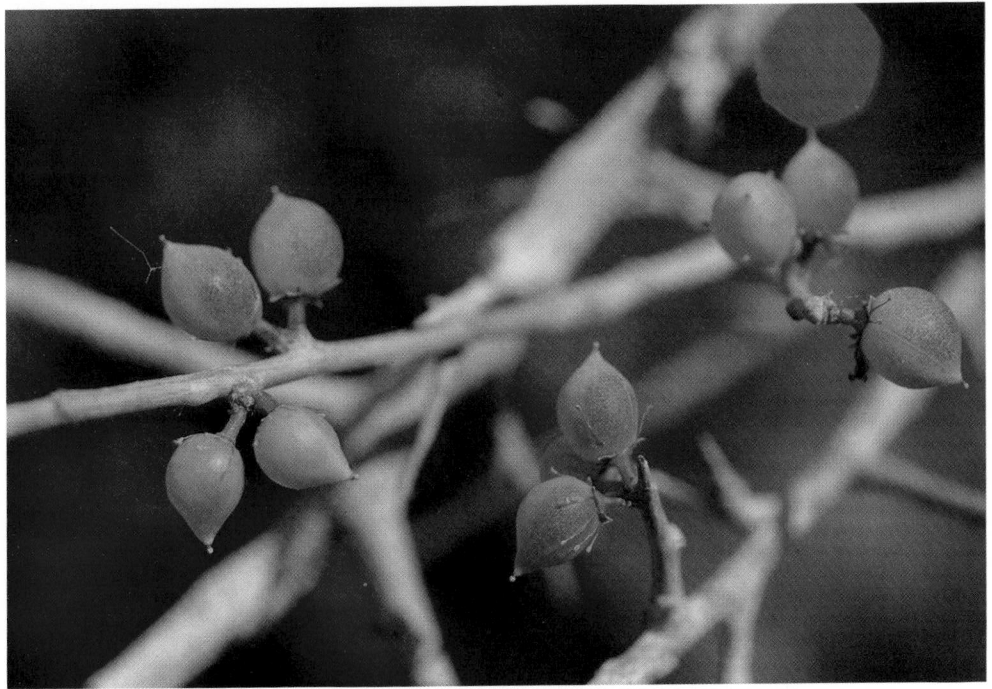

Myrrh

Commiphora abyssinica (Berg.) Engl.

Your robes are all fragrant with *myrrh* and aloes and cassia.

Psalms 45:8

Then, opening their treasures, they offered him gifts, gold and frankincense and *myrrh*.

Matthew 2:11

THE Scriptures describe myrrh, the most precious and popular resin, as an ingredient of holy ointments and as a cosmetic. It was in demand in ancient perfumeries and was employed in medicine; the ancient Egyptians used it as incense in their temples and as an embellishment for their dead. Thus it was among the important items in the trade with the great empires of the East (Revelation 18:13).

Myrrh is connected with the birth and death of Jesus. It was one of the gifts that the ''wise men from the East'' offered to the child Jesus (Matthew 2:11), and was also given to Jesus before his crucifixion (Mark 15:23). Nicodemus brought a mixture of myrrh and aloes with the linen cloths for wrapping the body of Jesus (John 19:39–40).

Mor is justly translated 'myrrh', which is identical with the species of *Commiphora abyssinica*; although other species of this genus may well also have been included in the biblical *mor*.

This species and a few similar ones are native to Arabia, Ethiopia and Somaliland. They are all thorny, branched shrubs or small trees growing on rocky ground. Their small leaves have three ovate leaflets and their fruit is similar to a small olive. The fragrant stems and branches exude drops of oily resin spontaneously, but when they are incised, the resin flows more heavily. It eventually solidifies (see 'Ladanum').

Further investigation is required to confirm the identification of this plant (*Commiphora abyssinica*) with myrrh.

Galbanum

Ferula gummosa Boiss.

And the Lord said to Moses, "Take sweet spices, stacte, and onycha, and *galbanum*, sweet spices with pure frankincense.

Exodus 30:34

I grew tall ... like cassia and camel's thorn I gave forth the aroma of spices, and like choice myrrh I spread a pleasant odor, like *galbanum*, onycha and stacte, and like the fragrance of frankincense in the tabernacle.

Ecclesiasticus 24:14–15

GALBANUM or galban, a gum resin mentioned twice in the Bible, is described in Exodus as an ingredient of the incense used in worship, and in Ecclesiasticus as a sweet spice, although it is actually a fetid gum. Despite the Greek, Aramaic and Syriac name *ḥalbane*, cognate with the Hebrew *ḥelbenah*, its identification is not yet firmly established.

It was undoubtedly imported into ancient Israel, since neither here nor in any neighboring countries is there any plant which produces this resin.

A yellowish or brownish gum resin, galbanum is obtained from a few species of *Ferula* growing in Iran and Afghanistan, but mainly from *F. gummosa*.

The galbanum (or one of its allies) is a tall herbaceous plant of the Carrot family, with large incised leaves, a relatively thick stem and rich umbels of small yellowish flowers. The gum exudes from the lower part of the stem and the rootstock, which can also be incised to release the milky fluid. Once exuded, it soon solidifies into lumps and takes on a waxy appearance and consistency. Used medicinally long ago as a carminative, expectorant and anti-spasmodic, it has become a rare commodity. It is exported by India.

Ceylon Cinnamon

Cinnamomum zeylanicum Nees

Take the finest spices: of liquid myrrh five hundred shekels, and of sweet-smelling *cinnamon* half as much.

Exodus 30:23

I have perfumed my bed with myrrh, aloes, and *cinnamon*. Come, let us take our fill of love till morning.

Proverbs 7:17–18

All articles of costly wood, bronze, iron and marble, *cinnamon*, spice, incense, myrrh, frankincense.

Revelation 18:12–13

THE tree of the Ceylon cinnamon is widely cultivated in tropical countries and its products are exported worldwide. The value of this plant was as well-known to the ancients as it is to us today. Its uses are manifold. The bark, from which a volatile oil in demand commercially is made, was also exported as quills to be used for flavoring sweets, in curry powder, incense, and perfume. Post-biblical literature, especially that of an exegetical nature, expanded on the plant and its fragrance.

The much-discussed identification of the biblical *kinnamon* as *Cinnamomum* has been clarified and confirmed by various scholars.

Since *C. zeylanicum* is native to Ceylon and the coast of India, cinnamon must have been brought here from a great distance. This is in accordance with the evidence that land and sea trade routes for drugs, perfumes and incenses not only existed between the Mediterranean and Indian coasts but also extended farther east, joining the very ancient 'silk route' between India and the Far East and reaching southeast Arabia, the main emporium of the Sabean kingdom for drugs and incense.

Cinnamon belongs to the predominantly tropical Laurel family, with 275 species mainly in south and southeast Asia. In its wild state it is a bushy evergreen about 6-10 m. tall, with a heavily-branching stem. The leaves are opposite, leathery, ovate to oblong, entire, 10–15 cm. long. The flowers are small and fetid, and the small fruit smells like terebinth.

Cassia

Cinnamomum cassia Blume

And of *cassia* five hundred, according to the shekel of the sanctuary, and of olive oil a hin.
Exodus 30:24

And he called the name of the first Jemimah; and the name of the second *Keziah*; and the name of the third Keren-happuch.
Job 42:14

Therefore God, your God, has anointed you with the oil of gladness above your fellows; Your robes are all fragrant with myrrh and aloes and *cassia*.
Pslams 45:7–8

CASSIA oil was a precious perfume, one of the ingredients of the holy oil used to anoint the 'Tent of Meeting' and the High Priest Aaron and his sons (Exodus 30:22–32). Cassia was also used as part of the incense burnt in the Temple. The oil is obtained by steam distillation from the plant's leaves and twigs and also from the immature fruits called 'cassia buds'. It is used as a flavoring agent and also in pharmacy.

In the quoted passages, the Hebrew *ketziah* and *kiddah* are translated as 'cassia'; the former is also applied as a personal name. The question as to whether *ketziah* and *kiddah* are synonymous or refer to different plants or drugs will never be resolved. Less problematic is the identifying of cassia (cognate with *ketziah*) as *C. cassia*; and there is little doubt as to the plausibility of the importation of these articles from East Asia. Recent investigations have produced evidence for the existence of very ancient trade routes between East and West Asia.

Cassia (or *C. obtusifolium* Nees var. *cassia*), is a tree often 10 m. tall, with rather large, 3-nerved, opposite leaves and small pale-yellow flowers, borne in panicles. It is native to East Asia, and is widely cultivated, especially in southeastern China, for its bark, buds and oil, which are exported to world markets.

Eaglewood

Aquillaria agallocha Roxb.

Aloe

Aloe vera L.

Your robes are all fragrant with myrrh and *aloes* and cassia.

Psalms 45:8

Nicodemus also, who had at first come to him by night, came bringing a mixture of myrrh and *aloes* about a hundred pounds' weight. They took the body of Jesus, and bound it in linen cloths with the spices, as is the burial custom of the Jews.

John 19:39–40

THE tall eaglewood trees native to East Africa and northern India, in great demand for their fragrance and oil, are undoubtedly the Hebrew *ahaloth*, rendered *aghal* in Sanskrit and *xylaloe* or *agallochon* in Greek ('aloes' in the RSV). This identification of the plant is much better founded than any other suggestion.

The genus *Aquillaria* comprises 20 species, a few of which supply the aromatic eaglewood from which a costly perfume is extracted. This perfume is listed in the Bible along with myrrh, cassia, cinnamon and other foreign spices.

In John it appears as a perfume for shrouds, in which instance it was probably an oil extracted from the succulent leaves of *Aloe vera* (in its broader sense also includes *A. succotrina* and *A. barbadensis*), which was widely used medicinally and as a substitute for embalming matter in ancient Egypt and elsewhere. Remnants of this probably cultivated aloe are still found in some Arab countries and also in Israel. It looks not unlike a small centaury plant with fleshy leaves forming a rosette. From the center of this rosette a stem bearing a spike of reddish-green flowers rises annually.

The eaglewood is a member of the *Thymelaeaceae* family, which comprises about 50 genera and 500 species, mostly in temperate regions. It is a tree up to 30 m. tall with entire alternate leaves and clusters of flowers with a colored perianth. The fruit is a two-valved capsule.

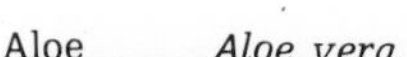

Aloe *Aloe vera*

Spikenard

Nardostachys jatamansi (Wall.) DC.

While the king was on his couch, my *nard* gave forth its fragrance. Song of Solomon 1:12

And while he was at Bethany in the house of Simon the leper, as he sat at table, a woman came with an alabaster flask of ointment of pure *nard*, very costly, and she broke the flask and poured it over his head. Mark 14:3

Mary took a pound of costly ointment of pure *nard* and anointed the feet of Jesus and wiped his feet with her hair; and the house was filled with the fragrance of the ointment.
John 12:3

IN the time of the Bible, spikenard (nard) was brought from India with some other drugs, such as cassia and cinnamon. In our days it is no longer valuable and has become all but obsolete.

Nerd, naird or *nard* is mentioned three times in the Song of Solomon and twice in the New Testament to designate an aromatic plant and the oil derived from it, which was used by the ancients in perfumery and as an ingredient of the incense in the Temple. The identity of the Hebrew name with *Nardostachys*, though disputed, is accepted by most translators; *nardos* is is also the word in Greek, *nardus* in Latin and *nardin* in Syriac and Persian. Moreover, the plant, which is native to Nepal and other parts of the Himalayan mountains, whence it was introduced into India, has the Veddasian name *narada* or *nalada.*

Spikenard is a perennial herb of the Valerian family, sometimes included in the genus *Valeriana.* Its leaves and short aerial stem are very hairy and its clusters of flowers are small. All of its parts contain an aromatic essential oil, especially the rootstock, whose fragrant oil is mixed with other oils to make the spikenard ointment, a precious salve once used in cosmetics and in medicine for the treatment of nervous disorder.

Turmeric

Curcuma longa L.

Saffron Crocus

Crocus sativus L.

Your shoots are an orchard of pomegranates with all choicest fruits, henna with nard, nard and *saffron*, calamus and cinnamon, with all trees of frankincense, myrrh and aloes, with all chief spices.

Song of Solomon 4:13–14

SAFFRON (in Hebrew, *karkom*) is mentioned only once in the Bible, in association with spikenard and cinnamon, spices imported from the Far East. Some commentators have identified it with *Curcuma longa*, the Indian turmeric of the Ginger family, others with true saffron, *Crocus sativus*, which was imported from neighboring countries. The first species was never grown in this country, and the second probably only in post-biblical times.

Since the Arabic name for turmeric is *kurkum* and for saffron *saferam* and *kurkam*, there is linguistic support for both renditions. *Karkom* thus appears to be a homonym for two different plants in different periods.

All Talmudic sources concerning *karkom* indicate a plant whose flowers (stigmas) were collected both for coloring and for healing purposes. In view of this and the fact that the garden saffron can easily be cultivated in Israel, while *Curcuma* cannot, there is no doubt that the sown *karkom* fields mentioned in the Mishnah refer to *Crocus sativus*.

Turmeric is a tall herbaceous plant, native to southern Asia and the East Indies, and cultivated in China, Bengal and Java for its rhizomes. These are filled with a yellow or orange substance, which when crushed into a powder called curcumin is used to color and flavor curries and to dye cloth. It contains an odorous, acrid, volatile oil used in pharmacy. It is sold in Arab markets as *kurkum* and is used both as a condiment and a medicinal drug.

The saffron crocus is a tiny plant with a subterranean corm, producing a bunch of narrow leaves and one or more rather large bluish-lilac flowers with six perianth segments, three stamens and a style branching into many thread-like yellow stigmas. These last provide the dye for food and beverages and are onerous to gather, 150 flowers producing only a single gram of saffron stigmas.

Saffron Crocus *Crocus sativus*

All of this points to the identification of the biblical *karkom* as turmeric and not as crocus, which is essentially used for color and not for flavor. But doubt arises when one considers another widely cultivated annual yielding numerous heads of orange flowers from which a dye is extracted. This is the safflower (*Carthamus tinctorius*), usually known as dyer saffron, a plant of the Composite family with an erect stem about 50 cm. tall. It probably originated in the Near East from a native plant common in the region. It was cultivated in Egypt from about 3500 BC for its orange flowers, which were used to dye cloth, and later for the high oil content of its seeds. The peculiarly aromatic flowers are still sold in the great bazaars of the Orient as a food-coloring substance.

Turmeric *Curcuma longa*

GLOSSARY

Terms explaind in the text are not included; numerals refer to number of illustration.

Achene A small, dry, single-seeded fruit (1).
Acute Sharp-pointed.
Alternate Arranged in two rows, but not opposite (2).
Annual Living one year only or less.
Anther Part of the stamen, containing pollen grains (3).
Arboreal Tree-like.
Astringent Pungent.
Axil Angle between stem and leaf.
Axillary Arising from the axil of a leaf.

Bathah A formation of plants made up mainly of low shrubs (from the Hebrew).
Bipinnate Divided twice into leaflets, in a feather-like form(4).
Bisexual Containing both a pistil and stamens.
Bract Small leaflet accompanying the flower.
Bulb A subterranean thickened shoot, serving as a storage organ, consisting of a short stem and a number of fleshy leaf bases(5).
Bulbiferous Bearing small bulbs.

Calcareous Of the nature of, or containing, lime.
Calyx The outer, usually green envelope of a flower (6).
Capillary Hair-like.
Capsule A dry dehiscent fruit, usually containing several seeds (7).
Caprifig The male individual of the fig.
Carminative Medicine for expelling wind.
Carpel One of the units composing the pistil (8).
Catkin A flexuous spike of flowers, usually falling as a whole (9).
Cohabitant Living together.
Community (plant) An assemblage of plants displaying a more or less stable composition of species.
Coniferous Producing seeds in cones.
Contractile Shrinking.
Cordate Heart-shaped (10).
Corm Bulb.
Corolla The inner, mostly colored, perianth of a flower(11).
Cotyledon The first leaf or leaves of the embryo.
Cross-pollination Pollination between two varieties or individuals.
Culm Stem of grass.
Cupule Cup-like structure.

Deciduous Losing its leaves in the autumn.
Dehiscent Opening to shed its leaves.
Dentate Toothed (12).
Dioecious Having separate male and female plants.
Diploid Having two basic sets of chromosomes.
Disarticulate Disconnect; separate into smaller fruits.
Dissected Cut.
Divaricate Spreading.
Domestication Conversion of wild plants (or animals) into cultivated ones.
Dry farming Non-irrigated cultivation.
Dwarf-shrub Low shrubby plant, not exceeding 50 cm. in height.

Endosperm Nutritive tissue accompanying the embryo.
Entire Without toothed or otherwise divided margins.
Escapee Plant which has escaped from cultivation.
Evergreen Retaining its leaves the whole year round.
Expectorant Medicine promoting expectoration (ejection of mucous matter).
Exserted Protruding.

Female (flowers, plants) Bearing pistils or pistillate flowers only.
Febrifuge Medicine that lessens fever.
Filiform thread-like (13).
Floret Small flower.
Fruit-setting Ripening fruit.

Gall A tumor of plant tissue caused by insect irritation.
Glabrous Without hairs.
Gland A small vesicle bearing oil or another liquid.
Glandular Furnished with glands.
Globose Ball-shaped.
Gummiferous Bearing gum.

Head A group of flowers crowded together to form an organized, generally flower-like structure (14).
Herbaceous Soft and green, having the texture of leaves.
Hexaploid Having six basic sets of chromosomes.
Hybridization Crossing between varieties.
Hydragogue Expelling water or serum.
Hydrophytic Plants displaying the habits of water plants.

Incised More or less deeply and sharply cut.
Indehiscent Not opening to release its seeds when ripe.
Inferior (ovary) Adnate to the floral receptacle and appearing below the floral parts (15).
Inflorescence A flowering branch or cluster of flowers; a flower system.

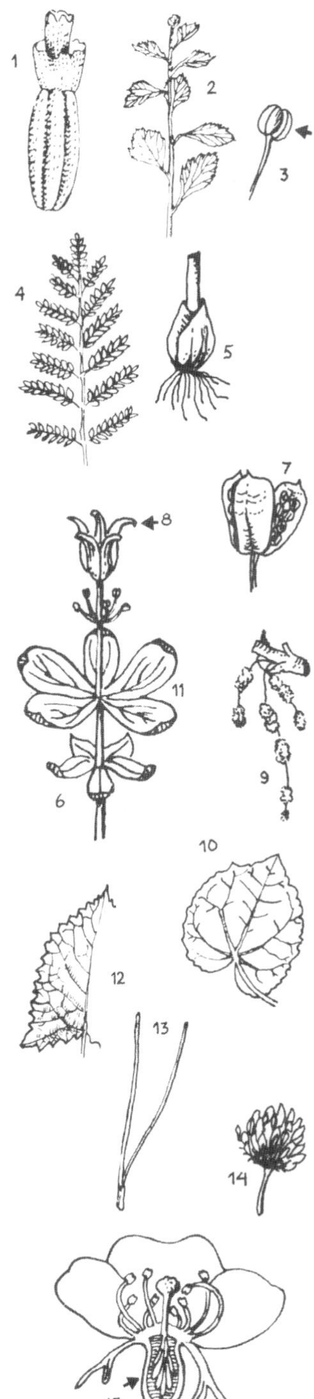

Joint A part of the stem between two adjacent leaf-bearing points.

Lanceolate Lance-shaped, widening towards base and tapering towards apex (16).
Latex Milky juice.
Leaf-break Unfolding of the leaves.
Leaflet A leaf-like structure of a composed leaf.
Leaf-setting Unfolding of the leaves.
Linear Long and narrow with almost parallel sides.
Lobe Any segment of an organ.
Lobed (leaf) Divided into segments but not into leaflets (17).

Male (flowers, plants) Flowers bearing stamens only; plants bearing male flowers only.
Maquis A formation of Mediterranean, mostly evergreen low trees or tall shrubs.
Marl Calcareous earth mingled with clay and sand.

Nectariferous Nectar-bearing.
Nutlet A small, dry, one-seeded fruit.

Oleiferous Producing oil.
Ovary Part of the pistil, bearing an ovule and ripening into a fruit (18).
Ovate (Ovoid) Egg-shaped.
Oviposit Lay eggs.
Ovule Small body within the ovary turning into a seed.

Palisade tissue Cells of column-like leaves bearing chlorophyll.
Palmate With divisions resembling a hand.
Panicle A branched inflorescence (19).
Papilionaceous Butterfly-shaped.
Parthenocarpy Production of fruits without seeds.
Perennial Living for more than two years and producing flowers each year.
Perianth A floral envelope not differentiated into calyx and corolla (20).
Pericarp The wall or shell of a fruit (21).
Perigone The envelop of a flower (22).

Petiole The stalk of the leaf (23).
Photosynthesis The process of producing chlorophyll.
Pinnate Composed of many leaflets arranged in two rows along a common stalk (24).
Pinnatifid Pinnately cut into lobes not reaching the mid-rib (25).
Pinnatisect As above, but with lobes reaching the mid-rib or almost so.
Pollination The transfer of pollen to the stigma.

Raceme A kind of flower cluster.
Rhizome A thick underground stem, producing roots below and shoots above (26).
Rootstock Subterranean branch of the stem.
Rosette Basal, circular cluster of leaves (27).
Rudimentary Imperfect, non-functional organs.

Scion A shoot or bud of plant used for grafting.
Segetal Living among crops.
Self-pollination Pollination of stigma with pollen from the same flower or flowers of the same plant.
Sepal One of the separate parts (leaflets) of the calyx.
Sessile Stemless.
Spathe A large, often colored, leaf-like organ (28).
Spike A simple inflorescence with an elongated axis and sessile flowers (29).
Spikelet A unit of grass inflorescence, bearing one to many florets.
Stamen A pollen-bearing organ of a flower (30).
Stigma Top part of the pistil, which receives the pollen (31).
Steppe A formation of dwarf-shrubs and herbs in arid or semi-arid areas.
Stipule A scale or leaf-like appendage at the base of a leaf stalk (32).
Stolon A creeping stem below or above the ground.
Strain A race; a group of individuals differentiated from other groups of the species.
Style The part of the pistil connecting the ovary with the stigma (33).
Subtended Extended under or opposite to.
Succulent Fleshy.

Tetraploid Having four basic sets of chromosomes.
Tuber Underground stem.
Tunic A fleshy or dry covering round a bulb.

Umbel An inflorescence arranged in the shape of an umbrella (34).
Unisexual Bearing stamens or a pistil only.

Valves Parts of the pericarp, separating from the fruit when mature (35).
Variety A group of plant individuals differing by certain characteristics from the typical form of the species.
Vesicular With small, bladder-like structures.
Viscid Sticky.
viticulture Cultivation of vines.

Whorl A number of leaves arranged around the stem (36).

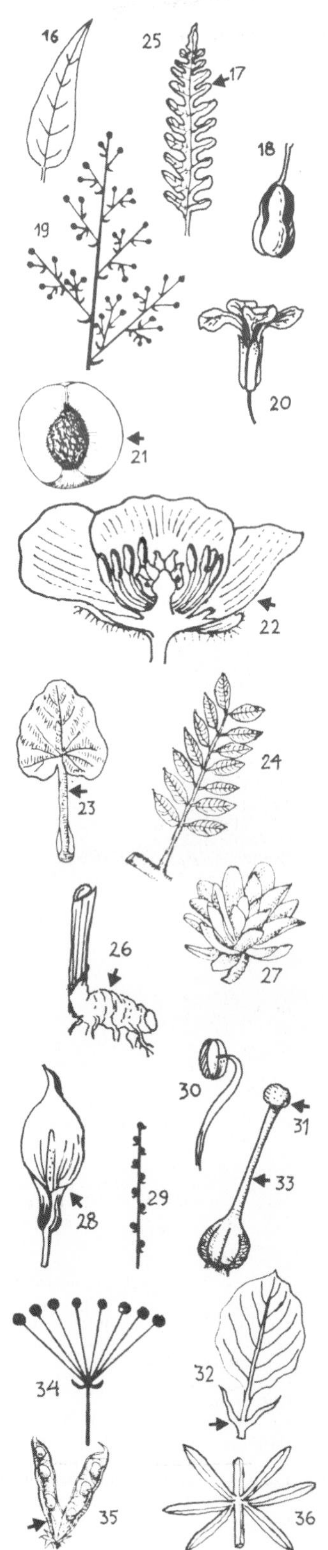

SELECTED BIBLIOGRAPHY

Bible and Bible Translations

Bible. Hebrew. **Pentateuch, Prophets, Hagiographa**. Jerusalem: Koren, 1973.

Bible. Hebrew. **The Mikraoth Gedoloth with Commentaries**. Jerusalem: Schoken, 1959.

Bible. Aramaic. **The Bible in Aramaic**, based on old manuscripts & printed texts. ed. A. Sperber, 4 vols. Leiden: E.J. Brill, 1959–1973.

Bible. Greek. **The Septuagint Version of the Old Testament**, with an English translation by Sir L.C.L. Brenton and with various readings & critical notes. Grand Rapids, Mich.,: Zondervan Publishing House, 1970.

Septuaginta; id est, Vetus Testamentum graece inuxta, LXX interpretes, ed. A. Rahlfs. 2 vols. Editio Quinta, 1952.

Bible. Latin. **Vetus Testamentum Latini** (Vulgate). Biblia Sacra Latina Veteris Testamenti Hieronymo interprete ex Antiquissima Auctoriate in Stichos Desripta. ed. Tischendorf. Wuppertal: F.A. Brockhaus, 1873.

Bible. Syriac. **Vetus Testamentum Syriace**. The Old Testament in Syriac according to the pshitta Version. Edited on behalf of the International Organization for the Study of the Old Testament by the Pshitta Institute, Leiden. Leiden: E.J. Brill, 1972.

Bible. Coptic. **Coptic Sacrorum Bibliorum**. Fragmenta Copto-Sahidica. 4 vols. Text in coptic (Sahidic) with preliminary notes in Latin and preface in German. Reprint of the 1885–1904 edition. Rome: J. Balestri 1970.

Bible. English. **Holy Bible, Authorized King James Version**. ed. C.I. Scofield, New York: Oxford University Press, 1967.

Bible. English. **Revised Standard Version**. Translated from the original languages, being the version set forth A.D. 1611, rev. A.D. 1881–1885 and A.D. 1901, compared with the most ancient authorities and rev. A.D. 1946–1952, 2nd ed. of the New Testament A.D. 1971. London: W. Collins Sons for the British and Foreign Bible Society, 1971.

The Apocryphal New Testament: being the Apocryphal Gospels, Acts Epistles and Apocalypses with other narrative and fragments, translated by M.R. James, 1st ed. Oxford: Clarendon Press, 1953.

Pseudepigrapha Series. Translated by H. Attridge, J.H. Charlesworth, R.A. Kraft, A.E. Purintum, R.S. Spittler, M.E. Stone, J. Strugnell, J. Timbie. New York: Society of Biblical Literature, 1972–1979.

General

Danby, H. **The Mishnah**. Oxford University Press, 1938.

Dioscorides, P. **De Materia Medica**. ed. M. Wellmann, 3 vols. Berolini: Weidmann, 1958.

Hastings, J. **Dictionary of the Bible**. Edinburgh: T. & T. Clark, 1909.

Herzfeld, L. **Handelsgeschichte der Juden des Altertums**. Braunschweig: J.H. Meyer, 1879.

Howes, F.N. **Vegetable Gums and Resins**. Waltham, Mass.,: Chronica Botanica. Co., 1949.

Josephus, F. **Works: the Jewish War & Jewish Antiquities**. Translated by H.J. Thackeray, 9 vols. Cambridge, Mass.,: Harvard University Press, 1966–1969.

Mandelkern, S. **Veteris Testamenti Concordantiae**. Berlin: Schocken, 1937.

Plinius, S.G. **Natural History**. Translated by H. Rackham, 10 vols. Cambridge, Mass.,: Harvard University Press, 1945.

Preuss, J. **Biblisch-Talmudische Medizin**. Berlin: S. Karger, 1923.

Smith, W. **A Dictionary of the Bible**,comprising its antiquities, biography, geography and natural history. London: J. Murray, 1863.

Botany & Related Studies

Balfour, J.H. **The Plants of the Bible**. London: Nelson and Sons, 1866.

Boissier, E. **Botanique biblique ou courtes notices sur les végétaux mentionnés dans les Saintes Ecritures**. Geneve: Depat com-Publ. Relig, 1861–1862.

Boissier, E. **Flora orientalis sive enumeratio plantarum in oriente a Graecia et Aegypto an India fines hucusque observatarum supplementum**. 5 Vols 1867–1881. Supl. ed. R., Buser, Georg Bibliopolam Basillae et Genevae. 1888.

Buschan, G. **Vorgeschichtliche Botanik der Kultur- und Nutzpflanzen der Alten Welt auf Grund prähistorischer Funde**. Breslau: 1895.

Celsius, O. **Hierobotanicon; sive, De plantis Sacrae Scripturae dissertationes breves**. 2 vols. Amsterdam: 1748.

Crowfoot, G.M. and L. Baldensperger. **From Cedar to Hysop: a Study in the Folklore of Plants in Palestine**. London: 1932.

Dan, J. and Raz, Z. **Soil Association Map of Israel**. Jerusalem: Ministry of Agriculture, 1962.

Evenari, M. Schanan, L. and Tadmor, N. **The Negev, the Challenge of a Desert**. Cambridge, Mass.: Harvard University Press, 1971.

Feldman, U. **Plants of the Bible**. Tel Aviv: Dvir, 1956 (Hebrew).

Feldman, U. **Plants of the Mishnah**. Tel Aviv: Dvir, 1960 (Hebrew).

Felix, J. **Plant World of the Bible**. Tel Aviv: Massada, 1968 (Hebrew).

Felix, J. **Agriculture in Palestine in the Period of the Mishnah and Talmud**. Jerusalem & Tel Aviv: the Magnes Press & Dvir, 1963 (Hebrew).

Flannery, K.V. "The Ecology of Early Production in Mesopotamia". ed. L.E. Sweet, **Peoples and Cultures in the Middle East**. American Museum of Natural History, Natural History Press, 1970.

Flückiger, F.A. **Pharmacognesie des Pflanzenreiches**. Berlin: Springer, 1891.

Fonck, L. **Streifzüge durch die biblisch Flora**. Freiburg: Herder Verlag, 1900.

Forsskal, P. **Flora aegyptiaco-arabica, sive descriptiones plantarum, quas per Aegyptium inferiorum et Arabiam Felicem detexit**.ed. Niebuhr. 1775.

Galil, J. and Neeman, G. **The Fig Tree**. Jerusalem: The Ministry of Education, 1979. (Hebrew).

Goor, A. and Nurock M.**The Fruits of the Holy Land**. Jerusalem: Universities Press, 1968.

Harlan, J.R. **Crops and Man**. Madison, Wisc.,: American Soceity of Crop Science, 1975.

Hehn, Y. **Kulturpflanzen und Haustiere in ihrem Übergang aus Asien nach Griechenland und Italien sowie im übrigen Europa**. Berlin: Gebrüder Borntraeger, 1911.

Keimer, L. **Die Gartenpflanzen im alten Ägypten**. Hamburg: Hoffmann und Campe, 1924.

Löw, I. **Aramaeische Pflanzennamen**. Leipzig: W. Engelmann, 1881.

Löw, I. **Die Flora der Juden**. 4 vols, Leipzig: Alexander Kohut Memorial Foundation, 1924–1938.

Moldenke, H.N. and A.L. **Plants of the Bible**. Waltham Mass.,: Chronica Botanica Co., 1952.

Post, G.E. **Flora of Syria, Palestine and Sinai**. 2nd ed. revised and enlarged by J.E. Dinsmore, Beirut: American Press, 1932–1933.
Reifenberg, A. **The Struggle between the Desert and the Sown**. Jerusalem: Publishing Dept., Jewish Agency, 1955.
Renfrew, J.M. **Paleoethnobotany**. London: Methuen L. Co., 1973.
Schweinfurth, G. **Arabische Pflanzennamen aus Ägypten, Algerien und Jemen**. Berlin: Reimer, 1912.
Simmonds, N.W. **Evolution of Crop Plants**. London: Longman, 1979.
Theophrastus. **Enquiry into Plants**. Translated by A. Hort. London: W. Heinemann, 1916.
Thompson, R.C. **A Dictionary of Assyrian Botany**. London: British Academy, 1949.
Thomson, W.M. **The Land and the Book**. London: T. Nelson & Sons, 1862.
Tristram, H.B. **The Natural History of the Bible**:being a review of the physical geography, geology and meteorology of the Holy Land, 8th ed., London: Society for the Promotion of Christian Knowledge, 1889.
Uphof, J.C.T. **Dictionary of Economic Plants**. New York: Cramer, 1968.
Waisel, Y. et al. (eds.) **Climatic Variations and Botanical History of Israel**. Proceedings of Seminar at the Tel Aviv University, 1971.
Woenig, F. **Die Pflanzen des alten Ägypten**. Amsterdam: Philo Press, 1971.
Zaharoni, M. and Berlinger, S. **Plants of the Bible**. Department of Education, Municipality of Haifa, 1969.
Zeybeck, N. **Styrax officinalis** L. Izmir: Scientific Reports Fac. Sci. Ege Uni. 1963.
Zohary, M. **The Plant Life in Palestine**. New York: Ronald Press Co., 1962.
Zohary, M. "Plants of the Bible", **Encyclopedia Biblica**. 7 vols., Jerusalem: Mossad Bialik, 1955.
Zohary, M. "Flora of the Bible", **Interpretors Dictionary of the Bible**, vol 1, 284–302. New York: Abingdon Press, 1962.
Zohary, M. **Geobotanical Foundations of the Middle East**. Stuttgart: Gustav Fischer Verlag, 1973.
Zohary, M. and Feibrun-Dothan, **Flora Palaestina**. Jerusalem: Israel Academy of Sciences and Humanities, 1966, 1972, 1979.
Zohary, M. **A New Analytical Flora of Israel**. Tel Aviv: Am Oved, 1976. (Hebrew).

Periodicals

Aaharonsohn, A. Über die in Palästina und Syrien wildwachsend aufgefundenen Getreidearten", **Verhandlungen der zoologischen-botanischen Gesellschaft, Wien**, Vol. 50 (1909) 485–509.
Birdwood, G. "On the genus Boswellia", **Linnean Society**, London, Vol. 22 (1870) 111–148.
Bodenheimer, F.S. "The Manna in Sinai", **The Biblical Archeologist**, Vol. 10 (1947) 2–6.
Braidwood, R.J. "Early Food Producers: Excavations in Iraqi Kurdistan", **Archeology**, Vol. 5 (1952) 157–164.
Burkill, L.H. "Habits of Man and the Origins of the Cultivated Plants of the Old World", **Linnean Society**, London, Vol. 164 (1951) 12–42.
Chaney, W.R. and Basbdirs, M. "The Cedars of Lebanon, Witness of History", **Economic Botany**, Vol. 32 (1978) 119–123.
Cohen, A. "To the Identification of Shamir and Shait", **Leshonenu**, vol. 23 (1959) 219–221 (Hebrew).
Danin, A. "A sweet Exudate of Hammada, Another Source of Manna in Sinai", **Economic Botany**, vol. 26 (1972) 373–375.
Eig, A. "Les Éléments et les Groupes Phytogéographiques Auxilliaires dans la Flore Palestinienne", **Fedde, Repertoriumm Specierum Novarum Regni Vegetabilis**, vol. 63 (1931) 1–201.
Fahn, A."Some Anatomical Adaptations of Desert Plants", **Phytomorphology**,vol. 14 (1964) 93–102.
Fahn, A. Wachs, N. and Ginzburg, C. "Dendrochronological studies in the Negev", **Israel Exploration Journal**, vol. 13 (1963) 291–300.
Feibrun, N. "New Data on Some Cultivated Plants of the Early Bronze Age in Palestine", **Palestine Journal of Botany**, vol. 1 (1938) 238–240.
Galil, J. "The Sycomore Tree in the Civilization of the Middle East", **Teva Va'aretz**,vol. 8 (1966) 306–318, 335–338 (Hebrew).
Galil, J. "The Sycomore Tree in Israel's Culture", **Teva Va'aretz**,vol. 9 (1966) 1–32 (Hebrew).
Galil, J. and Neeman, G. "Pollen Transfer and Pollination in the Common Fig (*Ficus carica* L.). **New Phytologist**,vol. 79 (1977) 163–171.
Hareuveni, E. "Researches in Names of Palestine Plants", **Leshonenu**,vol. 1 (1930) 239–246; vol. 2 (1931) 37–48 (Hebrew).
Hareuveni, E. "Recherches sur les Plantes de l'Evangile", **Revue Biblique**,vol. 42 (1933) 230–234.
Hepper, F.N. "An Ancient Expedition to Transplant Living Trees", **Journal of the Horticultural Society**, vol. 92 (1967) 435–438.
Lundgren, F. "Die Benützung der Pflanzenwelt in der alttestamentlichen Religion", **Zeitschrift für die Alttestamentliche Wissenschaft**, vol. 14 (1908) 1–191. Topelmann, Giesseu.
Sulman, F. and Tietz, G. "The Sex Hormones of the Mandrake", **Harefuah**, vol. 7 (1947) 1–4 (Hebrew).
Thimothy, B. "The Origin of the Manna", **Nature**, vol. 55 (1897) 400.
Townsend, C.C. "Papilionaceae in Flora of Iraq", **Ministry of Agriculture**, Iraq, vol. 3 (1974) 233–237.
Van Beek, G.W. "Frankincense and Myrrh", **Biblical Archeologist**,vol. 23 (1960) 70–95.
Warburg, O. "Heimat und Geschichte der Lilie", **Fedde, Repertorium Specierum Novarum Regni Vegetabilis**, Beihefte 167–204 (1929).
Zohary, D. "The Origin of Cultivated Cereals and Pulses in the Near East", **Chromosomes Today**, Eds. Wahrmann, J. and K. Lewis. 4 (1973) 307–20. Jerusalem: Keter.
Zohary, D. and Spiegel-Roy, P. "Beginnings of Fruit Growing in the Old World", **Scinece**,187 (1979) 319–327.
Zohary, M. "The Arboreal Flora of Israel and Transjordan and Its Ecological and Phytogeographical Significance", **Imperial Forestry Institute**, University of Oxford Institute, Paper 26 (1951).

AUTHORS OF PLANT NAMES MENTIONED IN ABBREVIATION

Ait. - Aiton
Alef. - Alefeld
All. - Allioni
Ant. - Antoine
Bge. - Bunge
Boiss. - Boissier
Carr. - Carrière
Coss. - Cosson
D.C. - de Candolle
Decne. - Decaisne
Desf. - Desfontains
Engl. - Engler
Forssk. - Forsskal
Jacq. - Jacquin
Karst. - Karsten
Ky. - Kotschy
Loud. - Loudon
Labill. - de Labillardière
Lindl. - Lindley
Moq. - Moquin-Tandon
Mansf. - Mansfeld
M.B. - Marshal von Bieberstein
Medic. - Medicus
Melv. - Melville
Mill. - Miller
Moll. - Mollinier
Nand. - Nandin
Nees. - Nees von Esenbeck
Oliv. - Olivier
Roxb. - Roxburgh
Schrad. - Schrader
Spreng. - Sprengel
Standl. - Standley
Thunb. - Thunberg
Trin. - Trinius
Wall. - Wallman

INDEX OF BIBLICAL REFERENCES

This index includes biblical citations to all the plants mentioned in this book. For easy orientation among the RSV's various renditions of one plant, cross references indicate each plant's common name as it appears in this book's contents and its various manifestations in all the quoted citations. Verses are given in order of appearance on page; numerals in brackets refer to page numbers. When several verses appear on one page, numeral follows last in sequence. Bold type numeral refers to page of the plant's main entry. For abbreviations used for the books of the Bible see end of this index.

Acacia *Is. 41:19* (15, 104, 112, 119); *Ex. 26:15; Josh. 2:1* (**116**). See 'Common Acacia', 'Shittim'.
Acanthus *Letter of Aristeas 70* (**165**) See 'Syrian Acanthus'
Adah *Gen. 4:23* (**149**, 166) See 'White Saxaul'
Almond *Gen. 43:11* (**65**, 194, 195); *Num. 17:8, Eccles. 12:5* (66, 98); *Jer. 1:11–12* (66); *Gen. 30:37* (66, 118, 129, 132); *Gen. 28:19; Josh. 16:2* (66). See 'Luz'
Aleppo Pine *Neh. 8:15* (60, **114**, 119, 123); *I Kings 6:23, 31* (114). See 'Olivewood', 'Wild Olive'.
Aloe *Song. 4:13* (64, 206); *Ps. 45:8* (200, 202, **204**); *Prov. 7:17–18* (203); *Jn. 19:39–40* (204). See 'Eaglewood'
Algum *II Chron. 2:8* (**125**) See 'Algum', 'Red Saunders'
Almug *I Kings 10:11–12* (**125**) See 'Algum', 'Red Saunders'
Apple *Song. 2:5, Joel 1:12, Josh. 15:33, I Chron. 2:43* (**70**); *Song. 2:3* (103). See 'Tappuaḥ'
Apple of Sodom *Josephus, Jewish Wars, Book IV, 8:4* (**122**) See 'Fruits'
Ardat *II Esd. 9:26* (**133**) See 'Daphne', 'Oleander'
Aroer *Deut. 2:36* (**117**) See 'Phoenician Juniper', 'Shrub'.
Aromatic Cane *Ex. 30:23* (**196**) See 'Calamus', 'Ginger Grass', 'Sweet Cane'.
Ashḥur *I Chron. 4:5* (**150**) See 'Sea Blite', 'Sheḥariah'.
Azekah *I Sam. 17:1* (**167**) See 'Boxthorn'
Balm *Gen. 37:25* (42, **192**, 194, 195); *Gen. 43:11* (65, 194, 195); *Jer. 8:22* (192). See 'Stacte', 'Storax'.
Balm *Song. 5:1* (**198**) See 'Spice'
Barley *Ruth 1:22* (39, **76**); *3:2* (39); *Deut. 8:7–8* (54, 74); *Ezek. 4:9* (75, 77, 82); *Josh. 6:8–9* (76); *Ex. 9:31* (78); *II Sam. 17:27–29* (84); *Job. 31:39–40* (160)
Bean Caper *Num. 33:9–10* (**148**) See 'Elim'
Bitter Herbs *Ex. 12:8* (**100**) See 'Dwarf Chicory', 'Reichardia'.
Black Cummin *Is. 28:27* (**91**) See 'Dill'
Black Mulberry *Is. 40:20; I Macc. 6:34; Lk. 17:5–6* (**71**) See 'Impoverished', 'Mulberries', 'Sycamine Tree'.
Black Mustard *Mk 4:30–32* (**93**) See 'Mustard Seed'
Bottle Gourd *Josh. 15:37–38* (**87**) See 'Dilean'
Boxthorn *I Sam. 17:1* (**167**) See 'Azekah'
Bramble *Judg. 9:14–15* (154) See 'Christ Thorn', 'Crown of Thorns'
Bramble *Num. 33:55; Prov. 22:5; Lk. 6:44* (**157**). See 'Thorns'
Brambles *Song. 2:1–2* (**160**) See 'Golden Thistle', 'Thistles', 'Thorns'.
Bread *Ex. 16:4* (**142**) See 'Manna'
Brier *Judg. 8:16* (**158**); *Is. 15:13* (**162**); *Micah 7:4–5* (**164**); *Ezek. 28:24* (**166**). See 'Holy Thistle', 'Globe Thistle', 'Gray Nightshade', 'Nettle', 'Spiny Zilla', 'Syrian Thistle', 'Thorns'.
Broad Bean *Ezek. 4:9* (75, 77, 82); *II Sam. 17:27–29* (**84**).
Bulrushes *Ex. 2:3* (136, **137**) See 'Papyrus'
Burning Bush *Ex. 3:2–6* (45, **140**) See 'Bush', 'Senna Bush'.
Bush *Acts. 7:30* (140) See 'Burning Bush, 'Senna Bush'.
Bushes *Job. 30:3–4* (144, 145) See 'White Wormwood'
Calamus *Song. 4:13* (64); *Ezek. 27:19–21* (**196**). See 'Aromatic Cane', 'Ginger Grass', 'Sweet Cane'.
Caperbush *Eccles. 12:5; Neh. 3:30; Num. 26:33; Josh. 17:3; I Chron. 7:15* (**98**). See 'Desire', 'Tzalaf', 'Zelophahad'.
Carob *Matt. 3:4; Lk. 15:16* (**63**). See 'Locusts', 'Pods'.
Cassia *Ezek. 27:29–21* (196); *Ps. 45:7–8* (200, 203, 204); *Ecclesiasticus 24:14–15* (201); *Ex. 30:24; Job 42:14* (203). See 'Keziah'
Castor Bean *Jon. 4:6–11* (73, **193**) See 'Plant'
Cattail *Ex. 2:3; Is. 19:6; Jon. 2:5* (**136**). See 'Reeds', 'Rushes', 'Weeds'.
Cedar *Is. 44:14* (113, **120**, 128) See 'Laurel', 'Pine'.
Cedar *Is. 41:19* (15, **104**, 112, 119); *Judg. 9:14–15* (48, 154); *Ps. 92:12* (48, 60); *I Kings 10:27* (68); *Is. 9:10; I Kings. 5:10–11* (74); *I Kings 4:33* (96); *Lev. 14:4* (96, 115); *II Chron. 2:3, 8* (104, 125); *Is. 35:2; II Kings 19:23; Num. 19:6* (104); *Lev. 14:6* (105); *I Kings 9:11; Zech. 11:1–2* (106); *Amos 2:9* (108); *Is. 60:13* (112); *Is. 44:14* (113, 120, 128); *Ezek. 31:8* (129)
Ceylon Cinnamon *Song. 4:13–14* (64, 206); *Ex. 30:23* (196, **202**); *Prov. 7:17–18; Rev. 18:12–13* (202). See 'Cinnamon'
Chick-pea *Is. 30:24* (**83**) See 'Provender'
Christ Thorn *Matt. 27:29* (134, **154**); *Judg. 9:14–15; Jn. 19:5* (154). See 'Bramble', 'Crown of Thorns'.
Cilician Fir *Ezek. 27:3–5* (**106**) See 'Fir'
Cinnamon *Song. 4:13* (64, 206); *Ex. 30:23* (196, **202**); *Prov. 7:17–18; Rev. 18:12–13* (202) See 'Ceylon Cinnamon'
Citron *Lev. 23:40* (45, 46, **123**) See 'Goodly Trees'
Common Acacia *Is. 41:19* (15, 104, 112, 119); *Ex. 26:15; Josh. 2:1* (**116**). See 'Acacia', 'Shittim'.
Common Oak *I Kings 13:14* (45); *Gen. 35:8; Hosea 4:13; Amos 2:9* (**108**); *Is. 44:14* (113, 120, 128). See 'Oak', 'Tabor Oak'.
Common Millet *Ezek. 4:9* (75, **77**, 82). See 'Millet', 'Sorghum'.
Common Myrtle *Is. 41:19* (15, 104, 112, **119**); *Neh. 8:15* (60, 114, 119, 123); *Esther 2:7* (119); *Is. 15:13* (162). See 'Hadassah', 'Myrtle'.
Common Poppy *Is. 40:6, 8; I Pet. 1:24–25* (**172**). See 'Crown Daisy', 'Dog Chamomile', 'Flowers of the Field', 'Flowers of the Grass', 'Scarlet Crowfoot'.
Common Rue *Lk. 11:42* (**90**) See 'Rue'
Coriander *Ex. 16:31* (**92**) See 'Coriander Seed'
Coriander Seed *Ex. 16:31* (**92**) See 'Coriander'
Cotton *Esther 1:6* (73, **79**)
Crocus *Is. 35:1–2* (15, 26, **176**) See 'Lily', 'Rose', 'White Lily'.
Crown Anemone *Mt. 6:28–30* (169, **170**); *Lk. 12:27* (170). See 'Lilies of the Field'
Crown Daisy *Is. 40:6, 8* (172); *Jas. 1:9–10* (175). See 'Common Poppy', 'Dog Chamomile', 'Flowers of the Field', 'Flowers of the Grass'.
Crown of Thorns *Mt. 27:29* (134, **154**, 156); *Jn. 19:5* (154, 156); *Mk. 15:17* (156). See 'Bramble', 'Christ Thorn'.
Cucumbers *Num. 11:5–6* (80, 85, **86**); *Is. 1:8* (86). See 'Muskmelon'
Cummin *Mt. 23:23* (41, **88**, 90); *Is. 28:25* (75); *Is. 28:27* (91)
Cypress *Is. 41:19* (15, 104, 112, 119); *II Chron. 2:3, 8* (104, 125); *I Kings 9:11; Zech. 11:1–2* (**106**); *Is. 60:13* (112); *I Kings 10:11–12* (125); *Is. 15:134* (162). See 'Evergreen Cypress'

Daphne *Josephus, Jewish Wars, Book IV, 1:1* (**133**) See 'Ardat', 'Oleander'.
Darnel *Mt. 13:24–25* (**161**) See 'Syrian Scabious', 'Weeds'.
Date Palm *Lev 23:40* (45, 46, 61, 123, 131); *Ps. 92:12* (14, 48, **60**); *Jn. 12:12–13* (60); *Neh. 8:15* (60, 114, 119, 123); *Deut. 34:3* (68); *Joel 1:12* (70); *Ecclesiasticus 24:14–15* (129); *Neh. 33:9–10* (148). See 'Palm'
Desire *Eccles. 12:5* (**98**) See 'Caperbush', 'Tzalaf', 'Zelophahad'.
Dilean *Josh. 15:37–38* (**87**) See 'Bottle Gourd'
Dill *Is. 28:27* (**91**) See 'Black Cummin'
Dill *Mt. 23:23* (41, **88**, 90); *Is. 28:25* (75)
Dog Chamomile *Is. 40:6, 8; I. Pet. 1:24–25* (**172**) See 'Common Poppy', 'Crown Daisy', 'Flowers of the Field', 'Flowers of the Grass'.
Dwarf Chicory *Ex. 12:8* (**100**) See 'Bitter Herbs', 'Reichardia'.
Eaglewood *Song. 4:13* (64, 206); *Ps. 45:8* (200, 202, **204**); *Prov. 7:17–18* (203); *Jn. 19:39–40* (204). See 'Aloe'
Eastern Savin *Ezek. 27:3–5* (**106**, 107) See 'Cilician Fir', 'Cypress', 'Evergreen Cyrpess', 'Fir'.
Ebony *Ezek. 27:15* (**124**)
Elim *Num. 33:9–10* (**148**) See 'Bean Caper'
Emmer *Deut. 8:7–8* (54, 74); *I Kings 5:10–11; Gen. 14:49; Judg. 15:5* (74); *Ex. 9:32; Is. 28:25; Rev. 6:6* (76); *Ezek. 4:9* (75, 77, 82); *II Sam. 17:27–29* (84); *Job 31:39–40* (160); *Mt. 13:24–25* (161). See 'Grain', 'Spelt', 'Wheat'.
Ethnan *I Chron. 4:7* (**146**) See 'Matan', 'Mattanah', 'Mattenai', 'Shaggy Sparrow-wort'.
Euphrates Poplar *Ezek. 17:5–6; Ps. 137:1–3* (**130**). See 'Willow'
Evergreen Cypress *Is. 41:19* (15, 104, 112, 119); *II Chron. 2:3, 8* (104, 125); *I Kings 9:11; Zech. 11:1–2* (**106**); *Is. 60:13* (112); *I Kings 10:11–12* (125); *Is. 15:13* (162). See 'Cilician Fir', 'Cypress', 'Eastern Savin', 'Fir'.
Fig *Micah 4:4* (48); *Deut. 8:7–8* (54, 74); *Gen. 3:6–7; Song. 2:11–13; Mt. 24:32* (**58**); *Num. 13:23* (62); *Joel 1:12* (70); *Matt. 7:15–16* (159)
Fir *Ezek. 27:3–5* (**106**) See 'Cilician Fir', 'Cypress', 'Eastern Savin', 'Evergreen Cypress'.
Flax *Ex. 9:31; Jn. 19:40* (**78**). See 'Linen'
Flower *Song. 2:12* (180) See 'Mountain Tulip'
Flowers of the Field *Is. 40:6, 8; I Pet. 1:24–25* (**172**); Jas. 1:9–*10* (175). See 'Common Poppy', 'Crown Daisy', 'Dog Chamomile', 'Flowers of the Grass', 'Scarlet Crowfoot'.
Flowers of the Grass *Is. 40:6, 8; I Pet. 1:24–25* (**172**); *Jas. 1:9–10* (175). See 'Common Poppy', 'Crown Daisy', 'Dog Chamomile', 'Flowers of the Field', 'Scarlet Crowfoot'.
Frankincense *Song. 4:13* (64, 206); *Jer. 6:20* (196); *Neh. 13:5; Lk. 1:8–10* (**197**); *Mt. 2:10–11* (197, 200); *Ex. 30:34–35* (197, 201); *Ecclesiasticus 24:14–15* (201); *Rev. 18:12–13* (203). See 'Incense'
Fruits *Josephus, Jewish Wars, Book IV, 8:4* (**122**) See 'Apple of Sodom'
Galbanum *Ex. 30:34–35* (197, **201**); *Ecclesiasticus 24:14–15* (201)
Gall *Lam. 3:19–20; Mt. 27:33–34* (**186**). See 'Poison', 'Poison Hemlock'.
Garden Rocket *II Kings. 4:39–40* (**101**) See 'Herbs'
Garlic *Num. 11:5–6* (**80**, 85, 86)
Ginger Grass *Song. 4:13* (64, 206); *Ex. 30:23; Jer. 6:20; Ezek. 27:19–21* (**196**). See 'Aromatic Cane', 'Calamus', 'Sweet Cane'.
Globe Thistle *Judg. 8:7; 8:16;* (**158**). See 'Briers', 'Holy Thistle', 'Syrian Thistle', 'Thorns'.
Golden Thistle *Job. 31:39–40; Song. 2:1–2; Is. 34:13* (**160**). See 'Brambles', 'Thistles', 'Thorns'.
Goodly Trees *Lev. 23:40* (45, 46, **123**) See 'Citron'
Grain *Gen. 41:49; Num. 18:27; Judg. 15:5* (**74**). See 'Emmer', 'Spelt', 'Wheat'.
Grapes *Amos 9:13; Gen. 49:11–12; Is. 16:10* (**54**); *Num. 13:23* (62); *Lk. 17:5–6* (71); *Mt. 7:15–16* (159); *Deut. 32:32–33* (186). See 'Vine'
Gray Nightshade *Prov. 15:19; Micah 7:4–5* (**164**). See 'Briers', 'Thorns'.
Hadassah *Esther 2:7* (**119**) See 'Common Myrtle', 'Myrtle'.
Hammada *Jer. 2:20; Josh. 21:29; Ezra 10:26; I Chron. 25:22; Josh. 19:21* (**151**). See 'Jarmuth', 'Jeremoth', 'Lye', 'Remeth'.
Gum *Gen. 37:25* (42, 194, **195**); *Gen. 43:11* (65, 194, 195). See 'Tragacanth'
Henbane *Josh. 15:11; Josephus, Antiquities, Book III, 7:6* (**187**). See 'Shikkeron', 'Shikrona'.
Henna *Song. 1:14* (169, **190**); *Song 4:13–14* (206).
Hairy Elm *Is. 44:14* (113, 120, **128**) See 'Rain'
Herbs *II Kings 4:39–40* (**101**) See 'Garden Rocket'
Hollyhock *Job 6:6–7* (**99**) See 'Mallow', 'Purslane'.
Holm Tree *Is. 44:14* (**113**, 120, 128) See 'Stone Pine'
Holy Thistle *Judg. 8:7; 8:16* (**158**). See 'Briers', 'Globe Thistle', 'Syrian Thistle', 'Thorns'.
Hyssop *Ex. 12:21–22; I Kings. 4:33; Ps. 51:7; Jn. 19:28–30* (**96**); *Lev. 14:4; Num. 19:61* (96, 104); *Lev. 14:6* (105). See 'Syrian Hyssop'
Impoverished *Is. 40:20* (**71**) See 'Black Mulberry', 'Mulberries', 'Sycamine Tree'.
Incense *Lk. 1:8–10* (**197**) See 'Frankincense'.
Ivy *II Macc. 6:7* (**121**)
Jarmuth *Josh. 21:29* (**151**) See 'Jeremoth', 'Hammada', 'Lye', 'Remeth'.
Jeremoth *Ezra 10:26; I Chron. 25:22* (**151**). See 'Jarmuth', 'Hammada', 'Lye', 'Remeth'.
Jointed Anabasis *Gen. 46:16* (**147**) See 'Shuni'
Keziah *Job 42:14* (**203**) See 'Cassia'
Ladanum *Gen. 37:25; 43:11* (42, **194**, 195). See 'Myrrh'
Lake Rush *Is. 9:14; 58:5* (**135**). See 'Reed', 'Rush'.
Laurel *Is. 41:19* (15, 104, 112, 119); *Is. 44:14* (113, **120**, 128). See 'Cedar', 'Pine'.
Laurestinus *Is. 41:19* (15, 104, **112**, 119); *60:13* (112); *Gen. 30:37* (66,118, 129,132). See 'Plane'.
Leafless Tamarisk *Gen. 21:33; I Sam. 31:13* (**115**). See 'Nile Tamarisk', 'Tamarisk'.
Leek *Num. 11:5–6* (**80**, 85, 86)
Lentil *Ezek. 4:9* (75, 77, **82**); *Gen. 25:34* (82); *II Sam. 17:27–29* (84).
Lily *I Kings 7:19, 26; Song. 2:1–2; Hos. 14:5* (**176**). See 'Crocus', 'Rose', 'White Lily'.
Lily of the Field *Matt. 6:28–30* (169, **170**); *Lk. 12:27* (170). See 'Crown Anemone'
Linen *Jn. 19:40* (**78**) See 'Flax'
Locusts *Mt. 3:4* (**63**) See 'Carob', 'Pods'.
Luz *Gen. 28:19; Josh. 16:2* (**66**). See 'Almond'
Lye *Jer. 2:22* (**151**) See 'Jarmuth', 'Jeremoth', 'Hammada', 'Remeth'.
Madder *Judg. 10:1; Gen. 46:13; I Chron. 7:1* (**191**). See 'Puah', 'Puvah'.
Mallow *Job. 30:3–4* (144, **145**) See 'Shrubby Orache'
Mallow *Job. 6:6–7* (**99**). See 'Hollyhock', 'Purslane'.
Mandrake *Gen. 30:14–15; Song. 7:13; Testament of Issachar 1:3–5; Josephus, Jewish Wars, Book VII 6:3* (**188**)
Manna *Num. 11:5–6* (85); *Ex. 16:31* (92, **142**); *Ex. 16:4* (142); *Jn. 6:30–31* (142). See 'Bread'
Matan *Jer. 38:1* (**146**) See 'Ethnan', 'Mattanah', 'Mattenai', 'Shaggy Sparrow-wort'.
Mattanah *Num. 21:18* (**146**). See 'Ethnan', 'Matan', 'Mattenai', 'Shaggy Sparrow-wort'.
Mattenai *Neh. 12:19* (**146**) See 'Ethnan', 'Matan', 'Mattanah', 'Shaggy Sparrow-wort'.
Melon *Num. 11:5–6* (**85**, 86) See 'Watermelon'
Millet *Ezek. 4:9* (75, **77**, 82) See 'Common Millet', 'Sorghum'.
Mint *Mt. 23:23* (41, **88**, 90); *Lk.*

Thistle *Gen. 3:17–18; Hos. 10:8; Matt. 7:15–16* (**159**); *Is. 34:13* (**160**). See 'Golden Thistle', 'Gray Nightshade', 'Spanish Thistle'.
Thorns *Eccles. 7:6; Hos. 2:6* (**156**); *Num. 33:55; Prov. 22:5* (**157**); *Judg. 8:7* (**158**); *Job. 31:39–40* (**160**); *Prov. 15:19* (**164**). See 'Bramble', 'Globe Thistle', 'Golden Thistle', 'Gray Nightshade', 'Holy Thistle', 'Syrian Thistle', Thorny Burnet'.
Thorny Burnet *Hos. 2:6; Eccles. 7:6; Mt. 27:27–30; Mk. 15:17; Jn. 19:5* (**156**). See 'Crown of Thorns', 'Thorns'.
Tragacanth *Gen. 43:11* (65, 194, **195**); *37:25* (194, 195). See 'Gum'
Turmeric *Song. 4:13–14* (**206**). See 'Saffron', 'Saffron Crocus'.
Tournefort's Gundelia *Ps. 83:13; Is. 17:13* (**163**) See 'Whirling'
Tzalaf *Neh. 3:30* (**98**) See 'Caperbush', 'Zelophahad'.
Vine *Micah 4:4* (48); *Deut. 8:7–8* (**54**, 74); *Jn. 15:1–2; Gen. 49:11–12* (54); *Song. 6:11* (64); *Joel 1:12* (70).
Grapes *Amos 9:13; Gen. 49:11–12; Is. 16:10* (**54**); *Num. 13:23* (62); *Lk. 17:5–6* (71); *Mt. 7:15–16* (159); *Deut. 32:32–33* (186)
Vinedresser *Jn. 15:1–2* (**54**)
Vineyard *Is. 16:10* (**54**); *Is. 1:8* (86); *Song. 1:14* (190).
Vintage *Is. 16:10* (**54**)
Wine *Amos 9:13; Gen. 49:11–12* (**54**); *Is. 16:10; Ruth 2:14* (73); *Judg. 6:11* (158); *Song. 5:1* (198).
Walnut *Song. 6:11* (**64**) See 'Nut'
Watermelon *Num. 11:5–6* (**85**, 86) See 'Melon'
Weeds *Jon. 2:5* (**136**) See 'Cattail', 'Reeds', 'Rushes'.
Weeds *Matt. 13:24–25* (**161**) See 'Darnel', 'Syrian Scabious'.
Wheat *Deut. 8:7–8* (54, **74**); *I Kings 5:10–11; Gen. 14:49; Num. 18:27; Judg. 15:5* (74); *Ex. 9:32; Is. 28:25* (75); *Ezek. 4:9* (75, 77, 82); *I Sam. 17:27–29* (84); *Job. 31:39–40* (160); *Mt. 13:24–25* (161). See 'Emmer', 'Grain', 'Spelt'.
Whirling *Ps. 83:13; Is. 17:13* (**163**) See 'Tournefort's Gundelia'
White Broom *I Kings 19:14; Job 30:3–4* (**144**)
White Lily *Is. 35:1–2* (26, **176**); *I Kings 7:19, 26; Hos. 14:5; Song. 2:1–2* (176). See 'Crocus', 'Lily', 'Rose'.
White Poplar *Gen. 30:37* (118, 129, **132**) See 'Poplar'
White Saxaul *Gen. 4:23* (**149**, 166). See 'Adah'
White Wormwood *Job 30:3–4* (144, 145); *Jer. 23:15* (**184**); *Amos 5:7* (184); *Lam. 3:19–20* (186). See 'Bushes'
Wild Gourd *II Kings 4:39–40* (101, **185**)
Wild Olive *Neh. 8:15* (**114**) See 'Aleppo Pine', 'Olivewood'.
Willow *Ezek. 17:5–6; Ps. 137:103* (**130**). See 'Euphrates Poplar'
Willows of the Brook *Lev. 23:40* (45, 46, 123, **131**) See 'Willow'
Willow *Lev. 23:40; Is. 44:3–4* (**131**). See 'Willows of the Brook'
Zelophaḥad *Num. 26:23; Josh. 17:3; I Chron. 7:15* (**98**). See 'Caperbush', 'Desire', 'Tzalaf'.
Zillah *Gen. 4:23* (149, **166**) See 'Briers', 'Spiny Zilla'.

Old Testament: Gen – Genesis; Ex– Exodus; Lev – Leviticus; Num – Numbers; Deut– Deuteronomy; Josh – Joshua; Judg – Judges; Ruth – Ruth; I Sam – I Samuel; 2 Sam – 2 Samuel; I Kings – I Kings; 2 Kings – 2 Kings; I Chron – I Chronicles; 2 Chron – 2 Chronicles; Ezra – Ezra; Neh – Nehemiah; Esther – Esther; Job – Job; Ps – Psalms; Prov – Proverbs; Eccles – Ecclesiastes; Song – Song of Solomon; Is – Isaiah; Jer – Jeremiah; Lam – Lamentations; Ezek – Ezekiel; Dan – Daniel; Hos – Hosea; Joel – Joel; Amos – Amos; Obad – Obadiah; Jon – Jonah; Mic – Micah; Nahum – Nahum; Hab – Habakkuk; Zeph – Zephaniah; Hag – Haggai; Zech – Zechariah; Mal – Malachi.

New Testament: Mt – Matthew; Mk – Mark; Lk – Luke; Jn – John; Acts – Acts of the Apostles; Rom – Romans; I Cor – I Corinthians; 2 Cor – 2 Corinthians; Gal – Galatians; Eph – Ephesians; Phil – Philippians; Col – Colossians; 1 Thess – 1 Thessalonians; 2 Thess – 2 Thessalonians; I Tim – I Timothy; 2 Tim – 2 Timothy; Tit – Titus; Philem – Philemon; Heb – Hebrews; Jas – James; I Pet – I Peter; 2 Pet – 2 Peter; I Jn – I John; 2 Jn – 2 John; 3 Jn – 3 John; Jude – Jude; Rev – Revelation (Apocalypse).

INDEX OF PLANT NAMES

Common names are given in Roman type, scientific names – in italics; bold type numerals refer to page of the plant's main entry.

SUBJECT INDEX

Names & Places; Historical, Geographical & Literary Terms.

ILLUSTRATION CREDITS

Numerals denote page number; unless otherwise indicated several photographs on one page are by the same photographer.

D. Darom: 18, 20, 31, 32, 39 (upper), 40, 56, 58, 63, 64, 65, 66, 69, 71, 74, 75, 76, 77, 78 (right), 79, 81 (bottom & upper left), 82, 83, 84, 87, 89, 90, 91, 92, 93, 96, 97, 98, 99 (upper right), 100 (bottom), 116, 118, 119, 120 (left), 121, 122, 123, 129, 131, 132, 134 (bottom), 135, 136, 137, 141, 144, 145, 146, 147, 148, 149, 150, 154, 155, 156, 157, 158 (left & right), 160, 161, 162, 167, 170, 173, 177, 179, 180, 184 (left), 185, 187, 189, 191, 192, 193, 199.

M. Zohary: 24 (upper), 30, 35, 47 (bottom right), 78 (left), 81 (upper right), 85, 86, 99 (bottom left & right), 100 (upper), 106, 112, 113, 115 (upper), 117, 120 (right), 128, 130, 133, 134 (upper), 140, 151, 158 (center), 159, 163, 164, 165, 166, 172, 174, 175, 181, 184 (right), 186, 188, 190, 194.

The publishers also wish to thank all the other photographers and institutions for permission to reproduce illustrations: A - Z Botanical Collection: 124 (bottom); Botanic Gardens, Tel Aviv University: 74, 76, 84 (bottom), 92, 129, 131 (upper), 191; W. Braun: 19 (bottom); Brooklyn Botanic garden, photo B. Kissam: 203, 204; A. Danin: 142, 143; A. Hay: 25, 47 (upper), 55, 59, 62, 67, 178; Heather Angel: 202; Israel Exploration Society (Jewish Quarter Excavations), photo Prof. N. Avigad: 49 (upper right); Israel Museum: 44 (upper left & right); Jacana, photo R. Koenig: 206, 207; T. Kollek Collection, photo Israel Museum: 49 (upper left); Y. Lev-Ari: 107 (right); G. Nalbandian: jacket, 19 (upper), 23, 24 (bottom), 38, 39 (bottom left & right), 44, 46, 49 (bottom), 61, 70, 171. Norbert: 57; S.A. Rao: 124 (upper); Royal Botanic Garden Edinburgh: 107 (left); Royal Botanic Gardens Kew: 196, 197, 200; A. Shmida: 195; the illustrations on page 201 and 205 are taken from the book entitled *Medizinal Pflanzen* by H.A. Koehler, 1877.

Grateful acknowledgment is also due to the following people for having placed at the publisher's disposal invaluable information or their own orchards, gardens and fields thus making possible the photography of some of the rarest biblical plants in their natural habitats: M. Bar-Daromah, Kibbutz Yavneh; U. Givoni, Savyon; D. Har-El, Kibbutz Native Halamedheh; I.C. Hedge, Curator of the Herbarium, Royal Botanic Gardens Edinburgh; B. Salant, Kibbutz Saad; A. Unreich, Kefar Saba; Prof. Y. Waisel, director of the Botanic Gardens, Tel Aviv University.

The author is indebted to Mrs. Stefania Grizi for typing the manuscript.